THE DOG

Copyright © 2010 Quarto Publishing plc

This edition published in 2020 by Chartwell Books,
an imprint of The Quarto Group
142 West 36th Street, 4th Floor
New York, NY 10018 USA
T (212) 779-4972 F (212) 779-6058
www.QuartoKnows.com

Chartwell titles are also available at discount for retail, wholesale, promotional, and bulk purchase. For details, contact the Special Sales Manager by email at specialsales@quarto.com or by mail at The Quarto Group, Attn: Special Sales Manager, 100 Cummings Center Suite 265D, Beverly, MA 01915, USA.

MHTWD

ISBN: 978-0-7858-3825-8

Library of Congress Control Number: 2019954449

Conceived, edited, and designed by
Quarto Publishing plc, an imprint of The Quarto Group
The Old Brewery
6 Blundell Street
London N7 9BH

Editorial Consultant Caroline Coile
Managing Editor Paul Docherty
Art Director Ivo Marloh
Project Editors Elise See Tai and Amy Head
Design The Urban Ant Ltd.
Picture Manager Veneta Bullen
Production Nikki Ingram
Publisher Samantha Warrington

Publisher's Note The photographs in this book feature dogs with undocked tails and uncropped ears. However, these practices still occur in some locations.

Printed in Singapore COS072020

10 9 8 7 6 5 4 3

THE DOG

FINDING YOUR FOREVER

David Alderton

CHARTWELL
BOOKS

*A terrier type:
mischievous and playful*

*A retriever type:
solid and dependable*

Contents

Introduction 6

How to Use This Book 7

Dogs for Beginners....................... 8

Family-friendly Dogs..................... 20

Good Mixers 32

Low-maintenance Dogs 44

High-maintenance Dogs 56

Small Dogs 68

Large Dogs 80

Dogs that Love to Run 92

Hypoallergenic Dogs.............. 104

Guard Dogs 116

Super-smart Dogs 128

Dogs with Talents 140

Weird and Wonderful Dogs 152

The Human Selector................................ 164

The Dog Selector 166

Glossary 169

Further Resources............................. 173

Index 174

Acknowledgments................................. 176

*A spaniel type:
lively and attention-seeking*

Introduction

It is vital not to be seduced into choosing a dog simply on the basis of its looks. All puppies look cute and are actually of a surprisingly similar size; but of course, some will grow much larger and have correspondingly bigger appetites than others. This in turn means that they are likely to be considerably more expensive to keep and will require more space.

There are also many other different factors that need to be considered when you are aiming to find your ideal canine companion. Nearly 400 different breeds exist worldwide, and these have been bred for a very diverse range of purposes, often over the course of many centuries. It is not just their appearance that is different, but they can vary markedly in temperament, too, and this trait is influenced by their origins. Then there are other considerations, such as the amount of grooming they require, their exercise needs, and the possible risk of inherited diseases, to bear in mind as well.

This book is very different from any other covering dog breeds. The dogs themselves are not listed in terms of breed groupings; instead, they are divided on the basis of key characteristics, such as those that are likely to be good mixers, or those that are athletic by nature. The aim throughout is to help you to find the breed, crossbreed, or mongrel that will be most suitable for you and your individual circumstances.

How to Use This Book

The aim of this book is to help match you with the perfect canine companion, by identifying the characteristics of a range of dog breeds and helping you decide which types of dogs should be a good match for your own character and lifestyle.

On pages 164–168 are two charts, The Human Selector and The Dog Selector. These quick-reference charts allow you to discover the types of dogs that you should be considering, having carried out an assessment of your own lifestyle. It is so important to be sure that the dog that you ultimately choose will be compatible in this regard. This initial selection will help to steer you in the direction of individual breeds that are likely possibilities, while eliminating others that will not be suitable. Alternatively, just browse the main chapters and note the dogs that interest you most.

All about you
These pages will help you consider things about yourself and your lifestyle and which breeds may be suitable for you

All about dogs
This chart lists all the dogs featured in this book in alphabetical order and provides a checklist for certain factors that may help you make your decision

About the dog
Each profile describes the breed in detail, providing background information about the dog's origins as well as information about its behavior and personality

At a glance
A set of bullet points are provided for each breed to help establish some of the dog's key attributes at a glance

Each of the main chapters of the book features ten breeds that have certain characteristics in common, such as dogs that are suitable for beginners or those with particular talents. The dogs included sometimes vary quite widely— for example, in size—but the information here is standardized, allowing you to compare the individual needs, temperaments, and appearances of the particular dogs in each category directly. These pages, along with the charts at the back of the book, should help you to reach a final decision as to which type of dog will be most suited to your lifestyle.

Breed features
Captions highlight some of the breed's features, such as coat color and body shape

Key characteristics
Each table includes information about the breed's personality, exercise requirements, and other characteristics

Dog types for young people who may be thinking of having a family soon; a single person with a child who is eager to have a dog; or an older person who has not had a dog before, but is looking for companionship.

English Toy Spaniel

Keeshond

Dogs for Beginners

Owning a dog for the first time can be slightly daunting, particularly as you are likely to have many questions relating to your new pet's feeding, grooming, and general care. For many new owners, however, training is likely to be an area of particular concern. As a result, the breeds covered in this section have been chosen to reflect their suitability for people who have little, if any, experience of dogs. The dogs' friendly, eager-to-please attitudes mean that they are very responsive in terms of training, so provided that you follow the basic rules, you should find that this process is straightforward.

Their exercise needs do differ, however, so it is important to choose a breed that is suitable for your lifestyle and surroundings. The Pug, with its modest exercise needs, will thrive in urban areas, whereas the Labrador Retriever will be much more suited to rural living. Their coat care needs are variable, too, ranging from the Whippet, whose requirements are very modest, to others like the Shetland Sheepdog and Keeshond, which need far more grooming. Unlike some breeds, however, this can be carried out easily at home.

Shetland Sheepdog

1. Boston Terrier

These stocky, broad-headed, and well-muscled dogs are ideal companions. They are intelligent, can be trained quite easily, are alert guardians in the home, and are also very affectionate. Their care is straightforward, and unsurprisingly, the breed has now built up a worldwide following.

History

The origins of the Boston Terrier can be traced back to a dog called Judge, who was the result of a Bulldog–English Terrier mating. He was brought from England to the U.S. in the 1870s, and kept by Mr. Robert Hooper, who lived in Boston, Massachusetts. By 1889, there were already 30 breeders whose bloodlines included descendants of Judge, and they formed the American Bull Terrier Club. Opposition from Bull Terrier owners forced a name change for the emerging breed, however, so it became known as the Boston Terrier after the area in which Judge lived. Recognition from the American Kennel Club (AKC) followed in 1893, with examples of the breed then being taken to Europe during the 1920s.

The matter of markings

You may be offered a mismarked puppy. Such individuals do not conform to the official breed standard, often because they have a dark rather than white foot, for example, but marking has no effect on health. Boston Terriers have an appealing face, which is reflected in their personality. They will form a close bond with members of their immediate family, and are eager to learn. These dogs are suited to urban environments, provided there are parks nearby where they can be walked every day. The short coat of the breed is very easy to maintain in good condition.

Upright ears
The ears are positioned close to the sides of the skull

Large head
The large head has a flat top, with no signs of wrinkling

Boston Terrier colors
Colors are brindle, black with white markings, or seal, which is black with a reddish cast

CANINE CHARACTERISTICS		NOTES
Personality	Affectionate and relaxed yet alert	
Size	Height: 15–17 in. (38–43 cm) Weight: 15–25 lb (7–11.3 kg)	
Exercise	Enjoys a daily trot around the park; likes to explore, though not especially athletic	Avoid exercise in the hottest part of the day
At home	Adapts well to domestic life; prefers to stay inside in bad weather	
Behavior	Not always so friendly around other dogs; may snore when sleeping, especially when older	Use short training sessions to improve the dog's concentration; take care around other dogs
Grooming	Weekly grooming required	Use a rubber grooming mitt and wipe the inside of the ears and any tear staining with damp cotton balls
Common health issues	Prominent eyes are susceptible to corneal ulcers; brachycephalic syndrome; large head means puppies may need a Caesarean birth	Avoid undergrowth when walking to protect the eyes

2. Labrador Retriever

The Labrador, the most popular breed of dog in the world today, is the archetypal family dog, being well suited to a home with older children who can compete with its high energy levels. It has a very responsive nature.

AT A GLANCE
- Good family dog
- Responsive to training
- Tolerant nature but active
- Straightforward coat care
- Can be prone to obesity

History

The origins of this breed lie in the Canadian state of Newfoundland, where its ancestors worked as fishermen's companions. One of their characteristics, still apparent in Labradors today, was a readiness to enter water. The short coat of the breed, which is easy to care for, is also a feature that dates back to its earliest days. A longer coat would have attracted ice in the freezing winters of its Canadian homeland. During the 1800s, the first Labrador Retrievers were taken to Britain, where they rapidly found favor as sporting companions, as the demand for gundogs that were bred to work on a one-to-one basis grew rapidly. Crossbreeding with other retriever breeds occurred, especially toward the end of the century as it became harder to obtain further stock from Canada. This served to improve their scenting skills.

Adaptability

Part of the reason for the Labrador's popularity today probably relates to its attractive appearance, but a more significant underlying explanation is the breed's adaptability and enthusiasm to work alongside people. Labrador Retrievers are used for a diverse range of tasks, from helping to locate survivors buried under rubble after earthquakes to seeking out drugs and explosives at airports and other localities. Even if you have not trained a dog before, training is quite straightforward with this breed because Labradors are so responsive, having been bred over generations to work closely with people.

CANINE CHARACTERISTICS		NOTES
Personality	Active, lively, and affectionate; loyal	Take care that the dog does not become overexcitable when playing
Size	Height: 22–25 in. (56–64 cm) Weight: 55–80 lb (25–36 kg)	Dogs can be much heavier than bitches
Exercise	Needs a walk once or twice a day, ideally in the countryside	Be careful around water, as this breed loves to swim
At home	Enjoys space to play, which a large yard can offer	Make time for play
Behavior	Eager to learn, responsive; enjoys the opportunity to retrieve toys	
Grooming	Minimal brushing required	Allow mud to dry, so it can be brushed out of the coat easily
Common health issues	Hip dysplasia; susceptible to obesity, especially with age	Ensure breeding stock has been screened for hip dysplasia

Labrador colors
The Labrador can be bred in three colors—yellow (from fox–red to light cream), chocolate, and black

Head and ears
The wide skull has ears positioned well back and set quite low

Short body
The Labrador Retriever has a relatively short body with a chest of medium width

3. Schipperke

This Belgian breed was originally called the Spitske, probably because it is descended from spitz stock, although some believe it has a Belgian shepherd dog ancestry. During the late 1800s, it became known as the Schipperke, meaning "little skipper." The name is pronounced *skeep-er-ker*.

AT A GLANCE
- Easy to look after
- Very responsive to training
- Enjoys playing
- Eager guardian
- Lively nature
- Generally long-lived

CANINE CHARACTERISTICS		NOTES
Personality	Very loyal; suspicious of strangers	Keep an eye on the dog around other people, especially children
Size	Height: 10–13 in. (25–33 cm) Weight: 12–16 lb (5.4–7.2 kg)	There is generally a marked contrast between the size and weight of dogs and bitches
Exercise	Needs plenty of exercise	Exercise at least once a day
At home	Does not need spacious surroundings	
Behavior	Alert to intruders	Train not to bark unnecessarily
Grooming	Male dogs may have more profuse coats	Brush weekly
Common health issues	Eye problems, notably Progressive Retinal Atrophy (PRA); metabolic disease MPS 111B	Ensure breeding stock has been screened for eye problems and metabolic disease

History

The Schipperke's actual origins have been lost, but its working role was originally as a guard dog and ratter on the canal boats that plied across Belgium and other parts of Europe. Before this, however, members of the breed took part in the first organized dog show, which was held during 1690 in Brussels, with the entrants wearing ornate collars created by the craftsmen who owned them. From these working roots, the Schipperke ultimately entered the highest echelon of Belgian society when a member of the breed was acquired in 1885 by Marie Henriette, Queen of Belgium. This put Schipperkes on the international stage, with the result being that they were first seen in England in 1887 and then in the U.S. during the following year. By the turn of the century, this lively companion had become the most sought after of all breeds in its homeland.

Triangular ears
The small ears are set high on the head and are held erect when the dog is alert

Appearance and character

The Schipperke is an unusual breed in that some individuals are born naturally without tails. By tradition, the only color associated with the breed is black, although occasionally other colors are seen, including blond and cream. One of the most appealing features of the breed is its devotion to those in its immediate circle. A Schipperke is ideal for someone living alone, as it forms a particularly close bond with its owner. It is an alert watchdog, as might be anticipated, and is quite happy living in an urban setting.

Long coat
The coat at the rear of the thighs forms longer areas called culottes

Black coat
Coloration is always black, but dogs of more than about seven years old may show signs of gray

4. Pug

These unmistakable small dogs have become increasingly popular over recent years, as more people appreciate the appeal of Pugs as household companions. They are friendly dogs, easy to look after, and generally do not yap excitedly like some small dogs.

History

There are many conflicting accounts that claim to explain the ancestry of these dogs, but almost certainly, Pugs originated in China and may be related in some way to the Pekingese. After their arrival in Europe, they became closely linked with the Dutch royal family. There is some dispute, however, over the origins of the name "Pug." The word meant "monkey," and so this reference is thought to have referred to the distinctive face of the breed. An alternative meaning, however, was something that was greatly loved, and this too might explain their name, because back then, just as now, Pug owners doted on their pets.

Modern times

Pugs have tremendous personalities and having been kept for centuries purely as companions, they thrive in domestic environments. They are tolerant, making the breed a good choice for a home where children are also present, but they must be handled carefully, with their prominent eyes being particularly prone to injury. Pugs are not a difficult breed to train. It is often recommended that they are exercised on a harness rather than a collar. Their flattened facial shape can result in breathing difficulties, often resulting in snoring and snuffling. It is very important not to allow them to become obese, which will make these traits worse. In spite of their size, Pugs have gained a reputation as eager, brave watchdogs.

CANINE CHARACTERISTICS		NOTES
Personality	Attentive and very friendly	
Size	Height: 11 in. (28 cm) Weight: 14–18 lb (6.3–8 kg)	Keep an eye on the dog's weight as it can easily become overweight
Exercise	Gentle strolls preferred; happiest ambling along	Avoid exercise in the hottest part of the day, as it is susceptible to heatstroke
At home	Alert watchdog	
Behavior	Quiet and tolerant; not active, though it has a playful side; learns rapidly	
Grooming	Minimal brushing and combing required	Wipe tear staining with damp cotton balls
Common health issues	Eye and respiratory problems; obesity increases the risks of diabetes and heart disease	Be aware of health risks linked to obesity

Expressive eyes
The Pug has dark, expressive eyes that contrast with the small, soft ears

Pug mask
The well-defined mask covering the muzzle is a breed feature of fawn Pugs

Curly tail
The tail is tightly curled and is at the level of the hip. A double curl is the ideal

5. Tibetan Spaniel

These small dogs do not require extensive exercise, making them an ideal choice for owners in urban areas. Tibetan Spaniels are also very friendly and responsive toward people whom they know well, which means they will develop into excellent companions.

AT A GLANCE
- Relatively unusual breed
- Modest coat care needs
- Intelligent, friendly nature
- Alert watchdog
- Long-lived

CANINE CHARACTERISTICS		NOTES
Personality	Alert; will bark to warn of strangers, but not noisy like some small dogs; forms a strong bond with owners	Keep an eye on the dog around strangers
Size	Height: 10 in. (25 cm) Weight: 9–15 lb (4–7 kg)	
Exercise	Needs daily exercise	Exercise every day to help the dog settle in its home
At home	Adapts well to apartment living; settles well indoors	
Behavior	Bitches may only come into season once, not twice, annually, unlike most dogs—this can affect the availability of puppies	Be patient and prepared to travel in search of a puppy
Grooming	Sheds heavily in spring and fall	Brush and comb daily
Common health issues	Progressive Retinal Atrophy (PRA); portosystemic shunt, adversely affecting blood circulation through the liver; generally one of the healthiest of the small breeds	Ensure breeding stock has been screened for PRA

History

The ancestry of the Tibetan Spaniel extends back over 3,000 years, based on representations of such dogs in early Asiatic art. They were commonly kept at monasteries, warning the monks of the approach of any visitors and also apparently turning the prayer wheels that the monks used. As a result, the breed became known for a time in the West as the Tibetan Prayer Dog. Its closest relationship with other smaller breeds originating in this part of the world may be with the Pekingese (see page 70), and indeed, it was also called the Pekingese Spaniel for a period. When first discovered by Western explorers visiting Tibet during the late 1800s, the dog was far more variable in appearance than it is today. Some individuals were smaller in size, while others— particularly those originating closest to China—had much shorter muzzles, making them more like Pekingese dogs.

Past influences

As a result of being kept over the course of many centuries in closed monastic communities, Tibetan Spaniels instinctively develop a strong bond with people around them, but they are far less inclined to accept strangers. Training presents no particular problems, and their coat simply needs to be brushed and combed regularly to maintain its good looks. This is not a breed that requires clipping or regular trips to a grooming parlor. The coats of male Tibetan Spaniels are usually more profuse than those of females.

Tibetan tail
The tail is set high and is well covered with longer hair, which falls over the body

Coat color
Any color, including white, or any combination is recognized for show purposes

Muzzle feature
The face has a noticeable feature, reflecting the change in angle from the top of the skull to the muzzle

6. Shetland Sheepdog

The Shetland Sheepdog, developed in the Shetland Islands off Scotland's northwest coast, was originally kept on farms. It has since adapted very well to a purely domestic existence, however, proving to be an easily trained and loyal canine companion.

Full mane
The frill and mane of hair are especially evident in the male dogs

Long face
The face tapers slightly along its length from the ears to the nose

Sheltie colors
Colors can be black, blue merle, and sable (ranging from golden to mahogany)—all with white areas

History

The Sheltie, as this breed is affectionately known, is effectively a scaled-down version of the Rough Collie. It has a versatile and adaptable nature, and frequently watched over the native sheep in the fields of the Shetland Islands, often without supervision. Although the risk of predation was relatively small compared with the risk to the crops on the mainland, these herding dogs had an additional task of protecting the crops from being eaten by the sheep. The crops were grown in unfenced fields, and so Shelties would bark loudly to deter incursions by sheep into these areas. Visiting seamen would buy puppies to take home, and demand rapidly increased during the early 20th century.

Changing roles

The Sheltie began to decline on its native islands, as the small farms there were amalgamated and reorganized. But luckily, its popularity started to increase farther afield, both as a show dog and companion. The Sheltie is a very suitable choice for a family with older children, or people on their own, being affectionate and easily trained; however, an owner should be prepared to brush the coat regularly. As a working dog, the Sheltie instinctively responds well to training, and its natural intelligence adds to its appeal as a companion. It must have plenty of exercise and can display a tendency to bark repeatedly.

CANINE CHARACTERISTICS		NOTES
Personality	Loyal and protective	
Size	Height: 13–16 in. (33–41 cm) Weight: 14–16 lb (6.3–7.2 kg)	Do not overfeed the dog, as it has a healthy appetite and can become overweight
Exercise	Needs lots of exercise, as the breed is descended from working stock; may run around you in circles, barking on occasion—this is an attempt to herd you!	Exercise at least once a day with a long walk or jog; keep away from livestock, as it may want to chase them
At home	Needs plenty of space; good guardian	
Behavior	Playful and responsive	
Grooming	Needs more intensive coat care when shedding in spring and fall	Brush regularly—this is essential for the coat
Common health issues	Eye disorders, including Collie Eye Anomaly (CEA)	Ensure breeding stock has been screened for eye disorders

7. Keeshond

The name of these energetic Dutch Barge Dogs is pronounced *kayz-hawnd*, with the plural form being Keeshonden. They are intelligent and responsive dogs, and also often get along well with cats. They have a distinctive, attractive coat.

Color combinations
Coloration is a variable combination of cream, gray, and black

Facial features
The Keeshond has a medium-length muzzle, which is proportionate to the skull. "Spectacles" extend around the eyes

Pale ruff
The ruff between the front legs is paler in color than the body

History

The Keeshond is one of the smaller members of the spitz group, characterized by its foxlike appearance. It has raised, pointed ears, a ruff of longer fur around the face, and a well-plumed tail curving forward over the back. The breed is named after a key figure in Dutch history, Kees de Gyselaer, who was the leader of the Dutch Patriot Party in the late 1700s. His own dog was also called Kees, but after his defeat, the breed became very scarce, as people did not wish to be associated with such an overt symbol of the former resistance movement. It took nearly a century for these native Dutch dogs to become popular again, and today, they can occasionally be seen on barges traveling on the country's canal network. When Keeshonden arrived in England during the early 20th century, they were known as Dutch Barge Dogs.

Past and present

Having evolved to live within the confines of a barge, this breed is quite happy in homes where space is at a premium. Its size also means that it will not take over in this type of environment. Another trait of the breed, tracing back to its working past, is its role as a watchdog, with these dogs being very alert to the approach of visitors. Keeshonden can be rather noisy as a result, and need to be trained when not to bark.

CANINE CHARACTERISTICS		NOTES
Personality	Attentive and very friendly toward its owners; reserved and watchful in the presence of strangers	Train not to bark unnecessarily
Size	Height: 17–18 in. (43–46 cm) Weight: 55–66 lb (25–30 kg)	
Exercise	Needs plenty of exercise	Provide the opportunity to explore regularly off the leash
At home	Relaxed and playful	
Behavior	Alert and intelligent nature; often gets along well with cats	
Grooming	Male dogs have a more profuse ruff of hair; weather-resistant coat	Brush and comb regularly—this is essential, especially when shedding
Common health issues	Possible heart defects; epilepsy	Ensure a new puppy has a veterinary examination to reveal any heart problems

8. Cocker Spaniel

Two slightly different breeds of Cocker Spaniel now exist, reflecting their origins as working gundogs. The traditional form is the English Cocker Spaniel, while the newcomer is the American Cocker Spaniel, which is now often seen outside the U.S.

AT A GLANCE

- Eager to be involved in family life
- Very friendly
- Eager to learn
- Affectionate
- Grooming is essential
- Active nature

History

The Cocker Spaniel was recognizable in its own right by the 1800s, having been bred from the larger Land Spaniel, which ultimately became the Springer Spaniel. Crossings with the English Toy Spaniel (see page 19) also contributed to its ancestry. It acquired its name from its quarry, which was traditionally woodcock, moorcock (red grouse), and heathcock (black grouse). Its purpose was to flush these birds from undergrowth and also to act as a retriever. The division that now exists between English and American Cocker Spaniels started to become apparent during the 1930s. Show stock in the U.S. became typified by its smaller size and more profuse coat. The muzzle of the American breed is also shorter, and the top of the head is more rounded in shape. This clear division between the two strains was then formalized by the American Kennel Club (AKC) in 1946, when the American breed was recognized as separate from the English breed.

Making a choice

In terms of temperament, there is really no significant difference between the breeds, each of which is known simply as "the" Cocker Spaniel in its homeland. However, the care of the smaller American Cocker is more demanding, thanks to its longer coat. Few breeds are more exuberant or easily taught than Cocker Spaniels, but they do need plenty of exercise if they are not to become bored around the home. Coat care is also important.

CANINE CHARACTERISTICS		NOTES
Personality	Enthusiastic, lively	Train not to be too excitable
Size	American Height: 14–15 in. (36–38 cm) Weight: 24–28 lb (11–13 kg) English Height: 15–17 in. (38–43 cm) Weight: 26–34 lb (12–15.5 kg)	
Exercise	Energetic; loves to explore and play	Exercise daily and allow time for play in the yard
At home	Small size means it integrates well; likes to be outdoors exploring in the yard	
Behavior	Intelligent nature aids training—this breed is eager to please!	
Grooming	American Cocker Spaniel needs more grooming than its English relative	Groom daily and watch for pieces of twig, etc., which may become caught in the coat after a walk outdoors
Common health issues	Eye and ear problems, especially in American Cocker Spaniels; possible Rage Syndrome linked with solid-colored English Cockers in some bloodlines, resulting in sudden displays of aggression	Only buy from a dependable breeder

Feathered ears
The Cocker Spaniel's long, well-feathered ears are set on the head alongside the lower part of the eye

Cocker Spaniel coat
Coloration can vary from pale cream to black, often with tan points or white areas

Strong hindquarters
Powerful hindquarters allow the spaniel to run well

9. Whippet

The athletic nature of the Whippet dictates that these hounds must have a daily run off the leash. This breed is a sprinter and is the fastest of all hounds (based on its size). It is also very affectionate and makes a delightful companion.

AT A GLANCE
- Friendly nature
- Soft, sleek coat
- No noticeable "doggy odor"
- Very elegant appearance
- Can be reserved with strangers

History

Developed in northeastern England, the Whippet has been dubbed the "poor man's racehorse." These dogs used to compete against each other, being raced along alleyways. Out in the fields, their pace enabled them to catch rabbits and hares. The breed's precise origins are unclear, but crossings involving terriers, including the Bedlington (see page 109), which arose in the same area, probably contributed to its ancestry. Manchester Terriers may have played a part as well, along with both Greyhounds (see page 52) and Italian Greyhounds (see page 48). Whippet racing as a sport became popular after the breed was taken to the U.S. in the 1800s. Originally, this began in Massachusetts, and then became popular around Baltimore in Maryland.

Temperament

Although the Whippet may simply appear as a scaled-down version of the Greyhound, these breeds are different in terms of their personalities. Probably as a result of its part-terrier ancestry, the Whippet is more vocal and has plenty of stamina. It also has a more assertive personality and a decidedly playful side, although in common with other sight hounds, the Whippet is likely to be reserved toward strangers. It is gentle by nature, but it must be kept away from vulnerable household pets, such as rabbits. Whippets are not greedy dogs in terms of their feeding habits, but they will use the height of their long bodies to stand up and steal food left within their reach on counters or table surfaces.

Whippet colors
The Whippet can be bred in any color but black, blue, and bicolors

Broad thighs
The muscular, broad thighs give propulsive power and good acceleration

Long tail
The tapering tail hangs low and curves up at the tip

Powerful feet
The feet have well-arched toes and strong nails

CANINE CHARACTERISTICS		NOTES
Personality	Gentle, affectionate; shy with those it does not know	
Size	Height: 18–22 in. (46–56 cm) Weight: about 28 lb (13 kg)	
Exercise	Needs the opportunity to run off the leash, preferably in open country; will chase wild animals	Take care around vehicles when the dog is off the leash
At home	Likes human company	Keep out of cold, wet weather
Behavior	Learns quickly, and enjoys running after a ball	Train a puppy to come to you, lessening the likelihood it will run off when out in later life
Grooming	Hair on the underparts may become thin, especially during molting periods; requires minimal grooming	Use a hound glove to give the coat a good gloss
Common health issues	Thyroid and heart problems	

10. English Toy Spaniel

Although a loyal companion, this breed's popularity has faded significantly in recent times as a direct result of competition from the Cavalier King Charles Spaniel, which is a modern recreation intended to capture the English Toy Spaniel's original appearance.

AT A GLANCE
- Suitable for a home with children
- Easy-going nature
- Attractive color choice
- Tolerant
- Adapts to city life
- Responsive

History

The English Toy Spaniel is better known in its homeland as the King Charles Spaniel, reflecting the fact that it was a favorite of King Charles II. It is unclear whether he brought some of these spaniels back in 1660 after being exiled in Europe, but the original strain was predominantly black in color, with tan markings. The English Toy Spaniel comes in four colors—black with tan markings, which is the Black and Tan, white, black, and tan markings, which is the tricolored Prince Charles, the red and white Blenheim, and the solid red Ruby. At one time, these were considered the colors of distinct breeds. Contemporary portraits of the English Toy Spaniel show a dog that, in the late 1600s, had a relatively long nose, but its appearance changed significantly during the 1800s. This resulted in the development of the much flatter face and somewhat smaller body, which is typical of the English Toy Spaniel.

At home

English Toy Spaniels are very affectionate dogs, and are an excellent choice for a home with younger children, because of their relatively tolerant dispositions. These spaniels are playful, too. They do not require a large amount of exercise, although regular checks are essential to monitor their weight, because these toy dogs are susceptible to obesity. The breed will settle well within urban environments, and its training is straightforward.

CANINE CHARACTERISTICS		NOTES
Personality	Can become rather dominant by nature if spoiled; highly affectionate and instinctively friendly	Avoid spoiling and offering treats
Size	Height: 10 in. (25 cm) Weight: 9–12 lb (4–5.4 kg)	Do not overfeed the dog, as it may become overweight
Exercise	Needs relatively short walks; not a particularly athletic breed	Avoid exercise in the hottest part of the day
At home	Quite happy indoors if taken out twice daily	Provide the opportunity for the dog to go to the toilet at other times
Behavior	Relatively quiet; gets along well with other dogs	
Grooming	Brushing and combing required	Wipe the inside of the ears and any tear staining with damp cotton balls
Common health issues	Heart disease; patellar luxation, affecting the hind limbs; snoring and snuffling in older dogs due to their facial shape	Patellar luxation may need corrective surgery

Compact body
The short, compact body appears square in profile with a broad back

Long hairs
The coat has heavy fringing of hair evident on the body, ears, and chest

Low tail
The tail is set low. Puppies may occasionally be born with a corkscrew tail

Dog types for a family with younger children or teenagers; people who want to compete with their dogs; and would-be owners who enjoy the countryside.

German Shorthaired Pointer

Golden Retriever

Family-friendly Dogs

An enthusiastic nature and a willingness to join in with family activities are characteristics of the members of this section. They are robust, too, with plenty of energy in most cases. The Bull Terrier, for example, has great stamina, and will enjoy playing for long periods, but you still need to choose carefully from this list, taking into account the age of your youngest child.

The Boxer is probably too lively for a home with toddlers, so select a small breed, such as the Shih Tzu or Miniature Schnauzer, which will not be inclined to jump up. If you are interested in competing with your dog, then the Bearded Collie would be ideal, both as a companion and a participant in either obedience or agility competitions.

Just because these breeds are well suited to family living, however, does not mean that their training is straightforward in all cases. There are gundogs here, such as the German Shorthaired Pointer and Golden Retriever, which are very responsive in this respect. Others, such as the Beagle and Hamiltonstövare, have much more wayward dispositions in spite of very friendly natures, so it is important to persevere.

Miniature Schnauzer

1. Beagle

This lively scent hound breed makes a great family companion, being full of energy and almost always eager to play. Beagles are very good-tempered as a general rule, and their size is not intimidating for younger members of the family.

History

These hounds were bred to hunt hares, pursuing them in packs accompanied by hunt followers on foot. Beagles are the smallest of the native British hound breeds, as reflected in their name, which is thought to derive from *breeds*, a Gaelic word meaning "small." A particularly dwarf form, known as the Pocket Beagle, existed for a period, becoming particularly popular in the 1600s, although this bloodline died out during the late 1800s. Beagles were first taken to the U.S. in 1876, and started to be seen regularly at shows from the mid-1880s onward. They have since become very popular as pet dogs. The patterning of each hound is slightly different, allowing them to be distinguished easily even when in a pack.

Determination

The Beagle's broad nostrils enable it to detect and follow a trail with great determination, which can be the downside of choosing this breed. Beagles can be very reluctant to stop once they pick up a scent. It is therefore very important to concentrate on training your Beagle to return to you when called. Another aspect of the Beagle's care that needs to be watched is its large appetite, as it will gorge itself on food if allowed to do so, and can soon become overweight as a result. Avoid leaving shopping bags on the floor, as these are likely to be raided for any edible contents.

Strong back
The short, strong back with well-sprung ribs affords good lung capacity

Typical color
Color is typically either tricolored or lemon and white, with individual patterning

Legs and feet
The straight forelegs with round, firm feet provide good grip when running

CANINE CHARACTERISTICS		NOTES
Personality	Exuberant, friendly, also a glutton	Watch food intake
Size	Height: up to 13 in. (33 cm) and from 13–15 in. (33–38 cm) Weight: 18–30 lb (8–14 kg)	Bitches are usually slightly shorter; the two height classes are regarded as different varieties
Exercise	Energetic; can be wayward off the leash	Exercise with a good daily run
At home	Can be an escape artist	Ensure gates and fencing are secure
Behavior	Obedience training can be problematic	
Grooming	Short coat needs little attention	Use a hound glove to give the coat a good gloss
Common health issues	Epilepsy; hip dysplasia; thyroid disorders	Ensure breeding stock has been screened for hip dysplasia

2. Bearded Collie

This is not a breed for city dwellers or those who dislike walking, but in rural surroundings, with plenty of opportunities to exercise, the Bearded Collie can make an ideal companion, being especially suitable for a home with energetic teenagers.

AT A GLANCE

- Exuberant
- Affectionate
- Demanding coat care
- Thrives in the countryside
- Training is essential
- Needs plenty of exercise

History

Its early origins are unclear, but the Bearded Collie may be related to the Polish Lowland Sheepdog, which was known in Scotland as far back as the 1500s. The extinct Old Welsh Gray Sheepdog could have made a contribution to the ancestral bloodline of these dogs, too. Their main task was to move stock, particularly cattle, in the days before mechanized transport. The breed's survival today is due almost entirely to the devotion of an enthusiast named Mrs. Gwendoline Willison, who obtained a pair of these nearly extinct sheepdogs in 1944. She developed the "Beardie," as it is affectionately known, at her Bothkennar Kennels in Buckinghamshire, England. Within 15 years, the breed had been taken to the U.S., where it soon became popular, and its future is now secure.

Starting out with a Beardie

Training a young Bearded Collie will take time, to ensure that it will develop into a responsive adult. Young individuals particularly can be very exuberant, and so are not ideally suited to a home alongside toddlers. These collies benefit from long walks, but do not overexercise young puppies. As a breed developed to work outdoors, the Beardie has a soft, insulating undercoat and a longer, weather-resistant top coat. Be prepared to devote plenty of time to grooming. It is quite normal for the coat coloration to lighten at maturity.

Expressive face
The Bearded Collie's intelligent nature is reflected by its expression, with the eyes being oval

Collie color
Color is of no significance. It can be solid, bicolored, tricolored, merle, or sable

Oval feet
The feet are oval shaped with arched toes, plus a good covering of hair

CANINE CHARACTERISTICS		NOTES
Personality	Self-confident; lively	
Size	Height: 20–22 in. (51–56 cm) Weight: 40–60 lb (18–27 kg)	
Exercise	Needs lengthy walks	Keep away from livestock, as it may want to chase them
At home	Energetic, and will not settle if given insufficient exercise; needs a large yard	Develop a routine for taking the dog out
Behavior	Puppies are slow to grow up compared with other breeds; bitches are reputedly harder to train	Train to prevent boisterous behavior
Grooming	Grooming is essential	Brush regularly to prevent coat from becoming matted
Common health issues	Susceptible to Addison's Disease, affecting the adrenal glands, which can be fatal if undetected	Watch for digestive upsets, which can be an indicator of the problem

3. Boxer

The Boxer's highly playful nature explains its name. These dogs will often jump up and wrestle each other, supporting themselves on their hind legs. They have a genuine enthusiasm for life, and can form a strong bond with older children particularly.

History

The Boxer is descended from ancient Mastiff stock, and may share a close relationship with the French Dogue de Bordeaux (see page 87). However, its recent development into the breed of today began in Germany during the mid-1800s. Crossings involving hound stock and the older, long-legged form of the English Bulldog may underlie its appearance. The Boxer's typical coat is bicolored, with white areas usually evident on the muzzle, chest, and feet. It is an intelligent breed, which served as a messenger dog in the trenches of the First World War, and today, Boxers carry out a wide range of tasks, including acting as guide dogs and herding stock.

Take care!

The Boxer is not a breed that will thrive in hot climates. It is susceptible to heatstroke, as is the case of other breeds that have short muzzles. Dogs lose heat by panting and cooling air through their nostrils, rather than sweating as we do. Boxers, with their particularly lively natures, should therefore not be exercised around midday, when the sun is at its hottest. They are also vulnerable to skin cancers, particularly in the case of white Boxers. White Boxers are not accepted for show purposes. As companions, Boxers are very loyal, but if challenged, they are unlikely to back down, so they need to be well trained to avoid conflicts.

Long forelegs
The Boxer's long, straight forelegs end in compact feet with well-arched toes

High-set ears
The high-set ears are positioned on the uppermost points of the skull

Boxer coat
The coat can be fawn or brindle. White markings must not exceed a third of the coat's area

AT A GLANCE

- Generally good with children
- Very lively nature
- Surprisingly agile
- Loves to play
- Easy-care coat
- Does not age well

CANINE CHARACTERISTICS		NOTES
Personality	Loyal, friendly; wary of strangers	Keep an eye on the dog around other people
Size	Height: 22–25 in. (56–64 cm) Weight: 66–70 lb (30–32 kg)	
Exercise	Needs a good run every day	Take care around other dogs, as it may seek to play with dogs it meets
At home	Displays a tendency to jump up to get attention	Try to reduce jumping up behavior
Behavior	Lively and responsive; intelligent	Be patient, as it can be easily distracted during training
Grooming	Grooming is very straightforward, thanks to the short coat	Groom when necessary
Common health issues	Highly susceptible to neoplasia; white Boxers are likely to be afflicted by deafness; heart problems; cancers of all types are common	

4. Miniature Schnauzer

This scaled-down version of the Giant Schnauzer (see page 126) makes a lively companion and settles well in the home, being just as happy playing with older children as going for a walk in a local park with the children's grandparents. It is the ideal breed for young and old alike.

History

Schnauzers originated in Germany, and the Miniature was originally bred selectively from the smallest individuals present in the litters of its larger relative. This process was started in Frankfurt by two breeders named Georg Riehl and Heinrich Schott. They also used another German breed, the Affenpinscher (see page 78), to complete the miniaturization process, resulting in the breed of today. It is possible that some other small breeds, such as the Pomeranian (see page 73), may have played a part, too, although there is no clear evidence to this effect. The Miniature Schnauzer was established by the late 1880s.

The coat

A particularly desirable feature of the Miniature Schnauzer for the house-proud is the fact that these dogs do not shed their hair like most breeds. Instead, their coat can be stripped either by hand, which is described as "finger stripping," or plucked by using a stripping knife, to keep it looking neat—this is a skilled task. An alternative option for pet dogs is for their coats to be clipped, but this will soften the coat. The most distinctive color variety is the so-called "pepper-and-salt" form, whose appearance results from alternating light and dark bands on the individual hairs forming the top coat. If a Miniature Schnauzer is clipped rather than stripped, however, this then causes the full effect of the banding to be lost.

High tail
The tail is set high and is carried erect, with the hocks extending out behind the body

Strong thighs
The thighs are well muscled and slanting

Catlike feet
The feet resemble those of a cat, being short and rounded with black pads

CANINE CHARACTERISTICS		NOTES
Personality	Alert, friendly demeanor	
Size	Height: 12–14 in. (30–36 cm) Weight: 13–15 lb (6–7 kg)	
Exercise	Not a great athlete; prefers to walk rather than race around	Exercise by throwing a ball for the dog to chase
At home	Small size is suitable for most homes; good watchdog	
Behavior	Relatively tolerant of other dogs; may not get along well with cats; will hunt any rats	Train not to be territorial, which is in its nature
Grooming	Nonshedding coat, but it requires some attention	Clip or strip the coat to keep it neat
Common health issues	Narrowing of the pulmonary artery, a congenital problem, indicated by a lack of energy and breathlessness	This condition may be corrected by surgery

5. German Shorthaired Pointer

This breed of gundog thrives in rural surroundings, with its stamina and general enthusiasm for life meaning it should prove to be an excellent choice for a family with older children. As with other pointers, its training is relatively straightforward.

History

The origins of the German Shorthaired Pointer, or "GSP," can be traced back to the 1600s. The breed was originally created by crossings between the rather slow Spanish Pointer and German bird dogs. With the aim of developing the breed into a more versatile working companion, crosses with the lighter and faster English Pointer took place in the 1800s. Standardization of the emerging breed gained momentum in 1870 with the foundation of a stud book for the Kurzhaar, as the breed is named in its homeland.

Working abilities

This breed's eagerness to work makes it a devoted companion. German Shorthaired Pointers learn rapidly. They enjoy country walks, where they will display their pointing skills readily, adopting the characteristic "frozen" stance to indicate the presence of game. They will also enjoy retrieving toys thrown for them. Friendly and enthusiastic, German Shorthaired Pointers form a close bond with members of the family. Liver and white examples of the breed have a highly individual appearance, although it is also possible to obtain liver-colored dogs.

Broad ears
The ears are broad in shape and positioned high on the head, lying flat

AT A GLANCE
- Versatile gundog
- Relatively large breed
- Not aggressive
- Easy-care coat
- Responsive to people
- Energetic
- Generally obedient

Liver colored
Coloration can be solid liver or any combination of liver and white

CANINE CHARACTERISTICS		NOTES
Personality	Intelligent, cooperative, and sensitive	
Size	Height: 21–25 in. (53–64 cm) Weight: 45–70 lb (20.4–32 kg)	Dogs can be quite a bit heavier than bitches
Exercise	High energy levels; possesses great stamina; needs to be off the leash at times	Do not overexercise puppies, as this can cause long-term joint problems
At home	Thrives on being allowed to participate in family life	Ensure gates and fencing are secure—this breed can jump well over fences and may disappear if bored
Behavior	Very responsive to training; likely to be destructive if bored	Try to involve all family members in training to encourage the dog to build a bond with each individual
Grooming	Grooming is straightforward, thanks to the smooth coat	Brush occasionally
Common health issues	Hip dysplasia, causing lameness	Ensure breeding stock has been screened for hip dysplasia

Compact feet
The feet vary from being rounded to spoon shaped, with well-arched toes

6. Petit Basset Griffon Vendéen

This breed is unsurprisingly often better known by its initials "PBGV," but its name is pronounced *Puh-TEE Bah-SAY Gree-FOHN VON-day-uhn*. Being a natural extrovert by nature, the PBGV is becoming increasingly appreciated as a companion breed.

History

Many of the world's breeds of hound were created in France, including the PBGV. This is a member of the Griffon Vendéen group, which consists of four distinctive breeds, distinguished by differences in their height. There are two Basset forms, yet whereas the PBGV is now very popular, its slightly larger cousin, known as the Grand Basset Griffon Vendéen, is virtually unknown outside its homeland. "Basset" refers to its short legs, with "griffon" describing its rough coat. The PBGV and its relatives were bred in the Vendée region of France, with the two basset forms being split as recently as 1950. They were first seen in Britain in 1969, and are now widely kept in many countries.

The popularity of the PBGV

These bassets make friendly, lively companions, proving to be great characters. They are always eager to be involved in family life, and will thrive on plenty of exercise. Their rough, wiry coat is easily maintained, having been developed to give them good protection from sharp vegetation when they are out running. A simple brushing will suffice to remove mud from the coat once it has dried. The PBGV's coat is not normally trimmed. Packs are traditionally kept to hunt rabbits and hares, so do not be surprised if your PBGV takes off in pursuit of any such creatures that it spots when out for a walk in the countryside.

CANINE CHARACTERISTICS		NOTES
Personality	Expressive, independent nature; can be stubborn on occasion; friendly and social, reflecting its pack hound ancestry	Take care with training, which can be problematic due to its stubborn nature
Size	Height: 13–15 in. (33–38 cm) Weight: 31–40 lb (14–18 kg)	
Exercise	Very energetic, needs a run off the leash every day	Ensure the dog gets enough exercise, as boredom will trigger destructive behavior
At home	May be too lively alongside young children	Keep an eye on the dog around small children and animals
Behavior	Not likely to have disagreements with other dogs when out	
Grooming	Minimal grooming required; tousled coat, harsh in texture and double-layered	Brush when necessary
Common health issues	Epilepsy; hypothyroidism; ear infections; can be susceptible to skin problems	

Low-set ears
The ears are set low and are covered in long hair, being oval in shape at their tips

Neck and back
The PBGV has a long, strong neck with a straight back from the withers to the croup

Solid legs
The PBGV's strong forelegs have a solid, well-boned appearance

AT A GLANCE
- Friendly nature
- Large personality
- Lively breed
- Gets along well with children
- Small size
- Needs plenty of exercise

7. Bull Terrier

This is a very distinctive breed, with its broad, egg-shaped head. Bull Terriers have a determined character to match their stocky, well-muscled frame. They are very loyal, but not particularly friendly toward other dogs, particularly other Bull Terriers.

AT A GLANCE

- Powerful
- Playful
- Determined
- Not friendly toward other dogs
- Easily groomed
- Very determined breed

Distinctive head
The distinctive head curves down from the forehead to the nose

Solid neck
The Bull Terrier has a very powerful, arched, long neck with no sign of free skin

Powerful frame
Exceedingly muscular shoulders and a short yet strong back form the terrier's frame

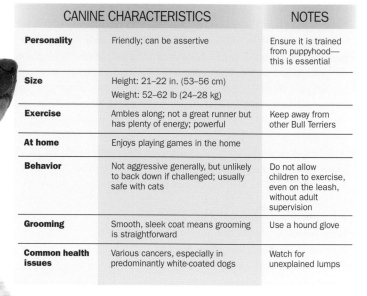

CANINE CHARACTERISTICS		NOTES
Personality	Friendly; can be assertive	Ensure it is trained from puppyhood—this is essential
Size	Height: 21–22 in. (53–56 cm) Weight: 52–62 lb (24–28 kg)	
Exercise	Ambles along; not a great runner but has plenty of energy; powerful	Keep away from other Bull Terriers
At home	Enjoys playing games in the home	
Behavior	Not aggressive generally, but unlikely to back down if challenged; usually safe with cats	Do not allow children to exercise, even on the leash, without adult supervision
Grooming	Smooth, sleek coat means grooming is straightforward	Use a hound glove
Common health issues	Various cancers, especially in predominantly white-coated dogs	Watch for unexplained lumps

History

This breed was originally created as a fighting dog in the 1800s, being pitted against others of its kind. It was bred from crosses between Black and Tan Terriers and old-style Bulldogs, which were taller and more athletic than the breed of today. The white coat, sometimes broken with black patches, which is quite common in the breed today, derives from crosses with Dalmatian (see page 95) stock, carried out in the 1850s to contribute to the Bull Terrier's stamina. White English Terriers, which no longer exist, also contributed to its ancestry. As the era of dogfighting drew to a close, the Bull Terrier became popular in the show ring.

Homes with teenagers

The Bull Terrier is most suitable as a pet for families with teenagers. This is mainly because this breed is very powerful, and its strength means that an adult Bull Terrier can be difficult for younger children to control if the dog starts to pull on the leash. Neutering is recommended to reduce any lingering aggressive instincts toward other dogs, while early socialization and firm training from an early age will help to ensure that a puppy develops into a well-adjusted and friendly older dog. The Bull Terrier has a very playful side to its nature, but be prepared to seek out strong toys as its powerful jaws enable it to destroy them easily.

8. Shih Tzu

The Shih Tzu's unusual name literally means Lion Dog, an image that is reinforced by the fact that the traditional color of the breed was golden–yellow. It was created purely as a companion dog, rather than being kept for working purposes.

AT A GLANCE

- Ideal urban companion
- Low exercise requirement
- Friendly
- Patient nature
- Needs plenty of grooming

History

The origins of the Shih Tzu, whose name should be pronounced *sher-zer*, lie in Imperial China. The Dalai Lama, who ruled Tibet, presented the Emperor of China with Lhasa Apso dogs (see page 75), which were taken to the Forbidden City in what is now Beijing. These small dogs then mated with the Pekingese (see page 70), which was resident there, and the Shih Tzu ultimately arose from such crosses more than 400 years ago. It was not seen in the West until the 1930s, and was taken to the U.S. for the first time some 30 years later. The Shih Tzu's popularity has continued to grow significantly since then.

Urban living

The Shih Tzu is a very determined breed, with a confident and extroverted demeanor. In spite of its small size, it is a dog with a real personality, and, particularly if acquired as a puppy, will prove very responsive toward its owners, forming a strong bond with them. This is probably because Shih Tzus have always lived alongside people, and so, being a true companion breed, they are well suited to being family pets. They will thrive in urban areas, where keeping a larger breed would simply not be a practical proposition. The only potential drawback to keeping a Shih Tzu is the amount of time that needs to be devoted to grooming the breed's profuse coat to prevent it from becoming tangled. The hair on the head is traditionally tied up.

CANINE CHARACTERISTICS		NOTES
Personality	Friendly and playful, in spite of sometimes having a rather reserved demeanor; watchful with strangers; affectionate	
Size	Height: 8–11 in. (20–28 cm) Weight: 9–16 lb (4–7.2 kg)	Mid-range in size is preferable
Exercise	Happy trotting around a park each day; not athletic, but likes exploring when out for a walk	Exercise daily and allow the opportunity to explore
At home	Suitable for apartment living; often likes to look out of the window	Spend time grooming to build a bond
Behavior	Can be fearless, and even climbs readily; sometimes rather assertive by nature; will seek out its owner's company	Train not to be too assertive
Grooming	Grooming takes time, as the coat is dense	Tie hair on the top of the head in a topknot if necessary
Common health issues	Congenital problems affecting the kidneys and the blood clotting system	Watch for urinary abnormalities and blood blisters

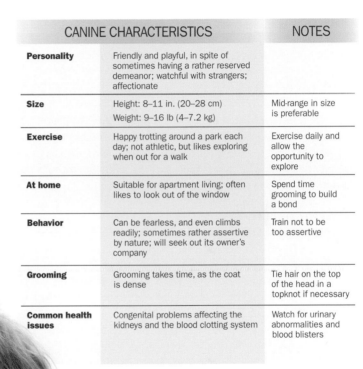

Prominent eyes
The prominent eyes are well spaced apart and are very dark in color

Puppy coats
The puppies' coats are less profuse than those of the adults

Shih Tzu colors
All colors are officially recognized, and patterning created by color combinations is common

9. Golden Retriever

The Golden Retriever is one of relatively few breeds that is defined by its coloration. Created as a gundog to work closely with people, members of this breed are instinctively friendly, and will settle very well in a family environment.

AT A GLANCE
- Attractive, beautiful appearance
- Confident companion
- Very responsive
- Gentle nature
- Eager to enter water
- Friendly

History

The origins of the Golden Retriever are rather mysterious. What is certain is that the breed was created on the Scottish estate of Lord Tweedmouth, whose aim was to create a retriever of waterfowl. He started on this quest in 1865, with the original cross being between a yellow Wavy-coated Retriever and a Tweed Water Spaniel, which produced four yellow puppies. An Irish Setter also made an early contribution to the bloodline. Although the breed was taken to North America—first to Canada in 1881 before being seen in the U.S. nine years later—it really did not start to attract a significant following until the 1930s.

Playful nature

Energetic and enthusiastic by nature, the Golden Retriever is an adaptable breed, but not one that adapts well to city life. These gundogs need space, where they can display the working side to their nature, playing with members of the family. One of their favorite games is chasing after a flying disk, which they can retrieve and bring back to be thrown again. Aside from reinforcing the bond between dog and owner, this type of activity also provides plenty of exercise for what is a very athletic breed. You will need to spend time brushing the double-layered coat, but this is not a particularly arduous or time-consuming task.

Golden color
Body color should be of an even shade— neither too light nor dark

Powerful hindquarters
The hindquarters are broad and powerful and the legs appear straight if viewed from behind

Compact feet
The medium-sized, round and compact feet have thick pads

CANINE CHARACTERISTICS		NOTES
Personality	Gentle; not suspicious of strangers; affectionate	
Size	Height: 21–24 in. (53–61 cm) Weight: 55–75 lb (25–34 kg)	Dogs are usually quite a bit heavier than bitches
Exercise	Needs a good daily walk, with the opportunity to explore off the leash	Avoid overexercising young dogs, especially taking them on marathon hikes
At home	Enjoys playing, and affectionate, too	Make time for play
Behavior	Will enter water readily if the opportunity presents itself; swims well; puppies can be boisterous; intelligent, as well as responsive	
Grooming	Combing as well as brushing required; bathing needed if the dog enters water; puppies, with their shorter coats, need less grooming than adults	Comb and brush regularly, and bathe when necessary
Common health issues	Susceptible to hip dysplasia; various eye problems	Ensure breeding stock that has been screened for hip dysplasia

10. Hamiltonstövare

This Scandinavian breed is unusual because, whereas most scent hounds pursue their quarry in packs, the Hamiltonstövare hunts on its own. It therefore develops a closer bond with its owner than many such breeds, and enjoys playing, especially chasing after balls.

History

This breed is named after its creator, Count Adolf Hamilton, who developed it during the 1880s. A wide variety of European hound breeds contributed to the Hamiltonstövare's ancestry, including Swiss and German hounds, as well as the English Foxhound, which it most closely resembles in appearance today. It is tricolored in appearance, with a relatively consistent pattern of markings. The black saddle area over the back contrasts with tan coloration elsewhere. There are also white areas on the face and chest, as well as the feet, with the tip of the tail also often being white, creating an attractive appearance.

Out and about

The Hamiltonstövare ranks among the most affectionate of the scent hounds, and this is another reason underlying the breed's increasing popularity outside its Swedish homeland. It is adaptable and settles well as a family pet, provided that it has lots of exercise, in view of its athletic disposition. A Hamiltonstövare will thrive in rural areas where it can be safely exercised off the leash each day. The only problem is training, because this breed generally pursues a trail single-mindedly, often ignoring entreaties to stop. There is no malice in this instinctive behavior, however, although it means that you will need to concentrate on the "stop, stay" aspects of training. These hounds are very genuine, having a natural enthusiasm for life, which adds to their appeal. Little time has to be devoted to grooming their short, sleek coats.

Wide head
The Hamiltonstövare has a long, relatively wide head with the ears set high and the eyes dark

Strong body
The back is strong and straight and the hindquarters are powerful

CANINE CHARACTERISTICS		NOTES
Personality	Lively	
Size	Height: 19–24 in. (48–61 cm) Weight: 50–60 lb (22.7–27 kg)	Dogs are usually slightly heavier than bitches
Exercise	Needs plenty of opportunities to run	Exercise daily off the leash
At home	Needs a large yard; not a breed that thrives in a small area	Ensure that the yard is secured and well fenced
Behavior	Enjoys relaxing and sleeping after being out for a run; not territorial, and usually happy around other dogs; will bay regularly, especially outdoors; active	Make time for play—it will love the opportunity to join in with games
Grooming	Grooming is straightforward, thanks to the sleek coat	Brush or use a hound glove to keep the coat neat
Common health issues	No widespread issues are recognized	

Tan and black
Tan and black coloration predominates with white largely confined to the body extremities

Dog types for people on their own; those eager to meet others who share their passion for dogs; those who appreciate a relaxed life; and city-dwellers, too.

Spinone Italiano

Good Mixers

Dogs of this type, which generally get along well with other members of their breed and other dogs, are an ideal choice if you are looking for a dog that can be exercised safely in an urban space, without becoming aggressive toward other dogs. Those such as the Havanese and the rare but increasingly popular Coton de Tulear are ideal for this role. Bred as companions, they lack the instinctive assertiveness of some other small breeds, including many terriers, and so are very unlikely to have an aggressive demeanor. This means that you can allow them to trot off the leash, without worrying that they may be aggressive.

Some of the other breeds in this section, such as the Scottish Deerhound, definitely do need more space, but, again, if you regularly go walking in the countryside, you can take your dog without being concerned that it may fight with others that it encounters. It is important that you allow a puppy included in this category to mix freely with other dogs, once it can go out safely with its vaccines completed. This should ensure that the young dog will grow up to be friendly and well socialized.

Cavalier King Charles Spaniel

1. Brittany

Although originally known as the Brittany Spaniel, the description of "Spaniel" was dropped, because in spite of its appearance, this French breed behaves more like a pointer. Its tail length may differ markedly between individuals, being a naturally variable characteristic.

AT A GLANCE
- Attractive coloration and appearance
- Good house dog
- Socialization is important
- Eager worker
- Lively nature

CANINE CHARACTERISTICS		NOTES
Personality	Affectionate, yet determined; gets along well with people	
Size	Height: 18–21 in. (46–53 cm) Weight: 30–40 lb (14–18 kg)	
Exercise	Needs plenty of opportunities to run; has masses of energy	Make time for lots of regular exercise
At home	Not suitable for urban life; often very active	Take the dog jogging with you—Brittanys make good jogging companions
Behavior	Responsive and learns quickly	Encourage socialization
Grooming	Brushing required; however, coat care is more straightforward than with most other spaniels	Brush regularly and check that the ears are clean
Common health issues	Some bloodlines can be afflicted by the blood-clotting disorder called hemophilia	Ensure breeding stock has been screened

History

A very versatile gundog, the Brittany was originally developed during the 1700s in the vicinity of the Argoat forests, in the area of France known as western Brittany. It will point, flush game, and retrieve, concentrating mainly on birds. There is now a slight divergence apparent between the appearance of the traditional French Brittany and the American form of the breed, which has become slightly larger. It is known in its homeland as the Épagneul Breton, and was first exhibited there in 1896.

Energetic companions

The Brittany is a breed well worth considering if you are interested in a smaller type of gundog. It is an energetic dog by nature though, and requires plenty of exercise, which means it is not suited to living in an urban environment. It can otherwise become bored and destructive, and will start misbehaving under these circumstances.

It is very important that Brittanys are well socialized from an early age, so that they will not be shy and withdrawn as they grow older. They will normally get along well with other dogs, as well as with members of their own breed. Training, whether as a working gundog or simply as a household companion, is quite straightforward, as Brittanys are very responsive. Keeping two Brittanys together means that they will play together for periods during the day, and this helps to use up some of their energy, although this is no substitute for a daily walk.

Broad hindquarters
Broad, powerful hindquarters, with well-bent stifle joints not turned outward

Hind feet reach
Hind feet should reach at least as far as the front paw footprints

Brittany colors
Coloration can be either orange or liver combined with white, with roan patterns being seen

Powerful feet
The powerful feet have arched toes and thick pads. The toes are not heavily feathered

2. Cavalier King Charles Spaniel

These delightful miniature spaniels have always been kept as companions, and are therefore well suited to domestic living. The traditional form is black and tan, but Blenheim (red and white), Prince Charles (tricolor), and Ruby (solid red) varieties also exist.

CANINE CHARACTERISTICS		NOTES
Personality	Tolerant; not aggressive; affectionate	
Size	Height: 12 in. (30 cm) Weight: 12–18 lb (5.4–8 kg)	Keep an eye on the dog's weight, as it is prone to obesity
Exercise	Needs modest exercise, happy with a walk around a park; not especially keen on running; prefers ambling	Take the dog for gentle strolls
At home	Settles well in the home; good with children, and a good family pet	
Behavior	Playful nature, but can be greedy with food; amenable with other dogs	Avoid food treats
Grooming	Frequent brushing and combing of the silky coat required	Brush, comb, and check the ears regularly
Common health issues	Hereditary heart problems; patellar luxation, affecting the kneecaps; syringomyelia, affecting the spinal cord close to the brain; some individuals suffer from a strange neurological syndrome, with the dog appearing to catch flies in its mouth	Patellar luxation may need corrective surgery

History

This breed is a modern recreation of the old style of English Toy Spaniel (better known in its homeland as the King Charles Spaniel), which was fashionable during the reign of King Charles II in the late 1600s. It was created during the 1920s, in response to a prize put forward by an American enthusiast named Roswell Eldridge, who was disappointed to find that the traditional long-faced form of this spaniel had died out during the Victorian era. This led ultimately to a situation where both long and short-faced examples were being shown together, when clearly they were becoming distinctive breeds. They were finally separated in 1945, and now the Cavalier is by far the more popular breed. Unfortunately, having been bred from a very narrow genetic base, bloodlines may be afflicted by a range of serious health disorders.

Ideal for city life

The gentle nature of these spaniels means that they not only make excellent household companions on their own, being ideal for a home with younger children, but they also live very well together. They are also social and friendly with other dogs that they meet when out walking. Their grooming needs are quite modest, and they do not require a lot of exercise, being quite happy to wander around a park each day. You must ensure that, particularly as they grow older, they do not put on weight as this can lead to a strain on the heart.

AT A GLANCE
- Instinctively friendly
- Settles well in the home
- Lives well with other dogs
- Modest exercise needs
- Susceptible to congenital health problems

High-set ears
The ears are set high on the head and tend to lie slightly forward when the dog is alert

Neck and chest
The relatively long neck extends to a moderately deep chest

Legs and feet
The straight legs are tucked under the dog, ending in compact feet with well-cushioned pads

3. Clumber Spaniel

The Clumber is one of the largest of the spaniels—it has a distinctive large head and a heavy body. It was among the original breeds that was recognized by the American Kennel Club (AKC) in 1883, although it has never been especially common.

AT A GLANCE
- Houndlike demeanor
- Social by nature
- Quiet temperament
- Tolerant and friendly
- Docile
- Unusual breed

CANINE CHARACTERISTICS		NOTES
Personality	Genuine, unflappable, determined, and instinctively friendly	
Size	Height: 20 in. (51 cm) Weight: 55–85 lb (25–38.5 kg)	
Exercise	Enjoys long walks and displays great stamina	Only choose this breed if you like long outdoor walks through the year
At home	Quiet by nature; not an effective watchdog	
Behavior	Loose lips mean that it sometimes dribbles; very social with other Clumber Spaniels and other dogs; rarely barks	Consider covering chairs to protect against the dribble
Grooming	Regular brushing of the coat is essential; the ears need checking, too	Inspect the coat for burrs or thorns if the dog has ventured into undergrowth
Common health issues	Ectropion, where the eyelids hang away from the eyes—this can lead to infection	This condition may need corrective surgery

History

The origins of the Clumber Spaniel may lie in France—its ancestors were reputedly given by the Duc de Noailles to the Duke of Newcastle in the late 1700s. The breed today bears the name of the duke's estate, which was located at Clumber Park, in the English county of Nottinghamshire. The breed became very fashionable among the English aristocracy, right up until the early part of the 20th century. It then went into decline, as faster field spaniels, such as the Cocker, became favored, but it has undergone something of a revival in recent years, particularly in show circles. There is a suggestion that the Basset Hound (see page 55) may have contributed to its development at some stage, as reflected by its relatively short-legged appearance.

Working together

The Clumber is also unusual for a spaniel in that it was originally worked in packs. These packs moved through the undergrowth, flushing out game birds. Even today, Clumber Spaniels may work like this in small groups, and unsurprisingly, given their ancestry, they get along well not only with their own kind, but also with other dogs. They are quiet and not aggressive by nature, with a reputation for working in a rather slow, methodical manner. Although the Clumber ranks as one of the rarer spaniel breeds, it is well worth seeking out as a companion, and is an ideal choice if you live in the country and are searching for a friendly, intelligent dog, or pair of dogs.

Head markings
White with lemon or orange markings are especially evident on the head

Body feathering
Some feathering is apparent on the underside of the body

Large head
The head is very large, with low-set, triangular-shaped ears

4. Spinone Italiano

These rough-coated Italian gundogs are descended from an ancient hunting background, but over recent years, they have started to become much more widely kept simply as pets. They have a very distinctive ambling gait, which adds to their appeal.

AT A GLANCE
- Very expressive face
- Quiet nature
- Affectionate
- Talented worker
- Gets along well with both children and other dogs
- Accepts visitors readily

CANINE CHARACTERISTICS		NOTES
Personality	Loyal, determined; demands affection; not aggressive	
Size	Height: 22–27 in. (56–69 cm) Weight: 71–82 lb (32.2–37 kg)	Dogs tend to be taller and heavier than bitches
Exercise	Needs daily exercise, preferably in rural surroundings off the leash	Exercise daily, as lack of exercise results in boredom and destructive behavior
At home	Needs spacious surroundings; enjoys playing	Provide the opportunity for play in the yard
Behavior	Learns rapidly; versatile	Encourage socialization
Grooming	Tousled coat is characteristic of this breed, and little grooming is required; rough hair helps to protect it against injury outdoors	
Common health issues	Cerebellar ataxia, affecting part of the brain may lead to a strange gait; bloat	Do not exercise after feeding, as this can cause bloat

History

Dogs closely resembling the Spinone Italiano existed as far back as the 1200s, and possibly even earlier, although the breed's precise origins are not known. It is probably linked with the smooth-coated Segugio Italiano, and the French Barbet may also have played a part in its development. Although developed primarily as a pointer, the Spinone Italiano can also serve as a retriever. Its dense, shaggy coat gives it great protection when it ventures into areas of undergrowth, as do its pendulous ears. Although still kept as a working dog, this breed is also now being seen with increasing frequency in the show ring.

Living together

This is a breed that has a genial, easy-going nature, especially in home surroundings, and it works hard in the field. However, its stamina must be appreciated and accommodated for if you choose one of these dogs as a companion. Regular daily exercise is vital, and it can actually help in this respect if you keep a Spinone Italiano with another dog because they will play together. Another member of the same breed would be ideal, given the innate intelligence of these gundogs, as they will be well matched. Puppies must be adequately socialized in any case, because otherwise, they can prove to be nervous in later life. Training is not especially difficult, as these gundogs learn quickly, but consistency is very important in this regard.

Long head
The head is long with a highly distinctive profile, combined with an intelligent expression

Coat color
Colors include solid white, white and orange, and white and brown, with chestnut shades preferred

Large feet
The feet are large and rounded, with short, dense hair between the toes

5. Coton de Tulear

This toy-sized dog is an attractive breed with a very distinctive coat. It was once very scarce and on the verge of extinction. Although it has undergone a welcomed revival in recent years, you may still have to be patient when seeking a puppy.

CANINE CHARACTERISTICS		NOTES
Personality	Laid-back, gentle, and social; very friendly toward people	
Size	Height: 10–12 in. (25–30 cm) Weight: 12–15 lb (5.4–7 kg)	
Exercise	Happy just wandering around a park, meeting other dogs	Allow time for exploring
At home	Content within an urban environment; will live happily in small groups	
Behavior	Enjoys playing games; makes a relaxed companion; can make a talented retriever	Make time for play
Grooming	Fluffy coat requires considerable care	Groom daily and bathe regularly
Common health issues	Overgrown nails may be a problem; generally healthy	Keep an eye on the nails, which may need regular trimming

History

The origins of the Coton de Tulear trace back to the mid-1700s when French settlers brought small dogs of Bichon stock with them to Réunion Island in the Indian Ocean. The breed's ancestors are believed to have passed through the port of Tulear, located on the larger neighboring island of Madagascar, on their way to Réunion, which helps to explain its name. They may have been bred with native dogs there, although certainly the Bichon family resemblance remains very strong in the breed today. The Coton de Tulear remained isolated and essentially unknown until the mid-1900s, when several examples of the breed were finally brought to Europe. They remained unknown in the U.S. until 1974, but a few more of these unusual dogs have since been brought here direct from their native island.

Jealously guarded

"Coton" means "cotton," and describes the fluffy, white appearance of this breed, which is a characteristic of members of the Bichon group. The Coton de Tulear is intelligent, playful, and very social, having been kept in family groups for centuries. These dogs have never been kept for working purposes, which helps to explain why they make such ideal companions. In fact, they were so highly valued on Réunion that not only was it very difficult to obtain stock to take abroad, but also, even on the island, ownership of the breed was restricted to members of the ruling families.

Appealing eyes
The appearance of the eyes contributes significantly to the dog's appeal

Friendly features
The lively expression helps to characterize the personality of this friendly breed

Random patterns
The patterning is random, but colored areas are often present on the head

6. English Setter

The ancestors of this breed were the so-called "setting-spaniels." These dogs used to indicate the presence of game birds by "setting," which is the old English word for "sitting." Their long, broad nostrils help them to detect their quarry.

AT A GLANCE
- Beautiful, elegant appearance
- Responsive nature
- Gets along well with other dogs
- Individual markings
- Active nature

History

Both the English Springer and Water Spaniel, as well as the Spanish Pointer, contributed to the ancestry of the English Setter. In the early 1800s, there used to be numerous local varieties of English Setters, which were known under their regional names. Some, such as the Newcastle Setter, reflected the area of the country where they had been created, whereas others, such as the Llewellin strain, commemorated the name of the breeder responsible for them. Sir Edward Laverack is regarded as being largely responsible for evolving the English Setter into the breed of today, over the course of half a century. He obtained his first pair of these gundogs in 1825.

Space needed

These elegant dogs have an unmistakable flecked appearance, which is described as "belton." They are very attentive and responsive to training. As household companions, they get along well with others of their kind, and even other breeds of gundog, such as the Labrador Retriever (see page 11). The most important aspect of their care is the need to give them sufficient space to exercise. Otherwise, they are likely to become bored and destructive in domestic surroundings. A large yard in a rural location would be an ideal playground for a couple of these setters, from where they can be taken out into the countryside for daily walks. English Setters possess a calm temperament, which they probably inherited from the pointer input into their ancestry, and are affectionate by nature.

Solid neck
The English Setter has a long, elegant neck, which is both muscular and lean

Deep chest
The chest is deep with the brisket extending down to the level of the elbows

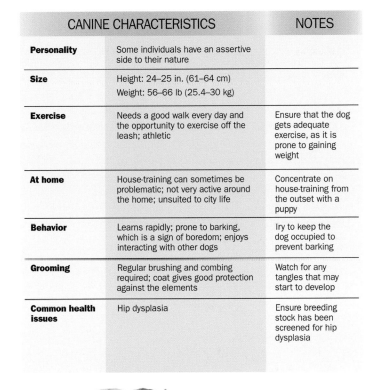

Straight tail
The tail joins at the level of the back, continuing in a straight line, tapering along its length

CANINE CHARACTERISTICS		NOTES
Personality	Some individuals have an assertive side to their nature	
Size	Height: 24–25 in. (61–64 cm) Weight: 56–66 lb (25.4–30 kg)	
Exercise	Needs a good walk every day and the opportunity to exercise off the leash; athletic	Ensure that the dog gets adequate exercise, as it is prone to gaining weight
At home	House-training can sometimes be problematic; not very active around the home; unsuited to city life	Concentrate on house-training from the outset with a puppy
Behavior	Learns rapidly; prone to barking, which is a sign of boredom; enjoys interacting with other dogs	Try to keep the dog occupied to prevent barking
Grooming	Regular brushing and combing required; coat gives good protection against the elements	Watch for any tangles that may start to develop
Common health issues	Hip dysplasia	Ensure breeding stock has been screened for hip dysplasia

7. Havanese

These gentle, friendly little dogs are descended from Bichon stock, as reflected by their appearance. What is harder to explain, however, is how the ancestors of the Havanese arrived in Cuba several centuries ago.

History

The ancestors of the breed may well have been taken to Cuba at an early stage, soon after the discovery of the New World, possibly by the Spanish from Tenerife in the Canary Islands. Alternatively, they could be descended from the Bolognese (see page 77), which represents another branch of the Bichon family tree. These dogs were a common sight during the 1600s at the royal courts of Europe. In Cuba, however, the emerging Havanese breed became popular with wealthy owners, but this changed after Fidel Castro's revolution in 1958. Symbols of the old way of life, including the Havanese itself, were no longer fashionable; but, luckily, Cuban refugees took a number of these dogs with them to the U.S., where the future of the breed was safeguarded.

Character

As befits a companion breed, the Havanese is a very suitable choice as a pet dog, having been bred exclusively for this purpose over the course of hundreds of years. It settles very well within the confines of even a relatively small home. Its exercise needs are also quite modest, so that it is ideally suited to living in urban surroundings, provided there is a park for daily exercise within walking distance. The Havanese is very social with other dogs, and is not aggressive by nature. It is potentially at risk, however, from larger dogs, which may seek to bully it, so be sure to watch over your pet when meeting strange dogs for the first time.

Large eyes
The dark brown, almond-shaped eyes are quite widely spaced apart

Havanese colors
All colors and combinations are acceptable for show purposes, including parti-colored individuals

Forward tail
The tail is normally carried forward over the rump, displaying a long plume of hair

CANINE CHARACTERISTICS		NOTES
Personality	Forms a strong bond with family members	Involve the dog in family life
Size	Height: 8–11 in. (20–28 cm) Weight: 7–13 lb (3–6 kg)	
Exercise	Needs a daily walk, but is not a very energetic breed	Exercise daily
At home	Active in the home; adapts well to an apartment	
Behavior	Learns rapidly, and quite easy to train as a result; social, and gets along well with other pets, such as cats; not prone to barking excessively	Keep an eye on the dog around other dogs
Grooming	Pet dogs can be clipped but show dogs need much more elaborate grooming; very occasionally, short-coated puppies are seen; coat tends not to shed	Groom daily and trim when necessary to keep the coat neat
Common health issues	Eye problems, such as Cherry Eye (prolapsed gland in the eye) and cataracts; deafness; skeletal weaknesses, such as patellar luxation	Ensure breeding stock has been tested for deafness; patellar luxation may need corrective surgery

8. Scottish Deerhound

These athletic giants make great jogging companions and need plenty of space, not just to exercise, but simply to curl up and sleep. The Scottish Deerhound also has a powerful tail that can knock fragile objects off low tables.

AT A GLANCE
- Needs lots of space
- Plenty of exercise is required
- May still possess hunting instincts
- Hardy nature
- Affectionate

History

Descended from rough-coated Greyhound stock, this breed was used to run down and overpower deer in the Scottish Highlands, but this role became less significant as firearms started to be used more widely during the late 1700s. Luckily, the Scottish Deerhound's popularity then spread farther afield, thanks to Queen Victoria's favorite artist, Sir Edwin Landseer. He portrayed these hounds in his work, to the extent that they became a symbol of Scotland, and thereby ensured their survival. Today, they are kept largely as companions, in addition to being seen in the show ring. Individuals displaying dark bluish–gray coloration are generally most common.

At home

The Scottish Deerhound is a very affectionate breed. It forms a close bond with its owner, and settles well as part of a family, although its large size means that there are more suitable, smaller breeds for a home where a toddler is present. The breed's friendly nature extends toward other dogs, and not just other Deerhounds. A sad aspect of owning a giant dog, such as a Deerhound, however, is that its lifespan is relatively short. Its life expectancy is rarely more than 10 years, whereas smaller breeds may live well into their teens.

CANINE CHARACTERISTICS		NOTES
Personality	Affectionate; thrives on human company; has a sensitive side to its nature	
Size	Height: 28–32 in. (71–81 cm) Weight: 75–110 lb (34–50 kg)	Dogs tend to be taller than bitches
Exercise	Needs a good run every day	Avoid overexercising young dogs
At home	Home needs to be partly designed around this breed; large floor area is essential	Offer food in three smaller meals a day, rather than one meal
Behavior	Instinctively inclined to chase; can reach up to tables and counters very easily to steal food	Consider muzzling the dog when it is running free, as it will chase small animals
Grooming	Long, wiry coat gives good protection against the elements	Groom regularly, and strip and trim to keep the coat neat
Common health issues	Susceptible to bloat	Do not exercise after feeding, as this can cause bloat

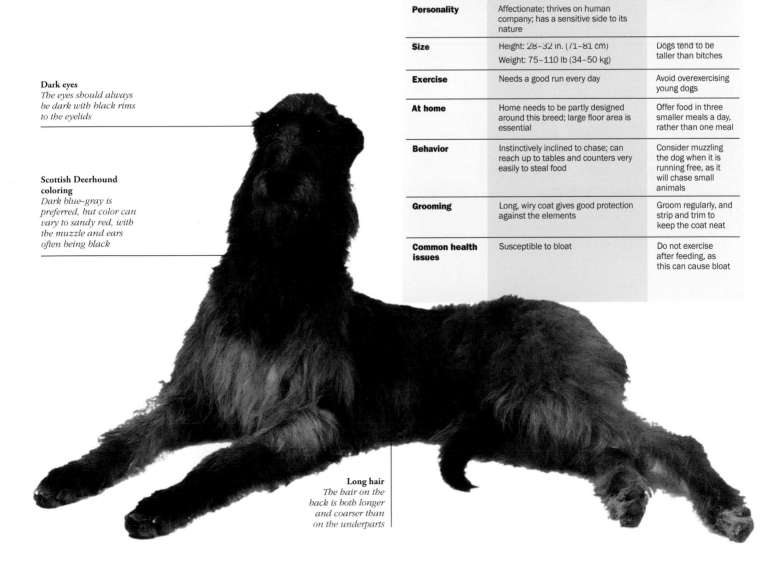

Dark eyes
The eyes should always be dark with black rims to the eyelids

Scottish Deerhound coloring
Dark blue–gray is preferred, but color can vary to sandy red, with the muzzle and ears often being black

Long hair
The hair on the back is both longer and coarser than on the underparts

9. Black and Tan Coonhound

A number of different breeds of hound originate from the southern U.S., although they may be uncommon elsewhere. They are often not standardized, being kept simply for hunting purposes, and they originally descended from European breeds.

Strong hindquarters
The hindquarters are powerful, with the feet positioned back, behind the body, when standing on level ground

Deep chest
The Black and Tan Coonhound has a deep chest that extends down to the level of the elbows

Black coat
Coal black coloration predominates, with the muzzle, chest, legs, breeching, and above the eyes being tan

AT A GLANCE

- Attractive patterning
- Devoted hunting companion
- Straightforward grooming
- Loud call when treeing
- Obedient by nature

CANINE CHARACTERISTICS		NOTES
Personality	Friendly, intelligent companion; forms a close bond with its owner	
Size	Height: 23–27 in. (58–69 cm) Weight: 55–75 lb (25–34 kg)	Bitches are generally shorter than dogs
Exercise	Needs the opportunity to run in safe areas away from traffic	Take care when off the leash, as the dog is not always easily controlled when free and may run off
At home	May drool, and often appears quite lazy; will spring into life when out in the countryside	Consider covering chairs to protect against the dribble
Behavior	Determined and active; can become willful	Train to prevent willful behavior
Grooming	Modest grooming needs, thanks to the short coat	Use a hound glove to improve the natural sheen of the coat
Common health issues	Susceptible to hip dysplasia; may put on weight rapidly if not getting sufficient exercise	Ensure breeding stock has been screened for hip dysplasia

History

The Black and Tan is the first coonhound breed to be developed in the U.S., originating during the 1700s in Virginia. It represents a cross between the English Foxhound and the Bloodhound (see page 144). The Bloodhound was used to track down escaped slaves, while Foxhounds were valued simply for hunting game. Crossings between the two breeds have resulted in the creation of a coonhound whose facial profile bears a distinct resemblance to its Bloodhound ancestor, although it has a more athletic build overall. These hounds have become specialized night-hunters, seeking raccoons, and are now ranked as the most common of the coonhound breeds.

Social with their own kind

It is hardly surprising that Black and Tan Coonhounds are social by nature and mix well with their own kind, given their ancestry. Foxhounds have been kept in packs for centuries, while Bloodhounds often worked at least in pairs. These coonhounds can run quickly and display plenty of stamina when pursuing their quarry. The aim is not to kill the raccoon, but to drive it up into a tree. The coonhounds then utter their distinctive bawling call at the base of the tree where the creature has taken refuge.

10. Tibetan Terrier

Contrary to what its name suggests, this Asiatic breed, unlike most terriers, was developed as a sheepherder rather than for catching vermin. In some respects, the Tibetan Terrier looks like a miniature version of the Old English Sheepdog (see page 61).

AT A GLANCE
- Friendly nature
- Benefits from daily coat care
- Not really a terrier
- Affectionate and intelligent
- Hardy dog

History

The Tibetan Terrier is closely related to another Tibetan breed, the smaller Lhasa Apso (see page 75), but its precise origins are unclear. Unfortunately, the first Western description of the breed, published in 1895, described it as a terrier, simply based on its overall appearance, and this erroneous name has stuck. It was only during the 1930s that these dogs were brought to the West, and it was not until 1956 that they reached the U.S. In Tibet, their long coats are traditionally clipped back at the same time as those of the sheep, and then, when mixed with yak hair, their hair is spun into cloth. Although many examples of this ancient breed are believed to have been killed during the era of Chinese Communist rule, Tibetan Terriers are still likely to be working with sheep in more remote areas of Tibet.

Gentle disposition

Although a herding dog, the Tibetan Terrier is perceived largely as a show dog and companion by enthusiasts in the West. As a working dog, some individuals may hop onto the backs of sheep in narrow passes, as a way of controlling them. Tibetan Terriers are gentle dogs, well disposed to their own kind, as well as to other breeds of a similar size. The long coat is not trimmed but is left in its natural state.

CANINE CHARACTERISTICS		NOTES
Personality	Loyal, protective, and sensitive; can be brave if challenged	
Size	Height: 13–16 in. (33–41 cm) Weight: 20–30 lb (9–14 kg)	
Exercise	Needs a relatively large amount of exercise, due to its working ancestry	Exercise at least once a day
At home	Alert watchdog	
Behavior	Lively and active by nature; agile; not adversely affected by warm weather	Do not encourage excessive barking
Grooming	Long coat means that regular brushing is required	Brush every couple of days; trim hair around the entrances to the ears—spraying the hair with water first may aid this task
Common health issues	Susceptible to eye ailments and congenital skeletal problems, such as hip dysplasia and patellar luxation, causing weakness in the kneecaps	Ensure breeding stock has been screened for these conditions; patellar luxation may need corrective surgery

Tibetan Terrier colors
All colors are recognized for show purposes, sometimes with dark tips to the ears and beard

Large feet
The feet are large and flat in shape, providing excellent grip

Hairy tail
The tail is of medium length and is heavily furnished with hair, sometimes being kinked near its tip

Dog types for less active people who live alone; a couple with a busy, irregular lifestyle; an urban dweller with a park nearby; or an on-the-go family with older children.

Japanese Chin

Italian Greyhound

Low-maintenance Dogs

Toy Manchester Terrier

There is no escaping the fact
that all dogs need to be walked
every day, and they should all
be groomed frequently, too. But
some breeds require less exercise
and grooming than others,
allowing you more time to
simply enjoy your dog's
company, particularly
if your lifestyle is busy.
Many of the breeds
in this section have been developed and
kept specifically as companions over
the course of many centuries, so they are
almost instinctively attuned to living in
domestic surroundings.

The dogs listed here vary significantly in
size. The Greyhound, for example, towers
over the tiny Chihuahua, highlighting the
size of the dog, as one of a wider range
of factors that you need to consider when
selecting a breed. This and various aspects of your
lifestyle are important, too. If space is limited, it will
generally be wiser to choose a smaller dog. The cost
of looking after a pet may also influence your choice.
Larger breeds have bigger appetites than their smaller
cousins, and boarding kennels charge higher fees for
looking after a larger dog. Make sure you compare the
individual attributes of each breed before reaching a
definite decision.

Chihuahua

1. Chihuahua

Chihuahuas have become very popular over recent years, with various celebrities having chosen them as pets. This breed ranks as the smallest in the world, with its name commemorating the Mexican state where it is believed to have originated.

AT A GLANCE

- Smallest breed in the world
- Lively nature
- Very vocal
- Easy-care coat
- Happy in apartment surroundings

Large ears
The Chihuahua has large erect ears that appear broader and flatter when relaxed

Apple dome skull
The apple dome skull is short with a slightly pointed muzzle

Chihuahua colors
The Chihuahua can be bred in any color—solid, patterned, or even splashed

History

The most likely explanation of the Chihuahua's origins is that it is descended from native dogs kept by American Indians in pre-Columbian times. Alternatively, it could be of European descent, with its ancestors being brought to the New World by early Spanish settlers. What is known, however, is that these small dogs started to attract the attention of American visitors to Mexico from the 1880s onward, and were soon highly sought after as companions. They were different in appearance at that stage, compared with contemporary Chihuahuas, having bigger ears and longer noses and looking more like fawns.

Heads up

Original strains of the Chihuahua are thought to have been smooth-coated, but there is now a long-coated version of the breed. It is best to select one of the smooth-coated variants, whose grooming needs are minimal. This small dog is not necessarily a good choice for a home with young children, because of an anatomical peculiarity associated with the breed. When you stroke the top of some Chihuahuas' heads, you will feel a softer rounded spot beneath the skin. This is a hollow in the top of the skull, known as the molera. It occurs even in human babies, but the edges soon grow together. In many Chihuahuas, however, this does not happen, leaving them vulnerable to injury as a result.

CANINE CHARACTERISTICS		NOTES
Personality	Much more dominant and assertive than its size suggests; terrier-like in this respect	
Size	Height: 6–9 in. (15–23 cm) Weight: about 6 lb (2.7 kg)	Avoid obesity—this can cause serious breathing problems
Exercise	Happy trotting around a park	Exercise with a short walk and provide the dog with the opportunity to explore
At home	Thrives on attention; can be fussy about food	
Behavior	May shiver with excitement; can get cold easily; quite noisy by nature	Do not encourage barking
Grooming	Very little grooming required	Comb and brush long-haired Chihuahuas regularly
Common health issues	Hydrocephalus, a build-up of fluid around the brain, causing an abnormally swollen head; may retain milk teeth	Brush teeth regularly to keep them in good condition

2. French Bulldog

This breed has a very distinctive appearance. Its large, raised ears led to these small bulldogs sometimes being described as "bat ears," although individuals with folded "rose" ears were also seen during the breed's early days.

AT A GLANCE

- Distinctive appearance
- Friendly, loyal nature
- Straightforward grooming
- Generally easy-going
- Not especially active
- Not a good swimmer

History

The French Bulldog was developed as a companion. It is thought to be descended from crosses involving Toy Bulldogs, which were popular with local lace makers in the English county of Nottinghamshire. Some of these skilled artisans emigrated to France, taking their dogs with them, and it was there that the breed of today evolved. Various local terriers may have contributed to its ancestry. The emerging breed gained a reputation for being very effective as a ratter. Toward the end of the century, French Bulldogs started to become fashionable pets in Paris, and attracted the attention of artists of the period, such as Toulouse-Lautrec, who immortalized the breed in their work.

What to expect

These are lively, small dogs that will thrive in urban surroundings. It is important, however, to ensure that they are not allowed to become overweight, as their breathing may become compromised. As a result of its short nose, the French Bulldog may snuffle and may also snore quite loudly. They are very playful dogs, making the breed an ideal choice if you have children; but, equally, they can become very devoted to an older owner, and their care is straightforward. Their distinctive tail is naturally short, and may look like a corkscrew in appearance. Known as the Frenchie, this breed is also quite easy to train. It is not noisy or excitable, and can be a useful guardian, being alert to the approach of strangers.

Bat ears
The French Bulldog has bat ears, which are broad at the base and rounded at the tips

Large head
The head is large and square shaped with dark, round eyes set low on the skull

Brindle colors
Brindle plus brindle and white combinations are common in this breed

CANINE CHARACTERISTICS		NOTES
Personality	Calm yet playful	
Size	Height: up to 12 in. (30 cm) Weight: 28 lb (13 kg)	Keep an eye on the dog's weight
Exercise	Enjoys walking around a park; not an athletic breed	Watch the dog around water as most French Bulldogs cannot swim
At home	Settles very well as a companion	Teach a puppy to play gently
Behavior	Very responsive; not prone to barking; may not get along with other French Bulldogs	
Grooming	Occasional brushing required	Watch for skin ailments
Common health issues	Brachycephalic syndrome; spinal ailments; Von Willebrand's Disease (VWD), a blood-clotting disorder; large head means puppies may need a Caesarean birth	

3. Italian Greyhound

There has always been a tendency in the dog world to scale breeds down, and the Italian Greyhound is a typical example. It makes an excellent household companion, and is available today in a very wide range of colors.

History

The greyhound lineage is one of the oldest that exists, and small versions of such dogs were known in the days of ancient Egypt. They were clearly highly prized as well, with their mummified remains having been found buried in the tombs of the pharaohs. Subsequently, miniature greyhounds became very popular as companions at the royal courts of Europe and appeared in paintings of the period. The trend toward miniaturization had nearly destroyed the breed by the late 1800s, however; but, luckily, careful breeding restored vitality, and Italian Greyhounds are now thriving again.

CANINE CHARACTERISTICS		NOTES
Personality	Does not readily take to strangers	
Size	Height: 13–15 in. (33–38 cm) Weight: 8 lb (3.6 kg)	The Italian Greyhound is the smallest sight hound
Exercise	May run at up to 25 mph (40 km/h) for short distances	Exercise daily with a good run off the leash; use a coat outdoors in cold weather
At home	Needs a warm, snug environment; can be hard to house-train	
Behavior	Attentive, not aggressive; territorial, as far as other dogs are concerned	Encourage socialization, otherwise the dog can be nervous when older
Grooming	Grooming is very straightforward—minimal grooming is required for the thin coat; hair thins when shedding, becoming almost bald, especially on the underparts	Brush occasionally when necessary
Common health issues	Eye problems; dental disease; epilepsy; fractures of the legs may also occur	

Long muzzle
The muzzle is long and relatively narrow

Strong thighs
The thighs are strong and well muscled, with the hind legs being parallel from behind

Deep chest
The Italian Greyhound has a deep, narrow chest with an arched, slender neck

A miniature athlete

In virtually every respect, the Italian Greyhound represents a Greyhound in miniature, even in terms of its gait. It has the same efficient stride, although, obviously, its stature means that it is no match for its larger cousin in terms of pace. Having been bred as a companion over the course of thousands of years, its hunting instincts are significantly reduced, while its size means that it will thrive in apartment surroundings. An Italian Greyhound will, however, require the opportunity to run around a park off the leash every day. Its sleek, short coat, and the lack of an undercoat, combined with its small body size, means that it is susceptible to the cold, and so it should always be taken out wearing a coat when the weather is bad. It is a quiet dog by nature, and very affectionate toward those it knows well.

4. Japanese Chin

This unique toy breed is noted for the decidedly feline side to its nature. The Japanese Chin moves very delicately and will use its paws to wash its face, just like a cat, and may even climb onto the back of a sofa and sleep there.

AT A GLANCE
- Very distinctive personality
- Playful nature
- Friendly
- Ideal for apartment living
- Grooming is needed

History

It is generally believed that the Japanese Chin's ancestors originated in China, with the breed evolving in Korea before being taken to Japan in about 732. These small dogs soon became the cherished companions of Japanese nobility, with the emphasis being on their size. The Japanese Chin became so highly prized in its homeland that the theft of any of these dogs was a crime that carried the death penalty. The breed was first seen in Europe during the mid-1600s, being introduced by Portuguese seafarers, and reached the U.S. for the first time in 1882, where it became known for a period as the Japanese Spaniel. After the Second World War, Western bloodlines were taken to Japan, to ensure the breed's survival in its homeland.

A natural performer

The Japanese Chin was developed as a companion breed, which would show off and entertain its owner and guests. This characteristic is still very apparent in these little dogs today, and they delight in being the center of attention. This means that a Japanese Chin will be an ideal choice for someone living on their own. One of their unusual behaviors is the so-called "Chin Spin," where the dog pirouettes in circles. They have also been known to sing, creating a very distinctive "boooing" call, quite unlike that of a bark or growl. Japanese Chins are normally quiet dogs, though, and generally accept strangers quite readily, although they often bark initially when a visitor arrives.

CANINE CHARACTERISTICS		NOTES
Personality	Calm and friendly; thrives on attention; has an independent side to its nature	
Size	Height: 9 in. (23 cm) Weight: 4–7 lb (1.8–3 kg)	Keep an eye on the dog's diet, as it is prone to gaining weight
Exercise	Needs modest exercise	Avoid exercise in the hottest part of the day
At home	May jump and climb	
Behavior	Learns rapidly, making training straightforward; may sometimes be a little stubborn	Take care with the eyes, which are liable to get scratched
Grooming	Regular grooming required	Brush and comb the coat every couple of days
Common health issues	Patellar luxation affecting the knees and heart murmurs are congenital problems; possible allergies to cereal products	Patellar luxation may need corrective surgery

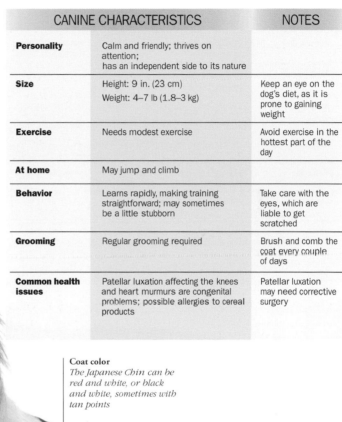

Coat color
The Japanese Chin can be red and white, or black and white, sometimes with tan points

Hairy tail
The tail is profusely coated with hair, with the hair forming a plume

Delicate legs
The legs appear straight and delicate when seen from behind, and end in hare-shaped feet

5. Toy Manchester Terrier

As its name suggests, this breed is a smaller version of the Manchester Terrier. This scaled-down version of the breed is closely related to the English Toy Terrier. Only the Toy version has naturally upright ears, called "candle-flamed" because of their appearance.

AT A GLANCE
- Sleek coat needs little grooming
- Well suited to urban life
- Compact size
- Loyal nature
- Alert

CANINE CHARACTERISTICS		NOTES
Personality	Big personality; lively and alert; loyal and friendly	Train firmly to avoid assertive behavior
Size	Height: 15 in. (38 cm) Weight: 12–22 lb (5.4–10 kg)	
Exercise	Likes to walk and investigate rather than run	Exercise with a daily stroll—this is essential
At home	Easy to accommodate; ideal for an older person	
Behavior	May bark repeatedly if bored; plays readily	Make time for play
Grooming	Minimal grooming required	Brush with a hound glove to improve the sheen on the coat
Common health issues	Eye and skin problems	Watch for repeated scratching, which may indicate a skin disorder

History

The ancestors of this breed were hunting terriers that were used to catch rats. Its distinctive coloration was inherited from the old Black and Tan Terrier, which was common in the northwest of England around the city of Manchester. Miniaturization meant that these smaller toy terriers, which retained their keen rat-killing instincts, could be used in contests held in public houses where large sums were sometimes wagered on the outcome of such contests. A terrier was placed in the so-called "ratting pit," and the time that it took to kill 300 rodents, purchased from local rat catchers, was recorded. Naïve visitors to such establishments could lose large sums of money, as these small, almost frail-looking dogs were highly effective. One of the most famous examples of the breed from that era was a dog named Tiny the Wonder, who killed all the rats in less than 60 minutes.

Small and friendly

Crossbreeding with other dogs, such as the Italian Greyhound (see page 48), has now created a friendly but no less determined breed that thrives in urban surroundings, just like its ancestors. Do not be fooled by the dog's size, because this terrier is very determined by nature, and will certainly dispatch any rats that it encounters without hesitation. Trim and attractive, the breed's sleek coat needs very little grooming. A Toy Manchester Terrier likes to explore when out on walks and is quite happy to trot alongside its owner. Unlike some terriers, it also generally gets along well with other dogs.

Sleek shape
The Toy Manchester Terrier has a sleek profile with distinctive black and tan coloration

Straight forelegs
The forelegs are straight with prominent "stopper" pads

Eager expression
The head is long, with an eager, alert expression on the face

6. Cesky Terrier

This unusual-looking breed's name is pronounced *ses-ki*. It is also sometimes known as the Czesky Terrier, having originated in what is now the Czech Republic. It has a friendly nature, but is not especially common.

History

This breed reflects the vision of its creator, František Horák. Living in what was then Czechoslovakia, he aimed to create a dog that would be ideally suited to hunting in the forests of Bohemia. In fact, the breed is also called the Bohemian Terrier for this reason. He started out with Scottish and Sealyham Terriers, with his initial breeding program taking 10 years. Other breeds, such as the Dandie Dinmont (see page 158), are thought to have made a more limited contribution. A further phase of crossings with Sealyham Terriers then occurred during the 1980s, and the breed has now been recognized as the Czech Republic's National Dog.

A different terrier

The Cesky Terrier is still relatively rare today, but is said to be a better companion than its ancestors. It is not excitable by nature and is relatively tolerant of children, although these terriers are more suited to a home with teenagers than young children. The breed still retains keen hunting instincts as far as rats are concerned, and thrives on exercise. Unlike other terriers, its coat care is very straightforward. These terriers are not stripped to remove hair, but simply need to be clipped over their bodies and tails, which are relatively long. The facial hair and the hair on the underside of the body is left unclipped. Puppies are quite different in appearance to adults, not just because of their shorter coats, but also because they are black in color at first.

CANINE CHARACTERISTICS		NOTES
Personality	Determined, somewhat independent; loyal	
Size	Height: 10–14 in. (25–36 cm) Weight: 12–18 lb (5.4–8 kg)	
Exercise	Good stamina; not an athletic breed	Exercise daily
At home	Alert guardian	Be aware that the dog may dig in the yard
Behavior	Calm, but enthusiastic in the field; lively hunting companion	Keep an eye on the dog outdoors, as it tends to be on the lookout for rodents
Grooming	Clipping and brushing required; no stripping is needed	Brush longer hair every two to three days
Common health issues	Scottie Cramp, from its Scottish Terrier ancestry—this affects movement, usually after exercise, but lasts only briefly	Watch for signs of the condition

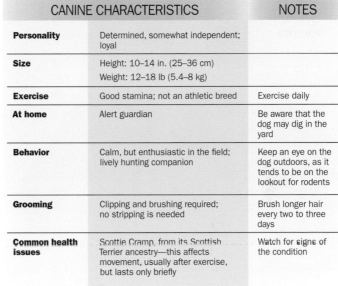

Distinctive features
The Cesky Terrier has a long head with a distinctive bushy beard, well-defined mustache, and eyebrows

Legs and feet
The thighs are strong and muscular, the hind legs are parallel, and the hind feet are smaller than the front feet

Gray to coffee
Coloration is either a shade of grayish–blue with contrasting furnishings or light coffee

7. Greyhound

As the archetypal athlete of the canine world, the Greyhound is a sprinter rather than an endurance runner. Quiet yet affectionate, this is a gentle breed that will settle well in a cat-free home with older children.

AT A GLANCE

- Loves to sprint
- Sedate temperament
- Suits urban living
- Loves to chase other animals
- Must be muzzled when out walking

Powerful hindquarters
The hindquarters provide the propulsive thrust for reaching top speeds

Greyhound coat
The Greyhound's coat may be solid black, gray, red, or fawn. It may also be brindled or spotted

Dewclaw check
Check that the dewclaws do not become overgrown

History

Images of Greyhounds have featured in cave paintings and on ancient Egyptian tombs dating back over 5,000 years, and their appearance has remained essentially unchanged throughout this period. The breed's relatively long nose and narrow head is typical of a sight hound. It relies on its keen eyesight to locate and pursue its quarry rather than tracking it by scent. The Greyhound's name is slightly confusing however, because this does not refer to its coloration. Instead, it derives from the meaning of the word "grey," in Old English, which corresponds to "ancient" and refers to the ancestry of these hounds.

Rescue a racer

The popular sport of Greyhound racing began in the U.S. in 1912. In a race, the hounds are released from traps in pursuit of a mechanical hare, which they chase around a track. At top speed, a Greyhound can run at about 43 mph (69 km/h) over short distances, but many fail to make the grade. As a result, there are always retired racing Greyhounds in need of good homes. They can develop into excellent pets, but should always be muzzled when taken out for a walk, as they are likely to chase after and seize small dogs and other animals.

CANINE CHARACTERISTICS		NOTES
Personality	Docile, not particularly extroverted; easy-going and friendly; not a possessive breed	
Size	Height: 27–30 in. (69–76 cm) Weight: 60–70 lb (27–32 kg)	Dogs are usually slightly taller than bitches
Exercise	Daily run off the leash is essential; does not need long runs	Use a coat outdoors in cold weather as Greyhounds have no dense underfur
At home	Suited to urban life with a park nearby, but will need space to stretch out indoors	Be prepared to sacrifice an armchair
Behavior	Once running, hard to persuade to return, but only covers a relatively short distance before stopping	
Grooming	Regular grooming required	Use a rubber grooming mitt to remove loose and dead hair weekly
Common health issues	Susceptible to bloat and gastric torsion; reputedly the only breed totally free from hip dysplasia; ex-racing dogs especially may be affected by lungworms	Do not exercise after feeding, as this can cause bloat and gastric torsion

8. Dachshund

These hounds come in a wide range of types—two weights and three coat textures—so there is probably a Dachshund to suit most people. They have an even greater range of colors, including dapples and merles.

CANINE CHARACTERISTICS		NOTES
Personality	Long- and short-haired varieties are quieter and more sensitive than the wirehaired type; miniatures are especially lively	Provide the dog with leadership
Size	Height: 5–9 in. (13–23 cm) Weight: 11–32 lb (5–14.5 kg)	This includes miniature and standard varieties
Exercise	Needs regular exercise and time to play	Walk regularly and play games in the yard or park; discourage jumping and rough play
At home	Likes occasional outdoor adventures but should sleep indoors	
Behavior	Often forms a strong bond with one person and acts aloof toward others	Encourage socialization early
Grooming	Grooming requirements vary depending on the coat type; less bathing required than most other breeds	Pluck coat of wirehaireds twice yearly; brush or comb long-haireds daily; rub down smooth-haireds regularly
Common health issues	Prone to intervertebral disk disease and obesity	Keep the dog on a healthy diet to avoid obesity; have regular eye tests

History

The Dachshund breed originated in Germany, which is why it is sometimes known as the "wiener dog," the "hot dog," or, even more often, the "sausage dog." Originally bred to hunt badgers, the Dachshund's legs have gradually become shorter. The Dachshund found a niche as an ideal family pet, steadily becoming one of the most popular hounds in the U.S. These days, your Dachshund is more likely to hunt for your TV remote control than a badger!

Be the boss

Their independent and mischievous natures make these little dogs a challenge to train. To prevent them from developing behavioral problems, such as separation anxiety, snapping, jealousy, and overzealous barking, owners must assert pack leadership. Dachshunds should be introduced to children and other pets at an early age and owners should try to ensure that this first encounter is a positive experience. Show them who's boss, and these dogs will be wonderful family companions with excellent temperaments.

Injury-prone back
The Dachshund's back is vulnerable to injury, so try to prevent it from jumping up or using the stairs

Dachshund coat
The Dachshund's coat can be solid red, sable, or cream. Two-color versions usually include tan and a shade of brown or gray, and three color coats have white mixed in. This is a smooth-coated individual

Eye check
This breed is prone to eye problems, so should have regular eye checks

Short legs
Some Dachshunds bred in Europe have longer legs

9. Welsh Corgi

There are two breeds of Welsh Corgis, named after the counties in Wales where they were developed. They can often be distinguished by their tails, as the Cardigan has a long tail, whereas the Pembroke tends to be without a tail. The Cardigan is also slightly larger.

History

Both breeds of Welsh Corgis were originally working farm dogs. Their task was to drive cattle along, nipping reluctant individuals on their legs. The short legs of these dogs ensured that they could move in and out around cattle without being kicked. Their origins are something of a mystery, but they have existed for more than a millennium, and the name "Corgi" is believed to be derived from the ancient Celtic word for "dog." The Cardigan breed is now slightly bigger than its Pembroke relative, and also has larger, more rounded ears. It is the Pembroke that has been kept by Queen Elizabeth II—she first obtained an example of this breed in 1933 in her childhood.

Not suitable for all

Even the Queen has been on the receiving end of the Welsh Corgi's working instincts, although her involvement with her beloved breed has helped to popularize it. The Welsh Corgi still retains a readiness to nip if frustrated, and this trait means that it is not recommended for a home with young children. This is not aggression as such, but an instinctive reaction, although it can be very upsetting and painful, especially for a child. Providing that you are aware of this behavior, however, and avoid any cause for your corgi to behave in this way, it does make a superb companion. Take care when exercising corgis, too, because they are not especially friendly toward other dogs.

CANINE CHARACTERISTICS		NOTES
Personality	Assertive in spite of its size; intelligent	Teach puppies to be handled, and to give up toys readily
Size	Pembroke Height: 10–12 in. (25–30 cm) Weight: 25–30 lb (11.3–14 kg) Cardigan Height: 11–13 in. (28–33 cm) Weight: up to 34 lb (15.5 kg)	
Exercise	Needs plenty of exercise, preferably in rural areas	Keep the dog away from other dogs, as they may not get along; avoid livestock, as it may try to herd them
At home	Enjoys playing	Do not encourage jumping or walking up stairs, which can cause an intervertebral slipped disk
Behavior	Retains working instincts; can display a somewhat independent streak	
Grooming	Straightforward brushing will generally suffice	Brush out mud on the legs and underside when dry
Common health issues	Progressive Retinal Atrophy (PRA) is a problem in some bloodlines; intervertebral disk disease	Ensure breeding stock has been screened for PRA

Corgi hindquarters
The corgi has powerful hindquarters, in spite of its short legs, with short hocks that aid mobility

Triangular-shaped ears
The ears are triangular in shape, emphasizing its alert nature

Broad chest
The chest is relatively broad with the ribs extending well back along the sides of the body

10. Basset Hound

The best known of the basset breeds today, the Basset Hound itself is the only example that has not been developed in France. Its name originates from the French word *bas*, meaning "low," which describes the stature of these hounds.

History

A short-legged mutation that arose among the hound breeds in France explains the appearance of these hounds. The forerunners of the Basset Hound itself were brought to England in 1866, but unlike other similar breeds, there is no corresponding long-legged variety in this case. They were used to hunt rabbits and hares especially, pursuing their quarry in packs, accompanied by huntsmen on foot. Crosses with Bloodhounds served to improve the emerging breed's scenting skills.

As a companion

Basset Hounds retain an effective ability to pursue a trail, and this can prove to be a problem with pet dogs, because they can move surprisingly fast, in spite of their relatively short legs. They are very genial companions, however, and have a wonderful deep baying call, which is normally uttered when they are pursuing a trail. This allows members of a pack to keep in touch with each other when they are moving through woodland rather than open country. Provided that you are aware of the Basset Hound's dedication to following its nose, this breed can make an excellent choice as a companion. Basset Hounds are remarkably tolerant with children, and their pack ancestry also means that these hounds will get along well, either together or in the company of other dogs. Their main vice is gluttony—be particularly careful not to leave food in shopping bags on the floor when you come home. Otherwise, you are likely to find that the bags have been raided!

CANINE CHARACTERISTICS		NOTES
Personality	Friendly, gentle nature; calm, phlegmatic disposition; dependable and trustworthy	
Size	Height: 14 in. (36 cm) Weight: 50 lb (22.7 kg)	Watch the dog's weight, as it can be prone to gaining weight, especially after neutering
Exercise	Needs a good daily run off the leash	Keep an eye on the dog off the leash as it can tend to stray
At home	Needs to have access to the countryside for walks; likes to sleep on sofas!	
Behavior	Good appetite	
Grooming	Grooming is very straightforward; occasional brushing required; can tend to smell	Use a hound glove to improve the sheen on the coat; bathe regularly
Common health issues	Intervertebral disk disease; ectropion, where the eyelids hang away from the eyes—this can lead to infection	Ectropion may need corrective surgery

Large head
The Basset Hound has a large head with broad, prominent nostrils, while the skull itself is clearly domed

Spine to tail
The tail continues on the line of the spine, but curves slightly along its length

Colors and patterns
The coat can be tricolored or lemon and white in color, with the patterning being of no significance

Dog types for people who have plenty of spare time; people who would like to learn new skills; people who are eager knitters; and those seeking a jogging companion, depending on the breed.

Samoyed

High-maintenance Dogs

Afghan Hound

The care needed by the different breeds featured here varies, being influenced largely by their backgrounds. Active breeds, such as the Samoyed, require a lot of exercise to prevent them from becoming bored and thus potentially destructive around the home. But the most important factor to bear in mind, before choosing a breed from this section, is its grooming requirements. It is perhaps ironic that all of these dogs were developed for working purposes rather than as pampered companions. Nevertheless, selective breeding down the years after they entered the show ring has modified their appearances, with the Afghan Hound, for example, now having longer hair over its body.

The coats of this group of dogs used to protect them from the elements when they were working outside. Maintaining this feature today in top condition is a skill that you may want to learn, although for most owners, it will be a matter of arranging a visit to a local grooming parlor. In between grooming sessions of this type, though, the dog's coat may not need a great deal of care. If you are interested in knitting, however, an Old English Sheepdog is likely to appeal—its hair is quite often made into garments.

1. Afghan Hound

Seeing these elegant hounds, it is often easy to overlook the fact that behind their beauty, there is a considerable amount of work required to achieve such an immaculate appearance. Training is also an issue, but the Afghan Hound is a great breed for an enthusiastic walker.

AT A GLANCE
- A beautiful appearance
- Runs quickly
- Hard to train
- Grooming is time-consuming
- Not always friendly toward other dogs

History

The origins of these elegant hounds lie within modern-day Afghanistan. In this area of open and frequently mountainous terrain, these dogs were originally bred to run down game, such as antelope and deer. One of the characteristics of the breed is its sure-footed nature, allowing it to maneuver at pace over rough ground. Afghan Hounds were first brought to the West in the late 1800s. There were discernible differences in their appearance at that stage, between strains from the mountainous region of the country, which were quite dark in color and had more profuse coats, and strains that lived in arid, desertlike surroundings, which were paler in color, and had shorter coats. These distinctions have since been lost.

At home

The Afghan Hound requires a tremendous amount of grooming. Today's strains have far more profuse coats than those that were originally brought to the West. It is also not a breed for an inexperienced owner, as these hounds can be very difficult to train. They do not regularly come when called, especially if there is something to chase. They may run after small fleeing animals, occasionally even small dogs, and injure them. Afghan Hounds really need to have the opportunity to run in the countryside, away from livestock, as a trot on the leash will not provide sufficient exercise.

Hound topknot
A topknot of silky hair is apparent on top of the head

Coat color
Any color or combination is acceptable

Hairy feet
The feet are covered in thick, long hair

CANINE CHARACTERISTICS		NOTES
Personality	Aloof; does not take to strangers readily	
Size	Height: 24–28 in. (61–71 cm) Weight: 50–60 lb (22.7–27 kg)	Dogs are quite a bit heavier than bitches
Exercise	Needs a good daily run off the leash—this is essential, otherwise it is likely to become bored and destructive around the home	Exercise daily off the leash
At home	A spacious yard provides additional space for exercise	Make time for play in the yard
Behavior	Very independent and hard to train; usually gets along well with family cats, but will chase other cats outdoors; may still display hunting instincts	Keep an eye on the dog around other dogs and small animals
Grooming	Lengthy daily grooming of the silky coat is essential	Groom daily and cut out any matted hair
Common health issues	Eye problems, such as cataracts; can develop "blue eye," a transient reaction to vaccination for infectious canine hepatitis	

2. Löwchen

Also known as the Little Lion Dog, because of its resemblance to a male lion when clipped, the Löwchen is a breed that does not shed its coat, and this means that it can be a good choice for allergy sufferers. It is also considered a member of the Bichon group.

AT A GLANCE
- Very distinctive appearance
- Nonshedding
- Rare breed
- Ideal companion
- Demanding coat care needs

History

Its Germanic name suggests that the Löwchen may have originated in Germany, but some people believe that it is actually a French breed. Its origins are thought to date back as far as the Middle Ages, and by the 1500s, Löwchens were being widely kept across Europe. It was traditionally clipped, but the reasons for this are not clear. It may have been for aesthetic reasons, accompanied by the belief that, as it looked like a lion, it would have a similarly strong constitution. Alternatively, it has been suggested that clipping meant Löwchens could be used by ladies as foot warmers in bed. Much more recently, however, the Löwchen's future has been in doubt. Its numbers had fallen to approximately 65 individuals by 1973, making it the rarest breed in the world at that time.

The breed today

Since 1973, the Löwchen has undergone a significant revival, and is now being seen more frequently again. This is partly because of the current increasing interest in nonshedding breeds—while all breeds shed some hair, the Löwchen does so at a much slower rate than others. Its popularity is also a reflection of its unique appearance and historical ties. Its coat care is more demanding than in many breeds, however, and this is likely to require professional grooming assistance. In the show ring, only the lion trim is acceptable. The coat itself is soft to the touch and is naturally wavy.

CANINE CHARACTERISTICS		NOTES
Personality	Lively, affectionate nature	
Size	Height: 10–13 in. (25–33 cm) Weight: 9–18 lb (4–8 kg)	
Exercise	Needs a good walk every day; quite active	Use a coat outdoors in cold weather for clipped dogs
At home	Enjoys human company; hair is not deposited around the home	Be sure to spend lots of time with the dog
Behavior	Quite extroverted, but not excitable or noisy	
Grooming	Single-layered coat; trimming and brushing required	Trim the coat every eight weeks or so and brush weekly
Common health issues	No widespread congenital illnesses recorded	Watch the ears for any signs of infection

High tail
The tail is set high and is carried forward over the back, but may be lowered when standing

Lion trim
The so-called "lion trim" can be a feature of this breed, as is the case with some Poodles. The longer hair on the front half of the body creates a manelike impression; hence its name

Color combinations
All colors and combinations of Löwchen can be shown, with none being excluded

Different-sized feet
The front feet are larger than the hind feet, with both being well arched

3. Chow Chow

This ancient Asian breed is unusual in a number of respects, including its bluish tongue. Its name may come from the Cantonese word meaning "edible," reflecting the fact that these dogs were widely bred in China as a source of meat.

AT A GLANCE

- Training is demanding
- Regular grooming is needed
- Enjoys good walks
- Loyal
- Historic breed
- Not ideal for a family pet

Blue tongue
The dark bluish tongue is a breed characteristic, irrespective of the coat color

Chow Chow scowl
The padded areas of skin on the brows create the impression of the Chow Chow's scowl

Shades of color
The Chow Chow can be cream, red (ginger to mahogany), shades of cinnamon, plus blue and black

History

The Chow Chow's origins have now been lost, but it has been suggested that the breed could be descended from crossings of Tibetan Mastiff (see page 89) and Samoyed (see page 66) stock, though this is questionable. The breed was first seen in Britain during 1780, when a pair was brought back from China. Later, in 1828, London Zoo obtained another pair, which were placed on public display. When Queen Victoria acquired the breed later in the century, however, Chow Chows became fashionable pets. In their homeland, in addition to being reared as food, Chow Chows have served as guardians and hunters' companions, and have also been used to pull carts.

Understanding owners

The Chow Chow is not a breed that is likely to win an obedience competition, as it possesses a very strong independent side to its nature. This makes training difficult, and the problem is reinforced by the fact that Chow Chows do not get along well with their own kind or other dogs. You need to have plenty of time to concentrate on training if you decide to take on one of these dogs, and this is not really a suitable breed for the first-time dog owner. Grooming is also time-consuming, particularly with the longer-coated form. Bear in mind, too, that the Chow Chow's facial shape may influence its behavior—the deep-set positioning of its eyes means that it cannot see well from the side. It may therefore react nervously if approached from this angle.

CANINE CHARACTERISTICS		NOTES
Personality	Independent, loyal; not one of the most affectionate breeds; watchful, especially with visitors; protective nature	Keep an eye on the dog around others
Size	Height: 18–22 in. (46–56 cm) Weight: 50–70 lb (22.7–32 kg)	
Exercise	Active	Try to exercise away from other dogs
At home	Very self-contained	
Behavior	Not a playful breed; strong-willed nature can create problems	Ensure that you undertake good training—this is vital
Grooming	Male dogs tend to have more profuse manes; weather-resistant coat	Brush and comb regularly
Common health issues	Prone to problems affecting the eyelashes and eyelids	These conditions may need corrective surgery

4. Old English Sheepdog

In spite of its name, this is not a particularly old breed, nor has it been used as a typical sheepdog. Its genial nature has meant that it has become a popular pet and makes a friendly companion. It has a distinctive appearance and ambling gait.

AT A GLANCE

- Very boisterous
- Coat care may be time-consuming
- Friendly, playful demeanor
- Possesses lots of energy
- Training requires patience

CANINE CHARACTERISTICS		NOTES
Personality	Outgoing; exuberant	
Size	Height: 21–25 in. (53–64 cm) Weight: 60–65 lb (27–29.4 kg)	
Exercise	Needs lots of exercise, as it has plenty of energy, typical of a working farm dog	Exercise with a good run every day
At home	Can be disruptive in the home when excited; useful guardian; not recommended for a house with toddlers, due to its size	Keep an eye on the dog around small children
Behavior	Has an independent streak; playful but rambunctious; extroverted	Be patient when training
Grooming	Grooming is demanding if not clipped; a clipped coat is more comfortable for the dog in the summer	Brush daily and clip to keep neat
Common health issues	Inherited cataracts; relatively free from congenital weaknesses	

History

Bearded Collie stock may have played a role in the Old English Sheepdog's ancestry, possibly along with the larger Russian Ovtcharka, which originated in the Ukraine. Ordinary drovers' dogs in the west of England, where the breed was created, would also have been involved in its development. The breed is sometimes called the Bobtail, because its tail was supposedly docked to confirm that it was a working dog. Old English Sheepdogs actually worked mainly with cattle, herding them from one field to another, and to market. What they did have in common with sheep, however, was that they were shorn annually, with their hair being made into clothing.

High-energy living

Old English Sheepdogs have tremendous amounts of energy, and so must have plenty of opportunities to exercise. Around the home, they can be quite clumsy, especially if they become excited. Their size is another factor, as objects can be easily knocked over. Training, too, is not particularly straightforward, due to their lively, active natures, and they are far from suitable for urban living. As might be anticipated, coat care is time-consuming. Unless you are keeping an Old English Sheepdog for show purposes, you can have it clipped. This will be a particular relief to your pet in the summer, and can yield up to 5 lb (2.2 kg) of hair that can be spun.

Head shape
The Old English Sheepdog has a square-shaped head with brown or blue eyes, or one of each color

Legs and feet
The hindquarters are rounded and powerful with the feet being small and rounded, too

Sheepdog coloring
The coat can be gray, grizzle, blue, or blue merle, with or without white

5. Kerry Blue Terrier

In spite of its name, this breed is really a shade of gray, with the extremities of its body bordering on black. Depth of coloration does, however, vary to some extent between individuals, with some being darker overall than others.

CANINE CHARACTERISTICS		NOTES
Personality	Bold, intelligent; can be stubborn	
Size	Height: 17–20 in. (43–51 cm) Weight: 33–40 lb (15–18 kg)	
Exercise	Good stamina	Exercise daily with a good walk; try to avoid other dogs
At home	Often eager to play; likes to chase balls; good guardian	Make time for games
Behavior	Has a reputation for disliking cats	Train to overcome the dog's dislike of cats
Grooming	Grooming is demanding; can obtain advice from an experienced grooming salon	Brush the coat daily and strip when necessary
Common health issues	Older dogs can suffer from tumors affecting the hair follicles—tumors appear as swellings at the base of the hairs	Watch for signs of the condition

History

Originating from County Kerry in the southwest of Ireland, this terrier is now regarded as Ireland's national dog. Its origins are unknown, although it is said that Kerry Blue Terriers are descended from a dog that survived a shipwreck in the Bay of Tralee. It may have been a Bedlington Terrier, if this story is to be believed, but the precise origins of the Kerry Blue have been lost. Other native Irish terriers were probably involved, and even possibly the Irish Wolfhound (see page 88). For many years, Kerry Blue Terriers were kept purely as farm dogs, hunting vermin as well as otters. Their versatility extends to herding stock on occasion and even acting as retrievers.

Small ears
The Kerry Blue Terrier has small, V-shaped ears that are carried forward above the level of the skull

Gray coat
Color can vary from blue–gray through to grayish–blue, ranging from deep slate to light blue–gray

Kerry Blues as companions

The popularity of the Kerry Blue Terrier is not as great as it used to be since its peak of popularity during the 1920s. This is possibly because of its very determined nature, although it makes an intelligent companion, always ready to learn. Nevertheless, these terriers can be stubborn and occasionally pugnacious, especially toward other dogs. Coat care is demanding, and you are likely to need professional assistance. All Kerry Blue puppies are born black and it takes a couple of years for their coat coloration to lighten. This color change is described by breeders as "clearing."

Straight forelegs
The forelegs are straight when seen from both the front and side angles

6. Soft-coated Wheaten Terrier

This is another versatile breed of terrier from Ireland. Such dogs were required to undertake a variety of tasks on the farms where they lived, and frequently worked on their own. More recently, they have also adapted to the show ring.

History

Working terriers similar to the Soft-coated Wheaten Terrier have been a common sight in parts of Ireland for more than two centuries, and it is likely that this could be the oldest of Ireland's four native terrier breeds. Until very recently, however, emphasis was placed firmly on its working abilities, and it was therefore not standardized for show purposes. It remained unrecognized by the Irish Kennel Club right up until 1937, and reached the U.S. for the first time in 1946. Even today, the breed is still quite scarce in the U.S.

Looks and personality

Unlike other terriers, the Soft-coated Wheaten has a soft and silky coat, which should ideally correspond in color to that of pale wheat. Puppies have darker coats than adults, and it can take 18 months for them to gain their adult coloration and for the single-layered coat to develop to its full extent. This breed's care is somewhat easier than that of other terriers, because the coat is neither stripped nor clipped for show purposes. Nevertheless, daily coat care is still essential, including other aspects of grooming, such as the ears and nails. Careful attention to the hair over the eyes, known as "the fall," is important, and you need to find a groomer who is familiar with the breed to achieve the best results. In terms of personality, these terriers like to chase, and have an ability to jump well. Training is possible, but more demanding than is the case with some other breeds.

CANINE CHARACTERISTICS		NOTES
Personality	Intelligent and lively; very independent, which makes training difficult; friendly	Be patient when training
Size	Height: 17–19 in. (43–48 cm) Weight: 30–40 lb (14–18 kg)	Dogs are usually a bit heavier than bitches
Exercise	Tends to pull on the leash	Exercise daily—this is essential
At home	Suitable for a home with older children; protective guardian	
Behavior	Quite playful	Work hard to train the dog from puppyhood
Grooming	Soft-textured coat; daily grooming is essential	Do not overlook the ears
Common health issues	Can be afflicted by renal dysplasia, which is an abnormal development of the kidney, and Addison's Disease, affecting the adrenal glands	Screening is possible

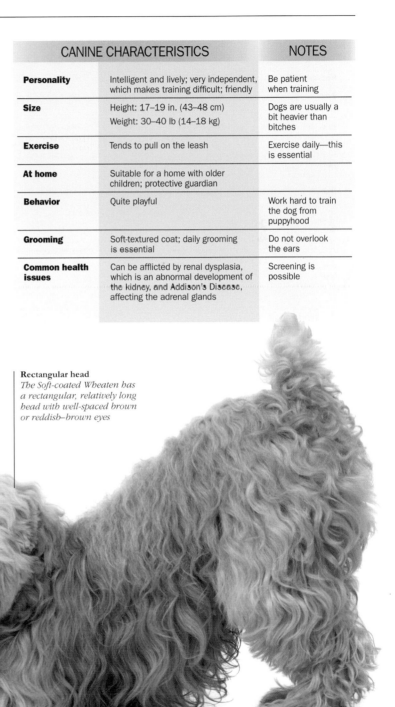

Rectangular head
The Soft-coated Wheaten has a rectangular, relatively long head with well-spaced brown or reddish–brown eyes

Playful nature
The characteristic play bow with the front legs flattened emphasizes the breed's playful nature

Powerful legs
The forelegs are straight and powerful with the pads on the feet being black

AT A GLANCE

- Intelligent companion
- Friendly toward the family
- Quite adaptable in many respects
- Distinctive coat
- Training can present problems

7. Puli

This breed's name is pronounced *poo-lee*, with the plural form being Pulik. It has an unmistakable corded, ropelike coat, although, especially in the U.S., there has been a recent trend toward showing Pulik with a brushed out woolly style of coat.

History

The original ancestors of the Puli may have originated in Tibet, and it is believed that there could be an ancestral link between this breed and the Tibetan Terrier (see page 43). Certainly, the Puli has existed in its current form for more than 1,000 years. The Puli worked as a sheepherder, with black being the preferred coat color, alongside larger flock guardians, such as Komondorok (plural form of Komondor) (see page 156), which had contrasting white coats and whose task it was to protect the sheep from attacks by wolves or would-be thieves. The corded coats of both these breeds were weather-resistant, giving good protection in the winter. In the spring, Pulik were shorn, just like the sheep they worked with, which kept them relatively cool in the hot summers of the Hungarian plains.

Coat care

A young Puli puppy has a tufted coat at first, but this will change naturally. The dense under layer will start to mat with the outer layer, which creates the breed's characteristic corded appearance. The cords themselves should be relatively thin and balanced in appearance, resembling rope, and delicate grooming is required to keep these dogs looking their best. Since the breed has started to be shown, the coat is now more profuse than in working stock, and it can trail down to the ground. In addition, a wider range of colors is now seen, although the black coat especially is liable to fade if exposed to bright sun for long.

CANINE CHARACTERISTICS		NOTES
Personality	Loyal and intelligent	
Size	Height: 14–19 in. (36–48 cm) Weight: 20–40 lb (9–18 kg)	
Exercise	Needs exercise every day, as this is an active working dog	Avoid sheep in particular, as the dog may want to chase them
At home	Alert guardian	
Behavior	Quick, responsive, agile; adept at anticipating what is required; playful; can be stubborn if training is neglected; thrives in agility and obedience competitions	Train from an early age
Grooming	Grooming is a time-consuming task —this applies to a woolly coat, too	Groom daily to form cords or brush to form a woolly coat
Common health issues	Hip dysplasia—though this is not a major condition in this breed	Ensure breeding stock has been screened for hip dysplasia

Corded colors
All shades of gray, rusty black, and black, plus black and white are recognized colors

Puli tail
The tail merges into the line of the back, and is carried above it

Cushioned feet
The well-rounded feet are cushioned by thick pads with the toes being arched

8. Gordon Setter

The Gordon Setter is also known as the Black and Tan Setter due to its distinctive coloration. However, these setters are less commonly seen today than in the past, which may be a reflection of their very active and industrious nature.

AT A GLANCE
- Beautiful coloration
- Possesses great stamina
- Very affectionate nature
- Even temperament
- Diligent when working

CANINE CHARACTERISTICS		NOTES
Personality	Diligent, determined worker; affectionate	
Size	Height: 23–27 in. (58–69 cm) Weight: 45–80 lb (20.4–36 kg)	Dogs are usually quite a bit heavier than bitches
Exercise	Needs long walks in rural surroundings	Exercise daily and allow the dog time off the leash to explore
At home	Size means that this breed is more suitable for older children	
Behavior	Dependable, and not excitable; responsive to training and tends to learn rapidly; eager to please	
Grooming	Regular brushing and combing of the longer feathering on the legs, tail, and ears required	Brush and comb regularly and do not neglect the ears
Common health issues	Progressive Retinal Atrophy (PRA), resulting in blindness, can be inherited	Ensure breeding stock has been screened for PRA

Low ears
The ears are set low, are level with the eyes, and are held close to the head

Long muzzle
The muzzle is relatively long, but is not pointed along its length

Deep colors
The Gordon Setter has defined black and tan markings

History

The Gordon Setter is named after the Duke of Richmond and Gordon, who was largely responsible for creating this breed during the 1820s. His aim was to develop a gundog that was more robust and had greater stamina than the other setters that existed at that time. Among the breeds that he used were various collies, and this led to the early Gordon Setters circling game birds when they detected them, in the manner of a working sheepdog, before "setting" (sitting) to indicate their presence.

Lengthy exercise needs

The Gordon Setter is a very attractive breed and still possesses the stamina that was sought after in the Duke's original breeding program. This means that it is incredibly active. It needs plenty of exercise, and should not be contemplated if you live in the confines of a town or city. Even in the countryside, long daily walks are essential if these setters are not to become bored and potentially destructive. In the right surroundings and with lots of time for exercise, these setters can prove to be excellent and responsive companions. A slight divergence now exists—as is the case with many gundogs—between those seen at field trials, and the slightly larger variety that is favored for show purposes.

9. Samoyed

Although the Samoyed is distinguished in part by its very elegant appearance, it was originally developed as a working breed over the course of centuries, surviving in a very harsh climate. Only relatively recently has it become known in the West.

AT A GLANCE
- Attractive appearance
- Very active
- Food intake needs controlling
- Grooming is time-consuming
- Friendly nature

Light-colored coat
The coat can be white, cream, biscuit, or white and biscuit

Triangular ears
The ears are erect, triangular, medium sized, well spaced, and rounded at their tips

Head and muzzle
The head is triangular shaped, with a tapering muzzle

CANINE CHARACTERISTICS		NOTES
Personality	Determined and friendly; confident in the show ring	
Size	Height: 19–24 in. (48–61 cm) Weight: 50–65 lb (22.7–29.4 kg)	Keep an eye on the dog's weight as it can be prone to gaining weight
Exercise	Needs plenty of daily exercise, as this is an active working dog; physically very strong	Avoid sheep, as the dog may want to chase them
At home	Can become bored without adequate exercise and is then liable to start chewing things up and causing damage	
Behavior	Independent side to its nature, potentially making training difficult; quite social with other dogs	Be patient when training
Grooming	Male dogs have more prominent ruffs around the necks	Brush and comb daily
Common health issues	Vulnerable to *diabetes mellitus* (sugar diabetes)	This condition can be controlled with regular insulin injections

History

The breed is named after the Samoyede tribe, whose homeland lies in northern Siberia. It is a typical spitz-type breed, with rather foxlike facial features, including raised ears and a ruff of longer fur around the neck, extending down between the forelegs. The plumed tail extends forward over the back, with the hair trailing down one side of the body. As with similar breeds, the Samoyed served as a sled dog, providing a vital means of transportation through its native region in an era before mechanization. It was also used as a reindeer herder.

Life in more temperate climes

The Samoyed, as its background indicates, is a very lively breed, and so you must be certain that you can fulfill its needs in this respect. It is also very strong, and must be properly trained, especially to stop it pulling when walking on a leash. Samoyeds are said to smile—this happens when these dogs are being attentive, as this results in the corners of their mouths becoming upturned. The genetic base of this breed in the West is very small, being derived essentially from just a dozen dogs brought to England in the late 1800s. A problem that has been encountered with the breed is its readiness to put on weight in domestic surroundings, because of its metabolism. This in turn can increase the risk of a Samoyed developing *diabetes mellitus*, to which these dogs are susceptible.

10. Borzoi

The Borzoi's name actually means "swift," being derived from the Russian word *borzyi*. It is a typical sight hound, as reflected by its long narrow head and Greyhound-like build, and has an elegant mode of running. It has also been described as the Russian Wolfhound.

History

It is likely that these aristocratic hounds are descended at least in part from Greyhound stock probably taken to Russia from the vicinity of the Middle East. Borzois have existed in a recognizable form for more than 500 years, and were a favorite of the Russian tsars. These hounds hunted in couples or trios, being able to outpace a wolf and drag it by its neck. They then simply pinned the wolf down on the ground rather than kill it. Hunts with Borzois were great ceremonial events. A number of these hounds were presented as gifts to other European rulers, and this helped to ensure the breed's survival after the Russian Revolution. Its links with the deposed aristocratic families meant that its numbers declined dramatically in Russia after 1917 and the Russian Revolution.

Racing along

If you have the space to exercise these graceful dogs, they are wonderful to watch when they are running in their typically elegant way. This can only be achieved in a rural setting however. They have much greater stamina than their Greyhound ancestor, thanks to crossings with indigenous, long-coated dogs in Russia early in their development. Having been bred to hunt as couples, Borzois will get along well together, and also in the company of other dogs of similar size and physique, such as Greyhounds. Their long, silky coat is another factor that needs to be considered before acquiring one of these hounds, as it will need regular attention.

Long head
The Borzoi's head is long, narrow, and slightly domed, with a prominent large black nose

Chest and legs
The chest is narrow but deep and the forelegs are straight

Silky coat
Any color or color combination can be exhibited, but the coat must be silky, not woolly

CANINE CHARACTERISTICS		NOTES
Personality	Friendly toward those it knows, but aloof with strangers; sensitive by nature	
Size	Height: 26–28 in. (66–71 cm) Weight: 60–105 lb (27–48 kg)	Dogs are quite a bit heavier than bitches
Exercise	Needs plenty of running off the leash every day; more inclined to return than some sight hounds	Exercise daily with a good run off the leash
At home	Will settle well if allowed to run regularly; not a guardian of property	Watch for the presence of cats in the area, which puppies, in particular, may chase after
Behavior	Quiet, not inclined to bark	
Grooming	Regular brushing and grooming required	Remember to check the ears
Common health issues	Some Borzois are born without some premolars, but this does not affect their health or eating	Check mouth for missing teeth if you want to enter shows, as this is considered a major fault

Dog types for elderly owners; city dwellers; and those whose mobility may be reduced, but who would still like to own a dog.

Pomeranian

Silky Terrier

Small Dogs

Just because a dog is small in stature does not mean that it is lacking in character in any way. In fact, the majority of the breeds covered in this section have been evolved specifically as companions over the course of many hundreds of years, and so they generally settle very well in the home. Their exercise needs are quite modest, and, as a result, they are ideally suited to living in urban areas. Their main drawback, perhaps, is that they are not always as sound as larger breeds, although screening of breeding stock should help to ensure that puppies are generally healthy.

Grooming some of these small breeds can be quite time-consuming as well, but provided that you establish a routine from puppyhood, the task should be straightforward. Although they are friendly with people of all ages, these smaller breeds are less suitable for a home where young children are present because they can be easily hurt by rough handling. The majority of these breeds serve as alert guardians, warning of people approaching the home, and, advantageously, their barking tends to suggest that they are significantly larger than is the case.

Pekingese

1. Pekingese

This breed is so-called thanks to the Chinese capital city of Peking, which was the name formerly given to what is now known as Beijing. The Pekingese is sometimes known affectionately just as the Peke, and has a very distinctive appearance.

History

The origins of the Pekingese are probably similar to those of the Tibetan Spaniel (see page 14), which this breed closely resembled when it was first seen in the West during the 1860s. Since then, the Pekingese's appearance has altered dramatically, with its face becoming significantly flatter in profile, while its coat has become more profuse. These dogs were a favorite at the Chinese Emperor's Imperial Court, being cared for by specially appointed eunuchs, and their theft was punishable by death. The Pekingese was first seen in England after the overthrow of the Chinese dynasty, when an individual of the breed was presented to Queen Victoria, who was a great dog lover. Virtually all the dogs used in the development of Western bloodlines were obtained around the turn of the 20th century. After the death of Dowager Empress Tzu Hsi, who bred the dogs, the breed soon went into decline in its homeland.

A true companion

These lively little dogs were known as "Sleeve Dogs," too, as they could be concealed within the billowing sleeve of a Chinese courtier because of their size. Yet another early name used for the breed was "Lion Dog," which refers to the long mane of fur surrounding the face—a feature still apparent today. What appears not to have altered significantly is the temperament of these small dogs. They are still excellent companions, albeit perhaps not for a home with young children, but are ideally suited for older owners, who will appreciate their loyalty.

CANINE CHARACTERISTICS		NOTES
Personality	Determined, loyal, stubborn, and confident	
Size	Height: up to 9 in. (23 cm) Weight: up to 14 lb (6.3 kg)	Keep an eye on the dog's weight
Exercise	A gentle trot around the park is adequate	Avoid exercise in the hottest part of the day to avoid heatstroke
At home	Happy trotting around in domestic surroundings alongside people, and around a nearby park	Do not encourage the dog to jump up—this can induce a slipped disk
Behavior	Courageous; will not back down readily when determined	
Grooming	Plenty of combing and brushing required	Brush and comb regularly and wipe any tear staining with damp cotton balls
Common health issues	Conditions affecting the prominent eyes, including prolapsed eyeballs and scratches; respiratory difficulties, linked to the flattened nose	

Pekingese face
The face is very large and wide, with a flattened muzzle

Coat color
All coat colors and patterns are acceptable, but areas such as the nose should be black

Coarse coat
The coat has a relatively coarse texture, being raised from the body, with a softer undercoat beneath

Front feet
The front feet are turned out slightly when the Pekingese is standing or moving

2. Yorkshire Terrier

Although it was originally kept for working purposes, the Yorkshire Terrier, named after the county of England where it was developed, is now maintained exclusively for show purposes and as a pet. Its small size has helped to ensure its popularity.

AT A GLANCE
- Small breed, full of character
- Extensive grooming is needed
- Suited to urban living
- Strong personality
- Modest exercise needs

History

The origins of this breed can be traced back to the mill towns in northern England where its ancestors were kept to hunt rodents. A variety of different terriers probably contributed to its ancestry, including another Yorkshire breed called the Leeds Terrier, which is now extinct, plus the Manchester Terrier, whose legacy can be seen in its color pattern. Other breeds that played a part include the Dandie Dinmont (see page 158) and Skye Terriers, although to a lesser extent. Two more Scottish breeds—the Clydesdale and Paisley Terriers—that featured in the Yorkshire Terrier's ancestry have since become extinct. They were brought south from Scotland by those seeking jobs in the Yorkshire mills at that time. The most famous member of the emerging breed, born in 1865, was a male dog called Huddersfield Ben, who is often described as its founding father.

Changing perspective

The original Yorkshire Terrier was a keen ratter and was bigger than it is today. Before long, a trend to create smaller pet "Yorkies" soon became apparent. They were very popular as ladies' pets in their early days, partly because of their long, soft hair, which trailed down the sides of the body. A Yorkshire Terrier needs constant grooming to look its best. The hair on the top of the head is traditionally tied up with one or two ribbons, to prevent it from trailing down into the eyes.

CANINE CHARACTERISTICS		NOTES
Personality	Intelligent, brave, tenacious, fearless	
Size	Height: 9 in. (23 cm) Weight: 7 lb (3 kg)	
Exercise	Likes to trot around and explore; not a breed well suited to running	Make time for play
At home	Attentive and lively companion	
Behavior	Always eager to investigate; still retains an instinctive rodent-hunting ability	Train not to bark unnecessarily
Grooming	Grooming is demanding; needs daily care	Keep the hair around the lips clean to prevent infections
Common health issues	Patellar luxation, affecting the kneecaps and causing lameness	Patellar luxation may need corrective surgery; be sure that both testicles descend into the scrotum—seek veterinary advice if not

Blue body
Blue coloration runs from the back of the neck to the base of the tail. The depth of blue on the tail is darker than on the body

Compact body
The body is well proportioned with a compact shape

Puppy color
Puppies are black and tan at birth, with blue then replacing the black. It should be a dark, steely shade of blue. Tan hairs lighten in color along their length

Little feet
The feet are rounded with dark nails

3. Maltese

These beautiful white dogs have soft coats and have been kept as companions for centuries. Even today, they retain their popularity, not just as a result of their attractive appearance, but also due to their appealing personalities.

History

As its name suggests, the Maltese is indelibly linked with the island of Malta, where its ancestors have lived for perhaps 1,500 years. It is possible that these small dogs were originally kept and traded around the Mediterranean region by the seafaring Phoenicians. They were known and favored by both the Greeks and Romans, and later retained their popularity as ladies' companions at the royal courts of Europe. Throughout this period, the Maltese seems to have changed relatively little in appearance. From the 1800s onward, the breed has become more widely known, and enjoys a widespread following today.

Appearance

Today, all examples of the breed are white, although some slight lemon or tan coloration may be present on the ears, whereas in the past, the Maltese's coloration was far more varied. The appearance of its coat has also altered. Early portraits of the dog portray it with a rather shaggy, wavy coat, whereas the Maltese now has a smooth, flowing coat with a characteristic silky texture. The coat is single-layered, with no hint of an undercoat, and extends right down to the ground around the body, obscuring the legs and feet. The hair on the head is often tied up with a ribbon, to keep it out of the Maltese's rather prominent black eyes. This hair blends in at the back of the head with the long hair on the ears.

Fine muzzle
The tapered muzzle has a black nose

Long hair
The long hair on the head can be tied into a topknot

Dark eyes
The eyes are very dark in color, are round in shape, and have dark rims, too

Feathered ears
The ears, which hang down the sides of the head, are set low and are heavily feathered

CANINE CHARACTERISTICS		NOTES
Personality	Very affectionate and gentle; takes delight in human company	
Size	Height: 10 in. (25 cm) Weight: 4–6 lb (1.8–2.7 kg)	Some individuals can be heavier
Exercise	Needs relatively modest exercise; happy with a walk in the park	Be aware that the coat can become quite muddy when outdoors
At home	Forms a strong bond with family members	
Behavior	Learns very quickly; has a brave side to its nature	Provide the dog with lots of attention and it will thrive
Grooming	A central parting extends down the back	Comb daily
Common health issues	Distorted eyelashes, where the eyelashes rub against the eyeball and cause severe irritation	This condition may need corrective surgery

4. Pomeranian

Miniaturization of larger breeds has been a common theme in the breeding of dogs over the centuries, and this explains the origins of the Pomeranian. The breed is descended from larger spitz stock, and has long been a popular companion.

History

The Pomeranian was closely linked with the royal courts of Europe in its early days, and ultimately, the breed became a particular favorite of Queen Victoria, who entered some of her beloved dogs at the first Cruft's Dog Show held in 1891. It is even said that when she died, her black Pomeranian called Turi was lying on her bed alongside her. By this stage, the breed had already undergone a noticeable reduction in size from the early examples that were brought to England by Queen Charlotte during the 1760s. In addition to becoming smaller, the coat length of these toy dogs was also increased, with the result being that the Pomeranian today is often described as the "Puffball," thanks to its appearance.

Scaled down

The Pomeranian is the smallest member of the spitz group, whose members are better known for their strength, acting as sled dogs in many cases throughout the far north. It bears the characteristics of the group, including the foxlike face with upright ears, longer hair over the body, while the hair on the lower legs is quite short, and a tail that curves forward over the body. There is also a mane of longer fur framing the face, extending down between the legs, although this is less noticeable in the Pomeranian because of the overall length of its coat. It makes a lively companion and is particularly valuable as a watchdog, like its ancestors, being alert to the approach of strangers.

CANINE CHARACTERISTICS		NOTES
Personality	Lively, affectionate	
Size	Height: 11 in. (28 cm) Weight: 4–5 lb (1.8–2.2 kg)	
Exercise	Enjoys a daily walk in the local park	In hot weather, exercise in early morning and evening when it is cooler, to avoid heatstroke
At home	Likes to be the center of attention; ideal companion for someone living on their own, particularly an older person	
Behavior	Can be relatively noisy; quite energetic	Train not to bark excessively
Grooming	Grooming is essential	Comb and brush daily and wipe any tear staining with damp cotton balls
Common health issues	Patellar luxation, affecting the kneecaps	Patellar luxation may need corrective surgery

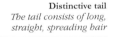

Distinctive tail
The tail consists of long, straight, spreading hair

Compact body
The body has a short, level back

Colors and patterns
Any color or pattern, such as black and tan, brindle, or part white, may be seen

Coat layers
The Pomeranian has a long, straight, somewhat shiny outer coat with a much softer, dense undercoat

5. Silky Terrier

This popular Australian breed was created purely as a companion, rather than as a working terrier. These dogs are now very popular both in this role and in show rings around the world, thanks to their attractive appearance and lively, friendly personalities.

AT A GLANCE
- Attractive small terrier
- Highly distinctive coat
- Responsive nature
- Grooming is very important
- Sturdy in spite of its size

History

The breed came into existence during the late 1800s, being developed mainly from crosses between the larger Australian Terrier and the Yorkshire Terrier (see page 71), which originated in England. It became common in the Australian states of Victoria and New South Wales, with its development being centered particularly around the city of Sydney. It is probable that Skye Terriers may also have been used, as reflected by the enlarged size of the Silky Terrier's ears. The breed became known in the U.S. after the Second World War, and has since become popular here, but it is less common in the U.K., where the Yorkshire Terrier remains the most popular toy breed of its type.

Past legacies

In the early days of the breed, these terriers were bred with both prick and drop ears. Since then, prick ears have become the dominant form, although, even today, puppies occasionally crop up with drop ears. Although Silky Terriers can be kept as apartment pets, they really thrive when given access to a yard, rather than just having to rely on being taken out for walks. The Silky Terrier's coat may not be as profuse as that of its Yorkshire Terrier ancestor, but it still needs regular grooming, to prevent it from developing mats. Bathing every two or three months, and the use of a canine shampoo, is important to maintain its attractive appearance, ensuring its highly distinctive coat remains in top condition.

CANINE CHARACTERISTICS		NOTES
Personality	Typical terrier—inquisitive and alert	
Size	Height: 9 in. (23 cm) Weight: 8–10 lb (3.6–4.5 kg)	The Silky Terrier has a relatively long body
Exercise	Likes to explore off the leash	Exercise daily and provide the opportunity for time off the leash
At home	Will hunt rodents if the opportunity presents itself; enjoys chasing after balls	Make time for play
Behavior	Can be upset by thunder and unexpected loud noises; generally gets along with other dogs	Provide the dog with lots of attention and it will thrive
Grooming	Lots of care is required for the silky coat; the coat is less profuse in puppies	Groom regularly and bathe every couple of months
Common health issues	Patellar luxation, affecting the kneecaps; epilepsy	Patellar luxation may need corrective surgery; epilepsy will need regular preventive medication to protect against epileptic fits

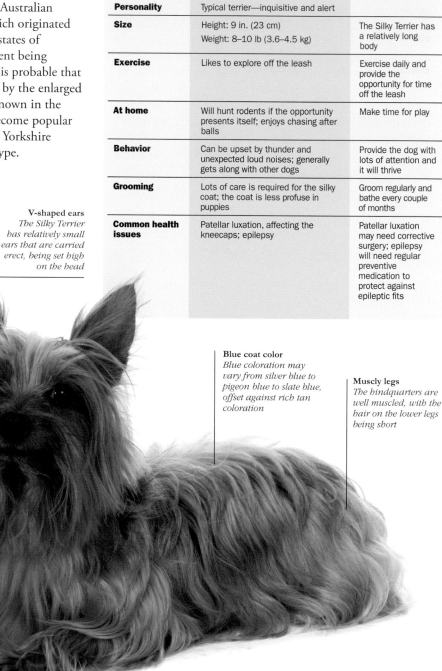

V-shaped ears
The Silky Terrier has relatively small ears that are carried erect, being set high on the head

Blue coat color
Blue coloration may vary from silver blue to pigeon blue to slate blue, offset against rich tan coloration

Muscly legs
The hindquarters are well muscled, with the hair on the lower legs being short

Catlike feet
The feet are small and catlike with dark-colored nails and thick pads

6. Lhasa Apso

The name of this particular Tibetan breed translates as "Hairy Lion Dog." The Lhasa Apso has developed in relative isolation over the course of centuries. It was kept as a companion breed, and has also served as a watchdog.

CANINE CHARACTERISTICS		NOTES
Personality	Generally quiet; protective; affectionate; watchful with visitors	Keep an eye on the dog around others
Size	Height: 9–11 in. (23–28 cm) Weight: 13–15 lb (6–7 kg)	
Exercise	Not especially active	Exercise with a daily walk
At home	Relates well to people and does not like to be left alone	Guard against separation anxiety when training a puppy
Behavior	Playful; calm disposition	
Grooming	Double coat demands intensive grooming; clipping of pet dogs is somewhat controversial with some breed enthusiasts; often dislikes bathing	Groom regularly and get a puppy used to grooming by starting early in life
Common health issues	Inguinal hernias	This condition may need corrective surgery

Development of the breed

Although normally long-coated, short-coated puppies appeared in some litters in the early days. A survey in 1960 found that six out of every hundred births on average were short-coated and were dubbed "Prapsos." Short-coated Lhasas are apparently even more rare these days. Much of the breed's appearance has been shaped by the landscape where it was developed. Its thick coat protects against cold night air, while the hair on the paws provides a cushion when walking on stony ground. Its relatively long body provides generous lung capacity, helping the dog to breathe in the thin mountain air of its homeland.

History

This breed is closely related to the Tibetan Terrier (see page 43), and was kept in Tibet's monasteries, where such dogs were jealously guarded, as they were believed to represent reincarnations of dead monks. For centuries, they were kept away from foreigners, although Tibet's ruler, the Dalai Lama, sent the occasional pair to the Chinese Imperial household as a gift. Lhasa Apsos remained essentially unknown in the West right up until the early 1900s, and in fact had nearly died out by the end of the First World War. A small breeding group was brought back to Britain in 1928, and they were introduced to the U.S. shortly afterward. But it was not until the later years of the 20th century that the Lhasa Apso started to establish a firm following. However, it is now scarce in its homeland.

Brown eyes
The medium-sized eyes are dark brown and very expressive

Coat color
The Lhasa Apso can be bred in all colors, sometimes displaying dark tips to the hair on the ears and beard

Long body
The body is longer than the dog's height, with the coat being heavy and very dense

Straight forelegs
The forelegs are straight in shape and well covered with long hair

7. Miniature Pinscher

This German breed is often affectionately called the Min Pin, although in its homeland, it is known as the Zwergpinscher. The description of "pinscher," meaning "terrier," refers to the shape of the ears, with these small dogs resembling terriers in appearance and behavior.

AT A GLANCE
- Sleek appearance
- Bold and loyal
- Alert guardian
- Minimal grooming is needed
- Small dog with a large personality

CANINE CHARACTERISTICS		NOTES
Personality	Bold, determined, and lively; quite fearless!	
Size	Height: 10–12 in. (25–30 cm) Weight: 12 lb (5.4 kg)	Keep an eye on the dog's weight
Exercise	Needs daily walks—this is essential, and needs to be allowed to wander off the leash in a safe, enclosed area	Train to return instantly on command, to avoid any conflicts
At home	Loves being part of a family; better suited to a home with older children	
Behavior	Very curious by nature; quick when playing ball	Make time for play
Grooming	Grooming is very straightforward and minimal, thanks to the short, sleek coat	Brush occasionally when necessary
Common health issues	Dislocated shoulders; generally very healthy	Dislocated shoulders will probably need corrective surgery

Powerful hindquarters
The hindquarters are well muscled and the thighs are strong

Toes and nails
The well-arched toes have deep pads and thick nails, with the feet looking quite feline

Red coat
Color can be red or stag red, where black hairs are intermingled, plus black or chocolate—both with red markings

Straight legs
The forelegs are straight and parallel, contributing to the breed's high stepping action

History

This is another breed that has been scaled down over time, to create the more refined and smaller dogs of today. The smooth-coated Dachshund (see page 53) and Italian Greyhound (see page 48) are both thought to have played a part in its development with crossings with the German Pinscher. It became officially recognized as a breed in its homeland in 1895 and was seen in the U.S. in 1920 for the first time. Its regal bearing and small stature has resulted in the breed being dubbed the "King of the Toys." The original role of this small dog was as a rodent killer on farms, but it is now a highly popular household pet.

Life with a Min Pin

One of the characteristics of the breed is its high-stepping gait, which has been likened to that of a trotting horse. These dogs may appear quite frail, but actually, they are very determined, bold individuals. Min Pins make excellent companions, with their big personalities, although they need to be trained carefully. Otherwise, you may find your pet squaring up to a much bigger dog in the park, as they are quite fearless in terms of their disposition. While they can be kept within the confines of an apartment, Min Pins are far happier having outdoor access where they can explore within the confines of a yard. They are quite adept escape artists, however, and this area must be securely enclosed. Their small size means that they can wriggle under a fencing panel or squeeze through a gap.

8. Bolognese

As a member of the Bichon group of breeds, distinguishable partly by its white coloration, the Bolognese has been a popular pet for centuries. It is perhaps the archetypal lapdog, thanks to its long ancestry, small size, and friendly disposition.

History

These small lapdogs have charmed many European rulers down the centuries. Queen Maria Theresa of Austria (1717–1780) loved her Bolognese so much that, when it died, it passed to the care of a taxidermist, and, today, it is displayed in a museum in Vienna. These small dogs were highly pampered, too, being fed on occasion from bowls made of gold. Although linked with the Italian city of Bologna, the actual origins of the breed are somewhat unclear. The most likely explanation is that they are descended from the Maltese (see page 72), with their ancestors being taken from Malta to Italy, where they ultimately became particularly popular in this region. Later, the actress Marilyn Monroe fell under the spell of the Bolognese.

Distinctive features

The breed today ranks as one of the rarer Bichons, differing in a significant way from its relatives. Its coat is described as "flocked," being particularly fluffy, and it is single-layered, with no undercoat present. The hair hangs down in ringlets, being longer over the body than it is on the face. The coat is not shed in a conventional way, which means that the Bolognese may be more suitable for those who suffer from allergies than some other toy breeds. The characteristic coloration of its coat makes an attractive contrast with its dark, expressive eyes and black nose. In the past, there were both black and black and white examples of the breed.

Expressive eyes
The Bolognese's expressive dark, round eyes with dark rims accentuate this breed's appeal

Hanging ears
High-set ears hang down each side of the head emphasizing its width

Black nose
The large black nose contrasts with the white coat

Long coat
The long coat, which does not curl, extends over the whole body

CANINE CHARACTERISTICS		NOTES
Personality	Intelligent, loyal; tolerant of children; does not take to visitors readily	Keep an eye on the dog around others
Size	Height: 10–12 in. (25–30 cm) Weight: 5–9 lb (2.2–4 kg)	
Exercise	Lively but not particularly energetic when out	Exercise with a relatively modest daily walk
At home	Excellent family companion	Make time for play
Behavior	Alert but not especially noisy, though it will bark when strangers visit	Train not to bark unnecessarily
Grooming	Regular combing required; coat is never trimmed or clipped	Comb regularly to prevent mats from developing
Common health issues	No significant problems recorded	

9. Affenpinscher

The name of this breed means "monkey terrier," referring to its unique facial appearance, which resembles that of a primate. The Affenpinscher has bushy eyebrows and a beard, with the coat itself having a rough texture and becoming shorter over the hindquarters.

Short hair
The hair on the head and underparts is generally shorter and less harsh than elsewhere

Symmetrical ears
Ears can be erect, semi-erect, or dropped but must be symmetrical

Black coat
Black individuals may display a rusty tan to their coat. The coat can also be silver, gray, red, beige, or black and tan

History

The Affenpinscher was developed in the area around Munich in southern Germany about 200 years ago. Native terriers played a part in its development, but how it developed its flattened face is unclear, as there are no corresponding native German breeds that could have fulfilled this role. This feature may have been introduced by matings with an Asian dog, or it might have occurred as the result of a mutation. Since then, there has been a tendency to develop this feature further, both by selective breeding and then crossings involving the Griffon Bruxellois.

Safety harness

The Affenpinscher enjoys going out for walks, but it is safer to exercise it using a harness instead of a collar. Even if the dog then pulls ahead, it is not at risk of injuring its windpipe (trachea), causing a condition called tracheal collapse, which can trigger fits of coughing and even gagging. Overweight dogs are most at risk of suffering from the condition.

CANINE CHARACTERISTICS		NOTES
Personality	Curious and bold; quite fearless by nature	
Size	Height: 10–12 in. (25–30 cm) Weight: 7–8 lb (3–3.6 kg)	Keep an eye on the dog's weight
Exercise	Likes to explore when out for a walk; good stamina and energetic	Take care when out as it may get into conflicts with larger dogs
At home	Quiet but may be excitable on occasion; possessive of toys and so not suited to a home with young children; territorial and may not take well to other dogs	Keep an eye on the dog around the home with other dogs
Behavior	Responsive to training; not fazed by traveling	
Grooming	Rough coat needs relatively little attention	
Common health issues	Slipped stifle, affecting the hind legs; prominent eyes are easily injured	Slipped stifle will probably need corrective surgery

10. Border Terrier

The Border Terrier is an active breed and makes a lively companion for those who enjoy the outdoors. Although it may be relatively small, it has great energy, and will only thrive in an environment where it can have plenty of exercise.

AT A GLANCE
- Very personable
- Intelligent
- Coat is likely to need professional grooming
- Active nature
- Eager digger
- High energy levels

Origins

The Border's origins set it apart from other terriers, and have influenced the temperament of the breed today. It was created in the border area between England and Scotland, more than 400 years ago, being particularly popular in the county of Northumberland. Its purpose was to run alongside the local packs of hounds to flush out foxes that went underground. As a result, not only does the breed today still display plenty of stamina, but it will also get along more readily with other dogs than many terriers.

The Border way of life

Border Terriers are not suitable for apartment living, and also bear in mind that they are great escape artists. They will have no difficulty enlarging a gap beneath a fence with their powerful paws, before squeezing through the gap, and disappearing. Do not leave one of these dogs in the yard unsupervised for any length of time, as it is likely to become bored and start digging and damaging plants. Border Terriers tend not to get along with cats; but, if you have a horse, it should soon learn to trot alongside as you ride, assuming you can find a safe locality where both animals can be exercised together. Border Terriers are also very playful, and this adaptable breed may now often be seen taking part in flyball and agility competitions.

Hazel eyes
The medium-sized, dark hazel eyes emphasize the breed's natural intelligence

V-shaped ears
The relatively small ears fall forward in the direction of the cheeks

Short muzzle
The relatively short muzzle has a prominent black nose

Straight legs
The Border Terrier has straight forelegs with small compact feet

CANINE CHARACTERISTICS		NOTES
Personality	Loyal, friendly, bold; can be reserved with strangers	
Size	Height: 10 in. (25 cm) Weight: 12–16 lb (5.4–7.2 kg)	
Exercise	Thrives outdoors and enjoys long walks, even in bad weather; ideal companion for an enthusiastic walker; has great energy	Exercise with long walks
At home	Likes to be fully involved in family life	Make time for play
Behavior	Responsive to training	Train not to chase cats from the outset
Grooming	Weather-resistant double coat; brushing is essential and the coat also needs hand stripping by an experienced professional twice annually	Brush daily
Common health issues	Can be born with a hole in the heart, causing blood to leak between its chambers rather than pump efficiently	This should be detected in a routine veterinary check—ensure that the puppy has been checked before buying

Dog types for people with large homes and plenty of space; people for whom their dog's food bill will not be a matter of concern; couples without children; and those living in rural areas.

Alaskan Malamute

Large Dogs

It is not just size that sets large breeds apart from their smaller relatives. They are obviously far more powerful, and so controlling them on the leash requires greater strength. They are therefore not suitable for children or frail owners. Some of these large dogs are fairly assertive by nature as well, in terms of their temperament, and so they require firm training from puppyhood, in order to ensure that they do not become dominant in the home.

Inevitably however, they also require considerable space indoors, and it is not sensible to keep any of these breeds without access to a large yard where they are able to have some exercise during the day. They must also have a good daily walk, although puppies must not be overexercised, and many, such as the Anatolian Shepherd Dog, which is used to working outdoors as a farm dog, possess considerable stamina. This section includes the two tallest breeds in the world, the Great Dane and the Irish Wolfhound, but it is a sad fact that large dogs generally have significantly shorter life spans than their small relatives, for reasons that are not fully understood.

Saint Bernard

1. Great Dane

This large, friendly German breed used to be much shorter in stature, but it now ranks among the tallest of all breeds. Height in dogs is always measured from the withers, the upper point of the shoulders, down to the ground.

History

Back in the Middle Ages, the ancestors of the Great Dane used to be kept in packs as hunting dogs, to pursue wild boar. They had a reputation for being much fiercer at that time. Then, in the 1800s, the breed was transformed into a much taller, lighter, and far more friendly dog, and was then recognized as Germany's National Dog in 1876. During the following decade, the Great Dane started to become well-known and popular in the U.K. and the U.S., both as a companion and as a participant in dog shows. In the U.S., its ears are often cropped, giving the dog a much more alert appearance. Uncropped ears, which are the norm in Europe, hang down the side of the head and some say give a friendlier appearance.

Living with a giant

Great Danes tend to be slightly shorter than Irish Wolfhounds (see page 88). The Great Dane is a friendly, genial giant, although it can be intimidating because of its size and its loud bark. It has a dignified temperament, with a rather aristocratic air. Although it gets along well with children, its size may overwhelm them. It is not a good choice where space is limited, particularly as its large tail is powerful, and objects can be accidently knocked over as a result of its enthusiastic nature.

Rectangular head
The Great Dane has a long head with the male dog having a more masculine appearance

Strong chest
The Great Dane's chest is broad, deep, and strong

Harlequin patterning
With harlequin patterning, black extends in variable patches over the white body

CANINE CHARACTERISTICS		NOTES
Personality	Loves human company; energetic	
Size	Height: typically 28–32 in. (71–81 cm) Weight: 100–120 lb (45–54.4 kg)	The tallest Great Dane was 42 in. (106 cm) tall, and weighed 238 lb (108 kg)
Exercise	Likes to have the opportunity to run off the leash—choose an area away from other people if possible	Avoid long walks with young puppies, as this can create joint problems later in life
At home	Settles well, but takes up a lot of space; needs an area to stretch out on the floor	
Behavior	Docile; likes to play; runs in brief bursts; may be too large for young children	Make time for play
Grooming	Simple brushing on occasion is all that is required	Teach puppies to be groomed early on, so that it does not become a struggle
Common health issues	"Wobbler syndrome," causing a loss of balance; osteoarthritis may affect older individuals, along with bone cancer; bloat	These conditions may need surgical treatment; do not exercise after feeding, as this can cause bloat

2. Anatolian Shepherd Dog

Originating in Turkey, there are at least three different regional strains of this breed in existence. These are known under separate names, such as the Akbash Dog found in western areas of the country, although these varieties have not been widely recognized outside their homeland.

History

The ancestors of this breed have been kept for centuries in Turkey, evolving in relative isolation in different areas there. This helps to explain the diversity in color and appearance that exists within the different bloodlines. These dogs have served as flock guardians, defending sheep and goats from attacks by wolves. They remained unknown in the West, however, right up until 1967, when an American serviceman named Robert Ballard obtained two puppies in a rural area near the Turkish capital, Ankara. It was in the U.S., therefore, that the breed was first developed as a show dog, although in the early days, regional differences were unappreciated.

The breed in the West

Today, there is growing appreciation of the varieties that exist, and more of an effort is being made to establish regional forms, based on their coloration. Most of the individuals that have followed are Kangal-type dogs, which are common in central Turkey. These individuals have black faces, compared with the Akbash variety, which has white hair on its head. Much rarer, not having made a significant contribution to Western bloodlines, is the Kars, which is localized to a remote area of eastern Turkey, and is significantly darker in terms of its overall coloration. None of these dogs can be recommended for a novice owner, as they need very careful training in order to integrate them successfully into the family home.

AT A GLANCE
- Very strong, powerful dog
- An amalgam of localized varieties
- Very determined
- Hardy nature
- Needs plenty of space
- Unusual breed

V-shaped ears
The ears drop down the sides of the head

Variable colors
Color and patterning can be variable

Muscular neck
The powerful neck has skin and fur combining to create a protective ruff

CANINE CHARACTERISTICS		NOTES
Personality	Forceful and determined; will not back down readily if challenged; dislikes visitors, even if they are welcome	
Size	Height: 27–32 in. (69–81 cm) Weight: 80–150 lb (36–68 kg)	There are regional variations
Exercise	Needs plenty of activity every day, although not a great runner	Exercise daily, but keep away from other dogs and livestock, as the dog may want to chase them
At home	Highly protective	
Behavior	Alert, courageous, and devoted; could pose a threat to people if not properly controlled	Keep a close eye on the dog around others
Grooming	Regular brushing required; may sometimes have double dewclaws on the hind feet	
Common health issues	Hip dysplasia, a weakness of the hip joints leading to lameness; entropion, where the eyelids are directed inward and rub against the eyeball; skin problems; cancer can be an issue in older individuals	Ensure breeding stock has been screened for hip dysplasia; entropion may need corrective surgery

3. Saint Bernard

This is one of the best known breeds in the world, thanks to the famous painting by Sir Edwin Landseer, which showed the Saint Bernard with a keg of brandy around the neck to revive a lost traveler that it had found in the snow.

CANINE CHARACTERISTICS		NOTES
Personality	Friendly and enthusiastic; good-natured with children; independent streak	
Size	Height: 26–28 in. (66–71 cm) or more Weight: 110–200 lb (50–91 kg)	
Exercise	Needs a good walk, including the opportunity to roam off the leash	Do not overexercise young dogs; avoid exercise in the hottest part of the day
At home	Often appears clumsy, especially in confined surroundings; may drool over furnishings	Consider covering chairs to protect against the drool
Behavior	Has a good sense of smell; usually not aggressive toward other dogs	
Grooming	Grooming is more straightforward for a smooth-coated dog	Remember to groom the bushy tail
Common health issues	Blood-clotting ailments; problems with the eyelids relative to the eyeball; bone cancer called osteosarcoma, affecting the legs, is common in older individuals	Testing is available for clotting deficiencies, if suspected; problems with the eyelids may need corrective surgery

Dark eyes
The eyes are medium sized and dark brown

Ear flaps
The ears are set high on the head, with the ear flaps being the shape of rounded triangles

Arched chest
The chest displays a clear arch and does not reach down to the elbows

Strong legs
The upper legs are very powerful and muscular, with the lower part being straight and strong

History

The breed is indelibly linked to the hospice founded by Saint Bernard de Menthon, in the 10th century, high in the Swiss Alps. The aim was to assist people who became lost and cut off by blizzards in this region. The monks used dogs of mastiff stock, and these may have been crossed with Bloodhounds to improve their scenting skills, although, initially, they were kept as watchdogs. The most famous Saint Bernard was a dog named Barry, who was credited with saving at least 40 lives between 1800 and 1812. He was passed to the care of a taxidermist on his death, and can be seen in a natural history museum at Bern. Overall, when Saint Bernards were working in the Alps, these dogs probably rescued some 2,000 people.

The breed legacy

In the 1800s when the winters in the Alps were severe, it was felt that Saint Bernards with thicker coats would help under these conditions, and so some crossings with Newfoundlands were made. The legacy from that period is still seen. Today, it is not uncommon for some Saint Bernards to display much thicker, longer coats than others, reflecting that period in the breed's past. They make trustworthy companions, but, today, they are not particularly effective guardians of property.

4. Great Pyrenees

Also known as the Pyrenean Mountain Dog, this breed's homeland lies in the Pyrenees, the region separating France and Spain. The Great Pyrenees is well protected against the cold, thanks to a dense double coat, with the thick undercoat trapping warm air next to the skin.

History

The Great Pyrenees was originally bred as a flock guardian, with its primarily white coloration allowing it to merge in alongside the flocks of sheep that it was protecting, largely against wolves. It was accorded the title of "Royal Dog of France" by King Louis XIV (1638–1715) for its bravery. The only defense that these dogs were given to fight off an attack by a pack of wolves, or indeed an angry bear, was a special iron collar, from which sharp nails protruded. Over time, however, both wolves and bears were exterminated, leaving the Great Pyrenees facing an uncertain future. Its attractive appearance led to these dogs entering the show ring. However, they were also traditionally used for cross-border smuggling of illegal goods in the Pyrenees, taking routes that were inaccessible to people.

Back from the brink

An unusual characteristic of the breed is the presence of double dewclaws on the hind feet. They have no functional significance, but these nails will need to be cut back on a regular basis, to prevent them from growing into the pads. This calls for a stout pair of clippers, and may be better undertaken by your veterinarian, partly because, if the dewclaws are cut too short, they will bleed. As with many giant breeds, these dogs will not thrive in a crowded home because they require space around them. They also need a well-fenced yard, where they can wander. Although they are not particularly energetic, they possess plenty of stamina, and will require long walks on a daily basis if they are not to become bored.

CANINE CHARACTERISTICS		NOTES
Personality	Friendly; aloof with strangers; watchful	
Size	Height: 25–32 in. (64–81 cm) Weight: 85–100 lb (38.5–45 kg)	Dogs weigh quite a bit more than bitches
Exercise	Needs good, long walks in the countryside	Avoid livestock, as the dog may want to chase them
At home	Needs lots of space and a yard; thrives in a stable home; settles well into family life	Allow time for exploring in the yard
Behavior	Attentive and adaptable; has lost the assertiveness of some similar breeds	
Grooming	Double coat; grooming is more demanding in spring when the coat is being shed	Brush regularly
Common health issues	Hip dysplasia, which can cause serious lameness; problems with eyelids; bloat	Ensure breeding stock has been screened for hip dysplasia; eyelid problems may need surgery; do not exercise after feeding, as this can cause bloat

White coat
The coat is white in color, or white with broken areas of gray, reddish-brown, badger, or shades of tan

Long feathering
The backs of both the front legs and the thighs have feathering of longer hair

Oval-shaped rib cage
The well-sprung rib cage extends down to the elbows

Double dewclaws
Double dewclaws are present on the hind feet, which are rounded with well-arched toes

5. Greater Swiss Mountain Dog

This breed is known in its homeland as Grosser Schweizer Sennenhund, and is a close relative of the Bernese Mountain Dog (see page 90). Although their coloration is identical, the Greater Swiss Mountain Dog can be distinguished quite easily from the Bernese by its larger size and smooth coat.

AT A GLANCE

- Striking patterning
- Good family dog
- Relatively little grooming is needed
- Very amenable to training
- Protective nature

White blaze
A prominent white blaze extends between the eyes, broadening over the muzzle

Typical expression
The animated expression typifies this breed. The eyes should be dark brown

Symmetrical markings
Markings on the head and elsewhere should be symmetrical

Powerful legs
The forelegs are long, straight, and powerful with rounded, compact feet

History

This breed was developed in the Swiss Alps and its ancestry almost certainly traces back to mastiffs. The dogs undertook a variety of tasks, but their main role was to pull carts, providing a means of transport. By the late 1800s, however, in the face of increasing mechanization, the breed had become scarce and was on the verge of extinction. Thanks largely to the efforts of an enthusiast named Professor Albert Heim, the breed was ultimately saved and has now become known to a much wider audience, first being seen in the U.S. in 1968.

For the family

This breed can make an excellent family dog, provided that you have the space available to accommodate it. You should also not be especially house-proud because Greater Swiss Mountain Dogs may dribble over furnishings. Avoid overexercising young puppies to protect them against joint problems later in life. A couple of short walks every day is much better than a longer daily hike. As with all large breeds in particular, never feed your dog before going out for a walk. This can trigger the build-up of gas in the stomach, known as bloat, which can be fatal.

CANINE CHARACTERISTICS		NOTES
Personality	Relaxed, loyal, and protective; reserved with strangers	
Size	Height: 24–29 in. (61–74 cm) Weight: 130–135 lb (59–61 kg)	
Exercise	Needs a good walk every day, rather than a brief run	Exercise with a good walk
At home	A family breed; prefers cooler climates; good with children	Help the dog to become part of the family
Behavior	Slow-maturing, like most large dogs; usually good with other dogs and cats	
Grooming	Brushing required and is needed more often when molting	Use a hound glove to emphasize the gloss on the coat
Common health issues	Hip dysplasia, causing lameness; distichiasis, the presence of extra eyelashes; bloat	Ensure breeding stock has been screened for hip dysplasia; distichiasis may need surgery; do not exercise after feeding, as this can cause bloat

6. Dogue de Bordeaux

A starring role in the Hollywood movie *Turner and Hooch* alongside Tom Hanks in 1989 led to this distinctive French breed becoming well-known on the international stage. Within France, it had simply been described as the Dogue for many years.

AT A GLANCE
- Impressively powerful
- Attractively colored
- Friendly toward members of the family
- Large appetite
- Adequate exercise is very important

History

Descended from mastiff stock, the Dogue has existed for centuries. Originally, it was kept as a fighting breed, and was also used in medieval battles. It was then developed into a guardian of property and served as a hunting dog. Members of the breed also worked as drovers for butchers, taking cattle to market. This enabled the Dogue to survive the upheavals of the French Revolution, although many of those kept as guardians at chateaux were killed along with their owners. Reputedly, crossings with smaller bulldogs were later used to rebuild its numbers. Most recently, the breed has become popular both in France and elsewhere as a companion.

The modern Dogue

The furrows on the face suggest that these dogs are always frowning, while the way in which the ears are set well back on the head indicates a breed with a fighting ancestry. The breed's coloration is fairly distinctive, ranging from fawn to red, sometimes with a black mask, and often there are white areas on the chest. The overall physique reflects the Dogue's strength, and although it may have calmed down considerably, it is not really suited to a first-time dog owner.

Dogue muzzle
The Dogue has a strong, thick, and relatively short muzzle, with broad jaws

Coat color
Color varies from a light to a dark red shade of fawn, often with a small white patch on the chest

Powerful chest
The chest is very muscular and powerful and extends down below the elbows

Strong feet
Well-muscled legs end in strong feet with thick, curving nails

CANINE CHARACTERISTICS		NOTES
Personality	Loyal to the family	Train to have a clearly defined subservient position within the family
Size	Height: 23–30 in. (58–76 cm) Weight: 80–120 lb (36–54.4 kg)	
Exercise	Needs good walks, but mental exercise, such as playing games, is also important	Do not exercise during the hottest part of the day, as the dog will be at risk of heatstroke
At home	Drools readily on furnishings, and often snores, particularly in old age; usually fine with younger members of the family; a very focused guard dog	
Behavior	Calm but sensitive, and will pick up its mood from its owner	Encourage socialization with other dogs at an early age while the dog is still a puppy
Grooming	Short coat needs very little attention, although more frequent brushing is required during molting	Wipe the skin folds regularly, as these areas can become infected
Common health issues	Hip dysplasia, causing a variable degree of lameness; heart conditions; epilepsy; large head means puppies may need a Caesarean birth	Ensure breeding stock has been screened for hip dysplasia; epilepsy can be controlled by medication

7. Irish Wolfhound

These massive dogs typically grow taller than any other breed, but are relatively light, certainly compared with mastiff stock. They can therefore gallop at speed, and have a good stride length, enabling them to cover a lot of ground with each step.

CANINE CHARACTERISTICS		NOTES
Personality	Affable, docile, and affectionate	
Size	Height: typically 30–34 in. (76–86 cm) Weight: 90–120 lb (41–54.4 kg)	Can be more than 84 in. (213 cm) tall when standing up on its hind legs; dogs are much heavier than bitches
Exercise	Needs a good daily run—this is essential	Do not overexercise young dogs, as this can lead to joint problems
At home	Takes up a lot of space; a secure paddock adjacent to your home would be ideal	Be prepared to sacrifice an armchair
Behavior	Young puppies in particular can appear rather clumsy at times—this should pass as their coordination improves; may get along well with much smaller dogs	Involve the dog in family life
Grooming	Tousled coat is remarkably weather-resistant	Brush or comb regularly
Common health issues	Hip dysplasia, causing lameness; Progressive Retinal Atrophy (PRA), leading to blindness; degeneration of the heart muscle, known as cardiomyopathy; tumors in the long limb bones, known as osteosarcomas in older individuals; bloat	Ensure breeding stock has been screened for hip dysplasia and PRA; do not exercise after feeding, as this can cause bloat

Pointed muzzle
The Irish Wolfhound has a long, slightly pointed muzzle with the skull being relatively narrow

Typical color
The coat is typically fawn, red, gray, black, or brindle, and even sometimes pure white

Shoulders and chest
Muscular shoulders emphasize the width of the chest, which is very deep

Strong forelegs
The forelegs are both straight and strong, with the feet being relatively large

History

The origins of this breed may extend right back to the sight hounds that were brought from the Mediterranean region to the British Isles perhaps as long as 3,000 years ago. These dogs were interbred with native mastiffs. The early wolfhounds were bold, not only defending sheep against attack from wolf packs, but they were also able to pursue wolves as well. By the late 1700s, the breed was facing an uncertain future, as the wolf began to die out throughout the British Isles.

Modern times

The modern Irish Wolfhound is a revival of the ancient bloodline. A Scotsman named Captain George Graham used examples that still survived, outcrossing to the related Scottish Deerhound (see page 41) and other large breeds, such as the Borzoi (see page 67) and even the Tibetan Mastiff (see page 89), to increase its numbers. The result is a friendly, athletic breed that makes a great companion if you have the space to accommodate it. In common with sight hounds of all sizes, however, it can be wayward in terms of returning when called once it is off the leash.

8. Tibetan Mastiff

Bred in the Himalayan region, the Tibetan Mastiff is a breed with a long history. It is perhaps closer in appearance to the original stock, which served as the parent of all mastiff bloodlines, than any other similar breed today.

AT A GLANCE

- Massive, powerful breed
- Unusual, catlike feet
- Only comes into season once a year
- Very loyal and protective
- Can be fierce especially when barking

CANINE CHARACTERISTICS		NOTES
Personality	Protective of the home and suspicious of strangers	Keep an eye on the dog around others
Size	Height: 25–28 in. (64–71 cm) Weight: 120–140 lb (54.4–63.5 kg)	Dogs are bigger overall than bitches
Exercise	Needs regular daily walks—this is essential	Ensure you are in firm control, especially in view of the dog's strength
At home	Not recommended for a novice owner; usually happy living with older children	
Behavior	Relatively slow to mature; bitches only come into season once a year, rather than twice, restricting the availability of puppies; naturally not well-disposed to other dogs	Ensure that the dog is well trained right from the outset
Grooming	Thorough, regular brushing of the double coat is essential; grooming also builds a bond between you and the dog	Clean the ears regularly to stop infections developing
Common health issues	Canine Inherited Demyelinative Neuropathy (CIDN), a progressive paralytic illness causing death by four months; hip dysplasia, causing lameness; thyroid problems, affecting the metabolism	Ensure breeding stock has been screened for hip dysplasia

Tibetan Mastiff ears
Medium-sized, V-shaped ears lie forward down the sides of the head

Coat color
The coat can be bluish-gray, brown or black, all often with tan markings, or golden colored

Coat length
Male dogs tend to have longer, more profuse coats than bitches

White patches
White areas on the breast and feet are not uncommon

History

It is widely believed that mastiffs as a group arose in Asia. The Tibetan first came to prominence during the late 1700s, where it was kept primarily as a fearsome guardian of both property and livestock. The breed was first seen in Britain during 1828, when one of these dogs was placed on display at London Zoo, having been given to George IV (1762–1830) as a gift. While black and tan still remains the favored color, Tibetan owners would also seek individuals of the breed that had a white "heart spot," said to signify bravery, on the chest.

At home with a Tibetan Mastiff

The breed's origins are unknown, although spitz-type stock, evident by the distinctively curly tail flopping forward over the back, certainly made a contribution. Tibetan Mastiffs are smaller compared with their size in the past, although they are still large, powerful dogs. Members of the breed are instinctive guardians, both of persons and property, and need proper training before they can be allowed to roam safely off the leash. It is worth remembering that their ancestors used to be tied up outside properties in their homeland, and would bark loudly rather than attacking, which is still a trait associated with this breed.

9. Bernese Mountain Dog

As their working ancestry suggests, these well-built dogs are powerful; but, today, they are kept as companions and for the show ring. They are still better known in Switzerland as Berner Sennenhunds, being closely associated with the area of Bern.

CANINE CHARACTERISTICS		NOTES
Personality	Tolerant, industrious, and calm by nature; confident; friendly and affectionate	
Size	Height: 23–28 in. (58–71 cm) Weight: 85–90 lb (38.5–41 kg)	
Exercise	Needs a good walk every day; tends to walk more at a trot	Exercise daily
At home	Gets along well with family members	
Behavior	Learns rapidly and is eager to please	Start training at an early age
Grooming	Regular brushing of the double coat required, but not difficult or especially time-consuming	Groom more often in spring when the dog is shedding
Common health issues	Hip dysplasia, causing lameness; Progressive Retinal Atrophy (PRA), leading to blindness; Von Willebrand's Disease, an inherited blood clotting disorder; puppies are occasionally born with a cleft palate and/or a cleft lip; cancer	Ensure breeding stock has been screened for hip dysplasia, PRA, Von Willebrand's Disease

History

This breed was relied upon to undertake a variety of tasks in its Swiss homeland. These included acting as farm dogs, herding, and guarding livestock and property. Their most important role was pulling carts and transporting goods. They have a long history in the region, and are thought to be descended from ancient Roman mastiff stock. By the 1890s, however, in common with other closely related Sennenhund breeds, the Bernese started to become scarce, as its working role declined in significance. Luckily, at this stage, a local innkeeper decided to try to rescue it from extinction, and began a breeding program.

Why the Bernese?

The Bernese's rich and contrasting coloration, combined with its symmetrical pattern of markings, has helped to underscore its popularity. The breed is now the most popular of the four sennenhunds, and can make a good household companion. These dogs have proved incredibly versatile, too. Bernese Mountain Dogs participate in a range of activities, including obedience and agility competitions, as well as herding and tracking events. There are even cart-pulling contests organized for the breed in the U.S., and their good nature sees them working as therapy dogs.

Straight muzzle
The muzzle is straight and strong with no pronounced dewlaps

Distinctive markings
The Bernese has very distinctive tricolored markings, with the patterning being symmetrical as far as possible

Legs and feet
The forelegs are straight and powerful with the feet being round and compact in shape

Powerful thighs
The thighs are powerful and well muscled

10. Alaskan Malamute

The Alaskan Malamute is named after the Inuit tribe known as the Mahlemut, who live in northwestern Alaska around Kotzebue Sound. It is an immensely powerful sled breed, and as with similar breeds, howls in a wolflike manner rather than barks.

History

The Alaskan Malamute's ancestry extends right back to early dogs, which were domesticated in Alaska thousands of years ago. Since then, it has come to provide a vital lifeline, as a means of transportation in the region. These dogs work in teams, pulling sleds that may be laden with goods and are controlled by the driver, or "musher."

Nature versus nurture

Few breeds are as well adapted to their environment as the Alaskan Malamute. Its strong shoulders, combined with its powerful body, provide the strength to pull the sled, while its broad chest allows for a good lung capacity, helping to get vital oxygen into the blood and to the muscles. Working in the bitter cold, where the temperature can fall well below freezing, it has a dense undercoat that serves to trap warm air next to the skin. The outer, weather-resistant top coat is dense, ensuring that snow cannot penetrate into this layer, with it being at its longest over the back. Finally, the Alaskan Malamute's powerful paws help to prevent it from sinking into the snow. These dogs need firm training. Neutering is important to control the inherent dominant attitude of males, which can lead to aggression toward other dogs. Individuals of this breed instinctively want to be top dog, and if unchecked, this desire can potentially create serious problems.

Almond eyes
The eyes are set obliquely in the skull, and are brown and almond shaped

Neck and chest
The strong neck connects with a muscular chest

Alaskan color
Coat color can vary from light gray to black, and sable to red, with white predominating. Pure white individuals are also sometimes seen

Powerful legs
Very powerful hindquarters provide propulsive thrust

CANINE CHARACTERISTICS		NOTES
Personality	Dominant, assertive, and determined; will pick up on any weakness	Provide the dog with leadership
Size	Height: 23–25 in. (58–64 cm) Weight: 75–85 lb (34–38.5 kg)	Dogs are quite a bit heavier than bitches
Exercise	Has incredible stamina, so good walks are essential; still used in sled racing—competitions may take place over ordinary ground with adapted sleds	Avoid exercise in the hottest part of the day, as the dog can suffer from heatstroke, due to the thick coat
At home	Can be restless, but will bond well with its handler; instinctively a "one-person" dog; not recommended for novice owners	
Behavior	Behavior can be challenging	Start training from puppyhood—this is essential
Grooming	Thorough brushing required; sheds more undercoat in spring	
Common health issues	Kidney disease; hemeralopia, being blinded by bright light; hip dysplasia; dwarfism or chondrodysplasia, where puppies are born with short legs	Ensure breeding stock has been screened for hip dysplasia

Dog types for people who like exercising, whether walking or running outdoors; those who want to participate in sled racing or cart pulling; and others in search of a gundog to train.

Dalmatian

Lurcher

Siberian Husky

Dogs that Love to Run

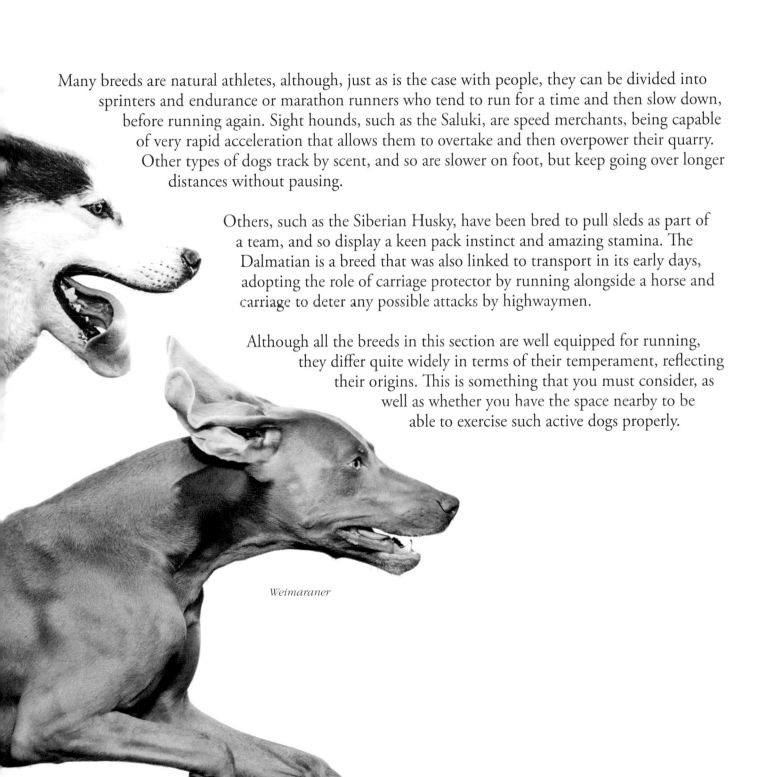

Many breeds are natural athletes, although, just as is the case with people, they can be divided into sprinters and endurance or marathon runners who tend to run for a time and then slow down, before running again. Sight hounds, such as the Saluki, are speed merchants, being capable of very rapid acceleration that allows them to overtake and then overpower their quarry. Other types of dogs track by scent, and so are slower on foot, but keep going over longer distances without pausing.

Others, such as the Siberian Husky, have been bred to pull sleds as part of a team, and so display a keen pack instinct and amazing stamina. The Dalmatian is a breed that was also linked to transport in its early days, adopting the role of carriage protector by running alongside a horse and carriage to deter any possible attacks by highwaymen.

Although all the breeds in this section are well equipped for running, they differ quite widely in terms of their temperament, reflecting their origins. This is something that you must consider, as well as whether you have the space nearby to be able to exercise such active dogs properly.

Weimaraner

1. Siberian Husky

This breed played a famous part in U.S. history. Back in 1925, a team of mushers and Siberian Huskies saved the town of Nome in Alaska from a diphtheria epidemic by getting through to the town with a supply of life-saving serum in appalling weather.

Friendly expression
The Siberian Husky has a friendly, alert expression. The almond-shaped eyes are brown, blue, or the dog has one of each color

Husky color
The coat can be any color or pattern, with markings on the head being common

Powerful thighs
The thighs are powerfully muscled with the hocks being relatively low to the ground

Straight legs
The front legs appear parallel and straight when seen from the front

History

The breed's origins are said to extend back over 3,000 years, to the region of Yakutsk, in Siberia. Originally known as the Chukchi, its name is thought to be derived from that of the Chukchi tribe, which originally kept these sled dogs as a means of transport. The dogs provided a vital lifeline for the people and the Chukchi used only their very best dogs for breeding. Furthermore, as the dogs grew up alongside children, they developed a friendly nature, which has lasted through to the present day. Although the Siberian Husky may be the smallest of the sled breeds, it is also the fastest, and can display remarkable stamina. It was taken to the U.S. in the early 1900s.

Racing the breed

The breed today is one of the most widely kept sled dogs, partly because of its size but also because of its friendly nature. Siberian Huskies are very active dogs, and are best kept in pairs if not larger groups, as they are instinctively social by nature, although there is a distinct pack order within the group. In many countries, sled racing is obviously not possible because of a lack of snow, but cart racing with Siberian Huskies is a popular pastime, and helps to display the breed's strength and determination. They are quiet dogs by nature, as befits a breed that still bears a striking resemblance to wolves, and they prefer to howl rather than bark. Blue-eyed individuals are not uncommon.

CANINE CHARACTERISTICS		NOTES
Personality	Responsive and friendly, but sometimes stubborn; appreciates a pack order	
Size	Height: 20–24 in. (51–61 cm) Weight: 35–60 lb (16–27 kg)	
Exercise	Needs plenty of daily exercise—this is essential; teams of Siberian Huskies can be used to pull carts	Exercise at least once a day
At home	Will settle well provided its exercise needs are met	Allow plenty of play at home to avert boredom
Behavior	Independent, and so training is very important	Train daily, even with older dogs
Grooming	Thick and dense coat protects against the elements	Brush weekly
Common health issues	Inherited eye conditions, including Progressive Retinal Atrophy (PRA)	Ensure breeding stock has been screened for eye conditions

2. Dalmatian

The Dalmatian ranks as one of the most distinctive of all breeds, due to its spotted appearance. It has become very well-known and easily recognizable thanks to the book by Dodie Smith, *101 Dalmatians*, which has also been made into various movies.

AT A GLANCE

- Striking individual appearance
- Very active and full of energy
- Easily groomed coat
- Good guardian
- Spotless at birth

History

Although the breed is named after the Dalmatian coast, which lies in the Balkan region of Europe, there seems little to link it to this area. While the origins of the Dalmatian are unknown, its appearance suggests that it is descended from a scent hound lineage. The first record of a dog of this type comes from the Netherlands, dating back to the mid-1600s. After this, the breed became very popular in England where its stamina was used in a unique protective role. The Dalmatian evolved as a coach dog that ran alongside a coach, or sometimes a rider on horseback, protecting the coach from attack. The breed also became linked with horse-drawn fire engines in the U.S. The Dalmatian was also a popular exhibit at the early dog shows in the 1890s.

Initially spotless

An unusual feature of the breed is that puppies are completely white at birth and only develop their spots from the age of two to three weeks. The patterning is highly individual—judges prefer those where the spots are well spaced over the body, and clearly defined. The spots (and nose) of an individual can be either liver–brown or black, but not both. As well as being attractive dogs, Dalmatians are very active by nature, and must be given plenty of opportunities to run off the leash.

CANINE CHARACTERISTICS		NOTES
Personality	Protective; loyal; intelligent and adaptable; reserved attitude toward strangers	Keep an eye on the dog around strangers
Size	Height: 19–23 in. (48–58 cm) Weight: 50–55 lb (22.7–25 kg)	
Exercise	Prefers open country rather than woodland	Exercise with a good daily run off the leash
At home	Alert; good guardian	
Behavior	Retains an eager hunting instinct; will hunt rats—has been used as a retriever	Keep an eye on the dog around small animals
Grooming	Simple brushing of the short coat is required; a very rare, long-coated Dalmatian can occur	Brush when necessary
Common health issues	Susceptible to bladder and kidney stones because of a metabolic deficiency, which can also cause gout; blue-eyed Dalmatians may suffer from deafness	

Strong legs
The front legs are strong, straight, and sturdy in appearance

Dalmatian tail
The tail continues along the line of the back, tapering toward its tip, and has a slight curve upward

Compact feet
The feet are round, and compact with thick pads and well-arched toes

Spotted coat
The spots on the sleek coat should be well defined

3. Weimaraner

The appearance of the Weimaraner is unique, thanks in part to its gray coat coloration, which can range from a light silvery shade to a darker mouse gray. The Weimaraner's expressive eyes can range in color from amber through to gray.

AT A GLANCE
- Sleek, striking appearance
- Unusual coloration
- Loyal companion
- Friendly nature
- Relatively easy to train
- Minimal grooming needs

History

This breed was created by the Grand Duke Karl August of Weimar in Germany, in the early 1800s. He sought to develop a hunting breed that excelled in all areas. As foundation stock, German Pointers were used and were crossed with Bloodhounds and French hounds to achieve improved scenting skills, pace, and stamina. Bravery was also important at that early stage in the Weimaraner's history, as the dogs were used to hunt wild boar and even bears. Since then, however, the breed has evolved into a bird dog. The dogs were so highly prized that they were not allowed to be bred freely, and strict controls on their ownership were imposed right up until the start of the 1930s.

A versatile companion

The Weimaraner is a very versatile gundog. It combines all the strengths of its ancestral breeds, being a pointer as well as a very good tracker and even a retriever. It is still highly sought after for this versatility today. In addition, its striking good looks and elegant gait mean that it is a popular dog in the show ring. The Weimaraner is well suited to being a household companion, especially in rural areas where it will thrive if given adequate opportunity to exercise with long daily walks. It is ideally suited to a home with energetic children, as it also enjoys playing. A spacious yard is important so that it can retrieve flying disks and run around enthusiastically chasing after balls.

Long ears
The ears are set high, have a lobular shape, and are slightly folded

Facial features
The Weimaraner has an eager, intelligent expression with the eyes being well spaced apart, ranging in color from light amber to blue–gray to gray

Gray coat
The coat is usually lighter on the head and ears than it is on the body

Firm feet
The feet are firm and compact with well-arched toes that also display signs of webbing

CANINE CHARACTERISTICS		NOTES
Personality	Friendly	
Size	Height: 23–27 in. (58–69 cm) Weight: 70–86 lb (32–39 kg)	
Exercise	Enjoys long walks; displays considerable stamina; athletic	Keep an eye on the dog around water, as it will enter water readily
At home	Becomes destructive if bored	Make time for play
Behavior	Energetic	
Grooming	Grooming is straightforward; a rare long-haired form of the Weimaraner exists	Brush when necessary
Common health issues	Puppies can be afflicted by umbilical hernias; susceptible to skin ailments	Ensure a puppy has a veterinary check for umbilical problems—this may need corrective surgery

4 Vizsla

The name of this ancient Hungarian breed is pronounced *Veesh-la*. The Vizsla's coloration is very distinctive, traditionally being a rusty–gold shade. Its nose should always be reddish, blending in with the color of the coat, as do its eyes and nails.

AT A GLANCE

- Thrives in warm surroundings
- Friendly nature
- Popular sporting companion
- Straightforward grooming
- Energetic

CANINE CHARACTERISTICS		NOTES
Personality	Gentle nature yet protective; likes being with people; loyal; sensitive; affectionate	Always offer encouragement
Size	Height: 21–24 in. (53–61 cm) Weight: 49–66 lb (22–30 kg)	
Exercise	Prefers open country; possesses plenty of stamina	Allow the dog to run off the leash
At home	Happy in a home with older children	
Behavior	Adaptable and responsive to training; lively	Involve the whole family in training
Grooming	Grooming is straightforward for the short-haired breed, but the lack of an undercoat means it is vulnerable to the cold; there is a rarer wirehaired form, which does have an undercoat	Groom when necessary
Common health issues	Hemophilia, a blood-clotting disorder, affects some male dogs; genetic weakness is associated with specific bloodlines	

History

It is thought that the origins of the Vizsla may date back over 900 years, with its name commemorating Vizsla, which was an ancient settlement found in the vicinity of the Danube Valley. By the late 1800s, however, the breed was close to extinction, with just a dozen surviving individuals still in existence. Crossbreeding with pointers probably then played a part in ensuring its survival, though the breed was imperiled again as a result of the First and Second World Wars. However, refugees fleeing from Hungary took some Vizslas with them during the 1940s, and they have since become more popular.

Training concerns

The Vizsla is a very adaptable breed, as reflected by the fact that having initially been valued as a pointer, working with falcons, it has since become a very effective retriever. The Vizsla forms a very close bond with its immediate family, although you need to ensure that it does not become a "one-person" dog, but will respond equally well to all members of the family. This potential difficulty can be overcome at an early stage by ensuring that more than one family member is involved in the young dog's training. Having been bred to hunt on the plains of Hungary, Vizslas require plenty of exercise.

Muscular neck
The neck is relatively long and muscular and broadens into the shoulders

Broad chest
The chest is broad and reaches down to the level of the elbows

Strong thighs
The thighs are well developed, with the hind legs appearing parallel when viewed from behind

Long legs
The long, straight forelegs end in rather catlike, rounded feet

5. Irish Setter

In any canine beauty contest, the Irish Setter could easily be the winner, thanks to its stunning chestnut–red coat coloration and elegant gait. As a result of its appearance, it is also known as the Red Setter. It is an affectionate dog and is a good choice for a family with teenagers.

History

Developed in Ireland, from crosses involving the Old Spanish Pointer and spaniels, this setter was called the Red Spaniel for a period early in its history. Back in the 1700s, the Irish Setter was just one of three varieties that could emerge in the same litter. The red form was actually less popular than the Irish Red and White Setter, because it was felt that the latter's white areas made it more conspicuous. The rarest variety was called the Hail, simply because its red body color was broken by small white spots that resembled hailstones in appearance. It is now essentially extinct, although very occasionally individuals crop up in litters. During the 1900s, occasional crossings with the Borzoi (see page 67) were used to give the Irish Setter a taller, rangier look.

Active by nature

Matings with the Borzoi probably did nothing to improve the rather wayward nature of the breed. Nevertheless, the Irish Setter has proved to be a highly competent gundog, with its natural enthusiasm being very evident when it is working. It is very important not to be seduced by the attractive appearance of this breed, but to appreciate that as a companion, it will require a lot of exercise. Young dogs often take longer to train than many other types of gundogs. Bored individuals will become destructive at home, and are likely to be disobedient when let off the leash, often disappearing into the distance.

CANINE CHARACTERISTICS		NOTES
Personality	Friendly and exuberant; dedicated worker	
Size	Height: 25–27 in. (64–69 cm) Weight: 60–70 lb (27–32 kg)	
Exercise	Needs plenty of opportunities to run	Choose a safe area, away from roads in case the dog runs off
At home	Loves playing	Make time for lots of play
Behavior	Can be inclined to run off quite readily; not a quick learner but a dedicated worker	Be patient when training
Grooming	Regular grooming of the longer hair required—the longer hair on the back of the legs and tail is called feathering	Brush and comb regularly
Common health issues	Puppies can be afflicted by a swallowing disorder—this can be linked to muscle weakness	

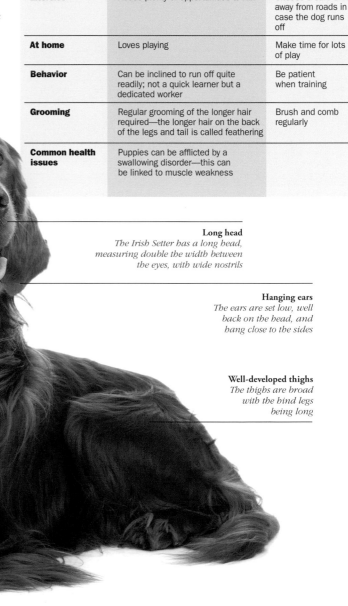

Long head
The Irish Setter has a long head, measuring double the width between the eyes, with wide nostrils

Hanging ears
The ears are set low, well back on the head, and hang close to the sides

Well-developed thighs
The thighs are broad with the hind legs being long

Small feet
The feet are relatively small with arched toes that lie close to each other

6. Lurcher

There is no standardization of these dogs, which are still kept primarily for working purposes. They are typically the result of crossbreedings between a hound and a herding dog, with the aim being to create a quiet and intelligent hunting companion.

History

The use of hounds for hunting in England dates back over a millennium. This activity was restricted to the nobility, but there were those who sought to use their dogs to run down and overpower prey, such as deer. While such activities carried serious penalties, this was not necessarily a deterrent. Lurchers were developed for this purpose, often being the result of matings between hounds, such as Deerhounds or Greyhounds, which gave them pace, and collies, whose purpose was to make their offspring more responsive. A variety of different breeds were used in these roles, however, to the extent that it could be argued that Lurchers represent the first designer dogs.

Defining a Lurcher

A Lurcher puppy that is bred from working stock will almost certainly display such instincts itself, although perhaps less so if it has been created from show bloodlines. Today, lighter-colored individuals are often more popular, for their looks, whereas, in the past, dark-colored individuals were favored because they were less conspicuous when working. The Lurcher is fast running and very responsive to its owner. It also often tends to have a natural intelligence, which makes it an attractive option if you are looking for a very active breed. The dog's variability in appearance also ensures that you end up with a truly individual dog, but you should always try to ascertain the dog's exact parentage. This will not only give you an insight into its likely adult size, but also its adult appearance. On occasion, puppies are back-crossed by matings with sight hounds, to improve the bloodline.

CANINE CHARACTERISTICS		NOTES
Personality	A genuine "trier" and full of enthusiasm; friendly nature and calm disposition	
Size	Height: variable Weight: relates to height	Lurchers are naturally slender with a Greyhound-like build
Exercise	Typically most active as darkness falls; needs the opportunity to run off the leash	Exercise off the leash daily
At home	Good companion; relates better to people than many sight hounds; not suited to a household with cats	
Behavior	Will chase after rabbits, cats, and even small dogs when out for a walk; will show stronger hunting instincts at dusk	Keep an eye on the dog around other animals
Grooming	Grooming needs depend on the crosses involved in the dog's background; wire-coated crosses, involving the Bedlington Terrier, are not uncommon	
Common health issues	Health issues are likely to relate to those of the parent breed; Progressive Retinal Atrophy (PRA) can be a particular issue	Find out what the dog's parentage is so that you have an idea of what to expect

Coat length
The length of the coat is variable. The texture in this case is wiry

Athletic build
The body is athletic and relatively long with good lung capacity

Powerful hindquarters
Powerful hindquarters provide power, contributing to the Lurcher's stamina

7. Belgian Shepherd Dog

Within Belgium, four different localized breeds of shepherd dog occur, but in some countries, all four varieties are grouped together. One of the breeds, the Belgian Sheepdog, as it is known in the U.S., is characterized by its long coat and solid black coloration, but it is known elsewhere as the Groenendael.

AT A GLANCE
- Intelligent breed
- Long-coated
- Industrious
- Needs mental and physical exercise
- Responsive to training
- Alert, lively nature

White muzzle
Whitening around the muzzle may become more pronounced in older individuals

White hair
A white area is likely to be present on the chest

Catlike toes
The toes are quite catlike, being elongated and well padded

CANINE CHARACTERISTICS		NOTES
Personality	Determined and loyal; can be suspicious by nature; reserved with strangers	Keep an eye on the dog around strangers
Size	Height: 22–26 in. (56–66 cm) Weight: 61–63 lb (27.7–28.5 kg)	Watch the dog's weight, as it can be susceptible to obesity
Exercise	Needs plenty of opportunities to run freely to help use up its natural energy	Encourage games, such as chasing a ball
At home	Good companion; must have access to a yard; easiest to settle in if obtained as a puppy	Provide the opportunity for play in the yard
Behavior	Friendly toward members of its own household	Encourage socialization at an early age
Grooming	Long coat needs brushing, as well as combing of the longer hair; longer ruff of hair around the neck and chest is most profuse in winter	Brush and comb regularly
Common health issues	Epilepsy	

History

The Belgian Sheepdog, or Groenendael, was named after the Château de Groenendael, lying to the south of Brussels, where the breed was created in 1885. It originated from a black, long-haired bitch who was mated with a similar dog. Introduced to the U.S. in 1907, today it is the most common of the four native Belgian breeds of this type. The others are the long-coated Tervuren, whose coloration is fawn, with black tips to the hairs, its short-coated counterpart, known as the Malinois, which is fawn and black, and the Laekenois, which is the most distinctive variety, being the only rough-coated variant. It is fawn in color.

Character of the breed

This breed has been used as a sheepdog, in police work, and as a guard dog, while it has also become popular in the show ring, in addition to being a companion. The breed's working ancestry means that these dogs are active and must also have mental stimulation to prevent them from becoming bored. They are natural workers, and usually learn quickly. Time spent on training will help to strengthen the bond between dog and handler, but training needs to involve more than one member of the family. The rather suspicious nature of the breed also means that socialization is important at an early stage in life.

8. Saluki

Also known as the Persian Greyhound, this ancient breed has an unmistakable sight hound appearance, thanks to its lean build, deep chest, and narrow waist. It also has long hair, called feathering, on the back of the legs, the underside of the tail, and also on the ears.

AT A GLANCE

- Ancient breed
- Very fast
- Great stamina
- Not the easiest breed to train
- Has a tendency to run off

History

The Saluki has origins that may stretch back over 10,000 years. The breed was created for hunting purposes in the Middle East, to run down gazelles—small, fleet-footed antelopes—as well as hares and foxes. Salukis were often used in association with birds of prey, being carried by riders on camels or sometimes horses. When the bird spotted quarry, circling overhead, the Salukis were then unleashed. Their role was not to kill their quarry, but simply to pin it down until an accompanying huntsman could dispatch it. This demanded not just pace, but also an ability for these hounds to work together.

An uphill task

Today's Salukis retain many of the essential characteristics of their ancestors. Unfortunately, this does mean they will take off after potential quarry, disappearing into the distance. It is hard to prevent such behavior, except by determined training, particularly as these hounds do require a good run every day if they are not to become bored and destructive at home. If you are likely to encounter small dogs that a Saluki might view as a target when out walking, it is safest to muzzle your dog beforehand. In spite of its independent streak, which becomes apparent when hunting, the Saluki is quietly affectionate toward people in its immediate circle at home, but does not take readily to strangers.

Head shape
The long, narrow skull has no pronounced stop between the eyes

Silky ears
The long ears are covered with silky hair

Solid neck
The neck is long, supple, strong, and powerful

Feathered toes
The toes are long and well arched with some feathering

CANINE CHARACTERISTICS		NOTES
Personality	Loyal; wary with visitors	Keep an eye on the dog around visitors
Size	Height: 22–28 in. (56–71 cm) Weight: 44–66 lb (20–30 kg)	Some strains are bigger than others
Exercise	Athletic; possesses plenty of stamina and energy	Exercise with a good daily run; avoid small animals
At home	Useful guardian; unlikely to get along well in a home with rabbits or even cats	
Behavior	Very fast when running; difficult to train not to run off; has an independent streak	Be persistent with training
Grooming	General grooming required; there is also a smooth-coated version of this breed, which is the more common type in the Middle East	Brush the coat and comb the longer hair on the ears and elsewhere
Common health issues	Can be susceptible to various eye problems; bone cancer can strike older individuals	

9. Pharaoh Hound

The Pharaoh Hound is another breed whose appearance has altered little over the course of thousands of years. It has been transformed from a breed used for hunting rabbits to one seen regularly at top shows worldwide today, reflecting its glamorous appearance.

AT A GLANCE
- Beautiful, striking coloration
- Sleek appearance
- Interesting history
- Friendly nature
- Easy-care coat
- Good with children

History

The Phoenicians who traveled and traded widely through the Mediterranean region are credited with taking the ancestors of the Pharaoh Hound to Malta and the adjacent island of Gozo from Egypt several thousands of years ago. Similar breeds are to be found on other Mediterranean islands nearby, notably Ibiza and Sicily. It was not until the late 1960s that the Pharaoh Hound started to attract an international following, being introduced to both the U.K. and U.S. at this stage. As people encountered the attractive coloration and also the friendly natures of these hounds, the breed's popularity soared. The Pharaoh Hound was originally kept for hunting rabbits.

Pace and pursuit

Although Pharaoh Hounds can make good family pets, do not allow them to come into contact with pet rabbits, as their hunting instincts are then likely to surface. This is also true when out for a walk. Try to choose a rural area away from rabbits and roads. If the Pharaoh Hound does race off after a rabbit—and it can be difficult to train your pet not to do so—then at least being away from traffic minimizes the risk of injury to your dog. The Pharaoh Hound's powerful feet allow it to chase rabbits even over rough and rocky ground. Its sleek coat may display some white areas, with the white area on the chest being called the "star."

CANINE CHARACTERISTICS		NOTES
Personality	Intelligent and affectionate	
Size	Height: 21–25 in. (53–64 cm) Weight: 45–55 lb (20.4–25 kg)	
Exercise	Needs plenty of exercise, with the opportunity to run off the leash every day—this is essential	Be aware that the dog will hunt rabbits, hares, or sometimes even smaller prey
At home	Settles well into a family alongside people of all ages	
Behavior	Alert and responsive; may not get along well with cats, as it may want to chase them; can be taught to chase balls easily; somewhat independent	Make time for play
Grooming	Grooming needs are minimal	Use a hound glove to create a shiny appearance to the coat
Common health issues	Although generally healthy, can react badly to some medicines and antiparasitic agents	Be alert to the risk of side effects with such treatments

Broad ears
The ears are broad at the base and very mobile, being carried erect when alert

Tan shades
Shades of tan or chestnut with small white areas are present on the body

Facial features
The face is long and lean with powerful jaws and an alert expression

Muscular neck
The lean, long, and muscular neck displays a slight curve

10. Norwegian Elkhound

This Scandinavian dog is a bold and versatile breed, which has a long history, dating back over 7,000 years. It is also sometimes referred to as the Gray Elkhound, to distinguish it from its more scarce black relative.

AT A GLANCE
- Ancient breed
- Lots of grooming required
- Intelligent
- Will not thrive in urban areas
- Thrives as part of a family

CANINE CHARACTERISTICS		NOTES
Personality	Determined, strong, bold, and loyal	Be firm but fair when training
Size	Height: 20–22 in. (51–56 cm) Weight: 48–55 lb (21.7–25 kg)	
Exercise	Needs plenty of daily opportunities to exercise but may run off	Pick a spot away from people and livestock, and practice training
At home	Developed to work on a one-to-one basis with its owner; can be a good watchdog	Make time for play to prevent boredom
Behavior	Brave	
Grooming	Brushing, especially of the ruff that extends down below the legs, is important—this will take longer during the molt	Brush regularly
Common health issues	Progressive Retinal Atrophy (PRA); hip dysplasia	Ensure breeding stock has been screened for these conditions

History

Ancestors of the Norwegian Elkhound were highly prized, with their remains being found in the graves of Vikings extending back 7,000 years. Further study has revealed that they were almost identical in appearance at that stage to the breed of today. Originally, these elkhounds were kept for hunting purposes, not just in Norway but also in neighboring Sweden. They could be used either on or off the leash. Those that hunted in woodland areas were allowed to venture off the track in search of their quarry. This was not comprised entirely of elk (moose), but could also include other large mammals, such as deer, bears, and wolves. Game birds, such as capercaillie, were also pursued by these elkhounds, although in more open country, the dogs were kept on leashes, being used simply to track scents.

Past and present

A strong and powerful build, combined with considerable determination, reveals the persistent and athletic nature of this breed. Norwegian Elkhounds are very reluctant to give up any challenge, and must have adequate exercise each day to prevent them from becoming bored and destructive around the home. The amount of time spent on grooming can also be quite high, particularly when these elkhounds are shedding their coats.

Pointy ears
The large, pointed ears are set high on the head. They are carried erect and are very mobile

Dark eyes
The oval-shaped, dark brown eyes are set well back on the head

Wedge-shaped head
The distinctive head shape has a good width between the ears, and the face has a lively expression

Curly tail
The thick tail is carried high. It is tightly curled and falls over the center line of the back

Dog types for people who suffer from allergies that cause symptoms such as breathing difficulties and runny eyes, plus house-proud owners or those who simply dislike housework!

Airedale Terrier

Portuguese Water Dog

Miniature Poodle

Hypoallergenic Dogs

Bichon Frisé

With a growing number of both adults and children developing allergies of various types today, there has been increasing interest in those breeds that are less likely to cause allergies. Hence, the description of them being hypoallergenic. In most cases, this is because the dogs do not shed their hair on a regular basis, unlike the majority of dog breeds. As a result, choosing a nonshedding breed should bring another advantage as well. Less time has to be spent cleaning around the home, removing dog's hair from carpets and furnishings, although there are now special vacuum cleaners to facilitate this task.

There is no absolute guarantee that any breed will not generate an allergic reaction. If you are in doubt, rather than acquiring a dog, it would be much better to allow a sensitive member of your household to meet dogs of the type that you are thinking of buying, and noting if there is any adverse reaction. Breeders of such dogs will not consider this strange, and would much rather experiment in this way, rather than sell a puppy that ends up being homeless soon afterward, through no fault of its own.

1. Poodle

Few breeds are more intelligent than the Poodle, with today's Miniature variety having originally found fame for this reason as a circus performer. Poodles are generally very playful dogs, are easy to train, and will bond readily with members of the household.

AT A GLANCE
- Choice of sizes
- Nonshedding coat
- Quick learner
- Very loyal
- Good companion
- Lively nature
- Ideal for city life

History

Today, the Poodle is a breed that occurs in three widely recognized sizes, with the Standard form being the largest. By a process of selectively breeding downward in size, the Miniature Poodle, as it is now called, was developed, although it was known as the Toy Poodle up until 1907. Further downward selection based on size led to the evolution of the Toy Poodle, which is the smallest variety. Just to complicate the issue further, however, some show organizations now recognize a new size division known as the Medium, which is intermediate between the Miniature and Toy Poodle varieties.

Strange looks

The unusual trim of the coat of the Poodle was actually of practical significance at first, in the case of the Standard Poodle. The Poodle was originally kept as a retriever, and would dive into cold water, to retrieve waterfowl that had been shot. The longer hair left around the leg joints provided warmth, while clipping the hair over the powerful hindquarters helped the Poodle to swim by reducing drag, and the pom-pom on the tail meant it could be spotted more easily in the water. There is no need to maintain your Poodle with an elaborate trim of this type, though. Pet Poodles, just like puppies, can have their coat styled in a "lamb" trim, where the coat of the legs blends in with the body, and is easy to maintain. Toy Poodles especially have become very popular urban companions, happily living in surroundings where a Standard Poodle would be cramped.

CANINE CHARACTERISTICS		NOTES
Personality	Responsive and adaptable; accepts children readily	
Size	Height: under 11 in. (28 cm) and 11–18 in. (28–46 cm) Weight: 6–70 lb (2.7–32 kg)	Poodles are recognized as separate breeds, based on their size
Exercise	Small Poodles need less exercise but still require a daily walk—exercise also provides mental stimulation	Exercise daily
At home	Socialization is important—Toy Poodles will bark quite frequently otherwise	Encourage socialization from an early age
Behavior	Playful and alert	Make time for playing games
Grooming	Grooming is usually undertaken at a grooming parlor	Groom and trim every four to eight weeks
Common health issues	Eye disorders, such as Progressive Retinal Atrophy (PRA); heart problems; epilepsy; patellar luxation; potentially suffers from a range of problems—the Standard Poodle is the most robust	Ensure breeding stock has been screened for PRA; patellar luxation may need corrective surgery

Dark eyes
The eyes are oval shaped

Hanging ears
The ears are set at or below the level of the eyes and hang close to the sides of the head

Poodle colors
Coloration should be both even and solid, ranging from white through apricot to black

Oval-shaped paws
The paws are relatively small with well-arched toes and thick pads

2. Portuguese Water Dog

This was the rarest breed in the world during the 1960s, but its numbers have grown, and it recently achieved massive international publicity when a Portuguese Water Dog named Bo was chosen for a pet by President Barack Obama and his family.

History

Known in Portugal as the Cão de Água, this breed is thought to share a common ancestry with the Standard Poodle. The first record of the dog dates back to the late 1200s, where a monk described how one rescued a drowning sailor. The dogs are traditionally associated with the Algarve region of Portugal where they were kept to work with fishermen. They would sit in the boat, bark when they spotted a school of fish, and leap overboard to steer them into the nets. Their bark was also invaluable in fog, helping the boats to determine where each one was, thereby preventing collisions. As technology took over, the number of the dogs declined, falling below 50 individuals at its lowest point.

Back from the brink

It was the breed's personality that ensured that it did not become extinct. Bred to work so closely in the company of people, the Portuguese Water Dog has an instinctive friendly character, which is very appealing. The fact that it is hypoallergenic is also a factor in its favor today. As with the other breeds covered in this section, however, there can be no absolute guarantee that a Portuguese Water Dog will not cause allergies, but it is less likely.

Domed skull
The skull is broad and has a domed appearance with a depression in the middle

Broad muzzle
The muzzle is wider at its base than the end and the nostrils are broad

Strong neck
The neck is straight and short

CANINE CHARACTERISTICS		NOTES
Personality	Playful and friendly; adapts readily to both obedience and agility competitions	
Size	Height: 17–23 in. (43–58 cm) Weight: 35–60 lb (16–27 kg)	
Exercise	Needs regular exercise, as it is an active dog	Keep an eye on the dog around water, as it may want to jump in
At home	Usually quiet in the home—barking signifies something of note; possesses distinctive tones to its bark	
Behavior	Very responsive to training; often tends to jump excitedly	Train not to jump up unnecessarily
Grooming	Brushing is required; styling can be either an even "lamb" trim, or a "lion" trim, where the rear half of the body apart from the tail is trimmed	Trim about every two months and brush daily
Common health issues	Eye problems, including cataracts and Progressive Retinal Atrophy (PRA); hip dysplasia	Ensure breeding stock has been screened for PRA and hip dysplasia

3. Chinese Crested Dog

This breed always provokes comment. Some people love its hairless appearance, whereas others regard its look as grotesque. Luckily, there is also a corresponding form of the breed with a full coat of hair, which is described as the Powderpuff.

AT A GLANCE
- Choice between hairless or nonhairless
- Climate influences care
- Dark pigmentation variable
- Tends to overeat
- Quiet nature

History

The origins of the Chinese Crested Dog are unknown. The breed probably arose as the result of a specific mutation in an isolated population of dogs somewhere in Asia. It became known in the West at an early stage, being originally described in 1686. Chinese Crested Dogs attracted prominence in the U.S. in the first part of the 20th century, thanks to the famous striptease artiste Gypsy Lee Rose, who owned several examples, reputedly choosing them because of their seminaked appearance. Both hairless and Powderpuff forms of the breed can crop up in the same litter. An unusual characteristic of the hairless form is that its skin feels relatively warm, which led to it being called the Fever Dog for a time, because of a belief that touching its warm skin could cure a fever.

Anatomical oddities

The hairless variety is not entirely hairless; areas of hair are restricted to the extremities of the body—these include the crest, for example, which describes the area of hair that extends between the ears. There is also a plume of hair on the tail, and the so-called "socks" on the feet. The actual pigmentation of the skin is highly individual, with some of these dogs being pinker in color than others. Its lack of hair does leave the Chinese Crested Dog at risk of both sunburn and feeling the cold. Along with the lack of hair, there is also a reduction in the number of premolar teeth in the mouth of the hairless Chinese Crested Dog, and they are often absent entirely.

CANINE CHARACTERISTICS		NOTES
Personality	Alert and playful	
Size	Height: 12 in. (30 cm) Weight: up to 10 lb (4.5 kg)	Keep an eye on the dog's weight, as it is prone to obesity
Exercise	Needs modest exercise	Avoid exercise in the hottest part of the day; use a sweater in cold weather and canine sun block in hot weather
At home	Forms a strong bond with people in its immediate circle	Ensure fencing is secure to prevent the dog's escape
Behavior	Not always well disposed to other dogs; not inclined to bark	Encourage socialization at an early age
Grooming	No discernible "doggy odor;" the Powderpuff requires brushing; the hairless variety requires little hair care	Brush a Powderpuff daily; massage a hairless dog's skin with oil
Common health issues	Dental problems; avascular necrosis of the hip joints, affecting the head of the femur; patellar luxation; susceptible to sunburn/skin cancer	Patellar luxation may need corrective surgery; watch the dog in hot weather

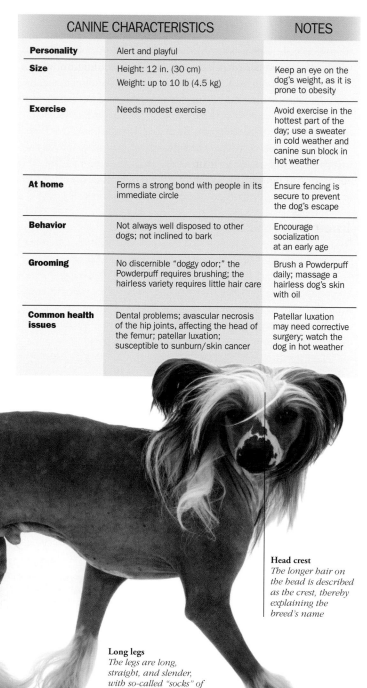

Slender tail
The tail tapers along its length to form a curve, extending to the level of the hocks

Color combinations
The Chinese Crested Dog can be bred in any color or color combination

Head crest
The longer hair on the head is described as the crest, thereby explaining the breed's name

Long legs
The legs are long, straight, and slender, with so-called "socks" of longer hair on the feet

4. Bedlington Terrier

There is no mistaking the attractive Bedlington Terrier, with its unusual pear-shaped head, not to mention its sloping hindquarters that give it an appearance that is described as the "roach back." As with most of the breeds in this section, it is likely to require professional grooming.

AT A GLANCE
- Highly distinctive appearance
- Tough, hardy disposition
- Unlikely to get along well with other dogs
- Good family pet
- Will hunt rodents

History

Originating from the county of Northumberland in the northwest of England, the Bedlington Terrier was in existence by the early 1800s. The breed is named after the village of Bedlington, which lay in a coal-mining area. It has a very distinctive appearance, like that of a lamb, which might suggest something of a delicate disposition, but in reality, these terriers are very determined and robust. Their ancestors include dogfighting stock and Rothbury Terriers, which were used for controlling vermin. Bedlingtons are not only recorded as hunting rats, but they would also take on larger and potentially dangerous quarry, including badgers, otters, and polecats.

The breed today

Since it was first exhibited back in the late 1800s, the Bedlington Terrier has become popular primarily as a companion rather than as a working breed. This in turn has seen the Bedlington Terrier evolve into a more placid dog, although it does not always get along with other dogs, let alone other members of its own breed. The Bedlington Terrier does rank among the fastest of the terriers, thanks to crossings involving whippets, and the breed's pace should not be forgotten when out on a walk. Its energy means that the Bedlington is a good choice for a home with children, and it has a decidedly playful side to its nature. Today, Bedlington Terriers are also frequently used to create Lurchers (see page 99), with this type of pairing involving Whippet blood. Bedlington Terriers are sensitive dogs by nature.

CANINE CHARACTERISTICS		NOTES
Personality	Quite calm; tends to be pretty relaxed about life	
Size	Height: 16 in. (41 cm) Weight: 18–23 lb (8–10.4 kg)	
Exercise	Needs a good run off the leash every day	Keep an eye on the dog around other dogs, as it may not get along with them
At home	Not a breed suited to apartment living; needs a yard; usually gets along well with older children in particular	
Behavior	Very active by nature; energetic; may chase cats and squirrels	Try to teach the dog not to chase other animals
Grooming	Brushing, combing, and trimming required	Brush and comb weekly; trim about every two months
Common health issues	Copper toxicosis, affecting the liver, is potentially fatal and is quite widespread	Ensure breeding stock has been screened for this condition—there is a specific DNA test

Low tail
The tapering tail reaches down to the hocks

Triangular ears
The ears have rounded ends, complete with silky tassels at their tips

Legs and feet
The forelegs are straight with the feet being long and hare shaped, supported on thick pads

5. Curly-coated Retriever

Ranking as one of the less common retrievers, the Curly-coated Retriever tends to be more independent by nature than other members of the group. It has a distinctive water-resistant coat, which is quite easy to keep in good condition.

AT A GLANCE

- Energetic and lively
- Attracted to water
- Can become bored
- Easy-care coat
- Plenty of exercise needed
- Responsive to training

History

The Curly-coated Retriever is regarded as being among the oldest of the retriever breeds. Its ancestry can be traced back to the old English Water Spaniel, a breed that is now extinct. Developed in England, another major influence in its past was the St. John's Newfoundland, whose descendants today are better known as Labrador Retrievers (see page 11). Other water-retrieving dogs, such as the Irish Water Spaniel (see page 113), probably played a part in its development along with the Standard Poodle (see page 106), which helped to ensure these retrievers had a more tightly curled coat. Its very unusual appearance saw the Curly-coated Retriever well represented in early dog shows; but, subsequently, both Labrador and Golden Retrievers became dominant in the show ring, while the breed declined as a working gundog, as the Flat-coated Retriever was preferred in this role.

Checking all is well

Today, there are signs that the Curly-coated Retriever's popularity could be increasing again. The introduction of Poodle blood did not just affect the breed's curled coat, but also brought with it a decreased likelihood of shedding. This in turn means that it is probably more hypoallergenic than other retrievers. As in all cases, though, allergy sufferers should spend time with a particular puppy or dog, to ensure that it has no adverse effect before committing to take on the responsibility of owning the dog. Individuals do differ in this regard, and there can be no guarantees about a dog's suitability.

CANINE CHARACTERISTICS		NOTES
Personality	Friendly toward people it knows well	
Size	Height: 23–27 in. (58–69 cm) Weight: not specified in this breed	
Exercise	Needs a good walk every day	Watch the dog around water as it may plunge in
At home	Lots of play at home is essential	Use play to prevent boredom
Behavior	Eager to learn and responsive to training; likely to become destructive if bored	Vary training routines to maintain concentration
Grooming	Very little grooming required; no undercoat; bitches may shed more heavily than dogs, especially when in heat	Bathe occasionally to decrease "doggy odor"; watch for matting
Common health issues	Hip dysplasia; eye ailments	Ensure breeding stock has been screened for hip dysplasia

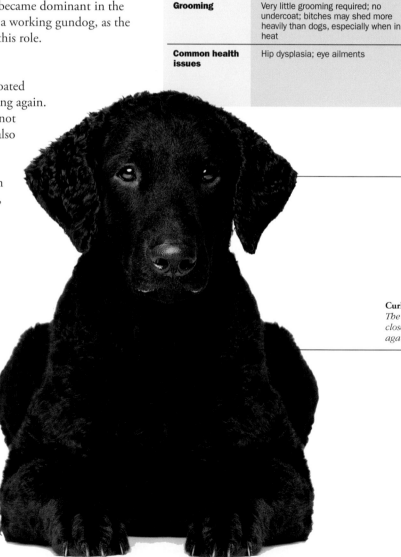

Large eyes
The almond-shaped eyes are relatively large in size

Curly coat
The tight, small curls lie close to the skin and protect against the elements

Liver or black
The coat is either liver or black in color. Some white hairs may be seen, often on the chest

6. Wire Fox Terrier

The Wire Fox Terrier has a very distinctive appearance and a lively temperament. The breed was exceedingly popular from the late 1800s through to the 1930s when other breeds started to become more fashionable. Today, it is relatively scarce.

CANINE CHARACTERISTICS		NOTES
Personality	Bold and inquisitive; quite independent	
Size	Height: up to 16 in. (41 cm) Weight: up to 18 lb (8 kg)	
Exercise	Energetic and active	Watch the dog when it is off the leash
At home	Will not thrive in urban surroundings; likely to dig in the yard; alert guardian	
Behavior	Playful; will readily hunt rodents	Make time for play
Grooming	Smooth and Wire Fox Terriers were not separated in the U.S. until 1984; brushing and professional grooming of the dense wiry coat is required	Brush several times a week; groom professionally three to four times a year
Common health issues	Eye problems, including Progressive Retinal Atrophy (PRA); epilepsy; patellar luxation, affecting the kneecaps	Ensure breeding stock has been screened for PRA; patellar luxation may need corrective surgery

V-shaped ears
The small ears are folded over at their tips and hang forward

Small eyes
The eyes are relatively small, dark, circular, and quite deep set

Head length
Male dogs have longer heads than bitches

Coat color
White should predominate in the coat, although color is not especially significant

History

Fox Terriers were originally bred to flush and drive foxes out of their dens so that they could be chased by hounds, and so the Fox Terrier had to have a bold, determined nature. Up until the 1870s, Wire Fox Terriers were grouped with smooth-coated Fox Terriers as a single breed. They were then split during the 1870s in England, and started to be developed on separate lines, although they are still very similar in some aspects of their appearance today. Coloration of these terriers was a significant feature. They were originally dark, but this sometimes led to them being chased by the hounds, as they were confused with the fox when they emerged from underground, so white became the dominant coat color.

A decline in fortune

The reason that the Wire Fox Terrier is less common today is probably a reflection of its temperament. If you choose one of these terriers, bear in mind that you are selecting a breed that is likely to prove rather stubborn and has a strong independent streak. It will also display other terrier traits, such as a desire to dig. Training can be difficult, too, although, in return, you will have an independent, lively character, rather than a lapdog. Fox Terriers are not recommended for a home with younger children, though, because they can sometimes be short-tempered.

7. Bichon Frisé

The name of this breed is often mispronounced. It should be *Bee-shon Free-zay*, which is a constriction of the French name for the breed—Bichon à Poil Frisé. Having been bred as a lapdog, the Bichon Frisé makes an excellent household companion.

AT A GLANCE
- Cute and cuddly
- Playful
- High grooming needs
- Settles well in an apartment
- Confident nature

History

The name of the breed gives a clue to its ancestry, with "Bichon" being an abbreviated form of "Barbichon," which literally means "Little Barbet"—the Barbet is a retriever breed, developed to work in water. The origins of this dog are also reflected in its alternative name of the Tenerife, being so-called after the largest of the seven Canary Islands that lie off the northwest coast of Africa. It is thought that the Spanish introduced these small dogs there when they settled on the islands back in the 1500s. The dogs must have changed in appearance at this stage, and were then taken back to Spain, where they were very popular pets among the nobility. The Bichon Frisé's popularity declined during the late 1800s, however, and it became a circus performer. Only since the 1970s, when it gained recognition in both the U.S. and the U.K., has it become widely known again, both in and out of the show ring.

The distinctive coat

The Bichon Frisé is closely related to similar breeds such as the Bolognese (see page 77) and the Havanese (see page 40), but can be distinguished from them by its double, curly coat. The drawback of this particular member of the Bichon family is that its coat care is far more demanding than that of its relatives; but the fact that the Bichon Frisé does not shed means that less time has to be spent on removing dog's hair left around the home.

White coat
White predominates, but shadings of cream, apricot, or buff may be evident near the ears or on the body

Round eyes
The round, dark eyes are surrounded by dark skin and reinforce the appeal of this companion breed

Front legs
The front legs are straight, with the elbows lying very close to the body

Catlike feet
The rounded feet resemble those of a cat

CANINE CHARACTERISTICS		NOTES
Personality	Intelligent, lively, and confident	
Size	Height: 9–12 in. (23–30 cm) Weight: 7–12 lb (3–5.4 kg)	Weight is not specified in the official breed standard
Exercise	Happy with a trot around the local park	
At home	Gentle, playful companion	
Behavior	Active and responsive; likes to stay close; not aggressive toward other dogs	Make time for ball games
Grooming	Brushing, bathing, and trimming required	Brush daily; bathe and trim regularly; groom professionally once a month or so
Common health issues	Blood disorders, including anemia and thrombocytopenia—these need urgent treatment	Watch for skin hemorrhages—these are more common in North American than European bloodlines

8. Irish Water Spaniel

In spite of its name, the Irish Water Spaniel is not a spaniel, as such breeds flush game out from undergrowth. Instead, it is a retriever, whose main function in its native Ireland was to plunge into water to retrieve shot waterfowl.

AT A GLANCE
- Unique coloration
- Loves water
- Active companion
- Modest grooming needs
- Good guardian
- Active and enthusiastic companion

History

The origins of this breed can be traced back to the Barbet and the extinct English Water Spaniel. The Standard Poodle (see page 106) may also have played a part in its development. By the mid-1800s, there was a distinctive split between the southern form of the old Irish Water Spaniel, from which the modern breed is derived, and the northern variety. The differences between the breeds were in terms of color—the latter was liver and white—and their ears. Northern Water Spaniels had short ears, largely free from longer hair, whereas those of the Southern Water Spaniel were bigger, with a more profuse covering of hair.

Unique attributes

The Irish Water Spaniel is really only a breed suitable for country areas, but be careful of allowing one of these spaniels to walk off the leash near water, as it may decide to plunge in for a swim. The dog is well protected thanks to its dense, curly, water-resistant coat, which also insulates it against the cold. In terms of coloration, it appears dark brown, or a unique shade called puce. The most distinctive characteristic, which sets the breed apart from all other retrievers, is its thin tail. The lack of feathering on this part of the body has led to it being described as a "rat tail."

CANINE CHARACTERISTICS		NOTES
Personality	Exuberant; intelligent and gentle; can be nervous	Encourage socialization from puppyhood to prevent nervousness
Size	Height: 22–24 in. (56–61 cm) Weight: 55–65 lb (25–29.4 kg)	
Exercise	Loves to swim—feet display signs of webbing, emphasizing the dog's strong affiliation with water	Try to find a lake or pool where the dog can swim safely or book sessions at a canine hydrotherapy center
At home	Settles well in a home with older children	
Behavior	Young puppies can be clumsy; older dog possesses a deep, intimidating bark	Train to prevent the dog from becoming overexcited
Grooming	Nonshedding coat; swimming helps to keep the coat well curled	Comb the coat to prevent matting; trim to keep neat
Common health issues	Cancer, especially lymphomas	

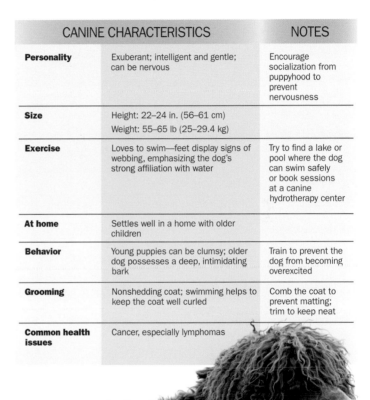

Distinctive tail
The highly distinctive tail has no curls along much of its length. It tapers to a point

Almond eyes
The eyes are relatively small and almond shaped, with a topknot of hair above them

Long ears
The long, low-set lobular ears lie close to the head and are covered in curls of hair

9. Airedale Terrier

Few dogs have proved to be as versatile as the Airedale Terrier. It saw active service during the First World War as a messenger dog, and has also worked as a police dog, in addition to retrieving ducks, tracking deer, and killing rats.

CANINE CHARACTERISTICS		NOTES
Personality	Intelligent, independent, and determined; can be forceful if not properly trained	Encourage socialization to accept visitors
Size	Height: 21–23 in. (53–58 cm) Weight: 50–70 lb (22.7–32 kg)	A larger hunting strain, the Oorang Airedale, is known in the U.S.
Exercise	Thrives on a good daily walk, preferably in the countryside	Keep an eye on the dog around other dogs
At home	Territorial; good guard dog	
Behavior	Learns quickly and highly adaptable by nature	Vary training to maintain the dog's concentration
Grooming	Hard, dense, wiry coat looks at its best if hand stripped, although clipping is more straightforward	
Common health issues	Dermatitis—hand stripping can help in cases of dermatitis; bloat	Do not exercise after feeding, as this can cause bloat

Folded ears
The V-shaped, folded ears lie down the sides of the head

Skull and eyes
The skull is long and flat, with the eyes being small and dark in color

Shoulders and chest
The shoulder blades are flat, with the chest being deep, extending to the elbows

Legs and feet
The forelegs are straight and well muscled, with the feet being small and rounded

History

The Airedale originates from the Aire Valley in the English district of Yorkshire, where it was bred in the mid-1800s to hunt otters. Its ancestry is believed to include the Otterhound, which imparted size and tracking skills, combined with the Bull Terrier (see page 28), which contributed strength and determination, as well as the old Black and Tan Terrier, which is now extinct. The Black and Tan Terrier reinforced the Bull Terrier's strength and determination, and introduced the rough coat, as well as possibly encouraging its affinity with water. The Airedale is the largest of Britain's terrier breeds, and although there was a move to reclassify it in the U.S. because of its size, this was unsuccessful.

Powerful personality

The Airedale can have a very forceful personality at times, as might be expected in the case of a breed that was originally involved in dogfighting in its early days. This can make it something of a liability today, as this terrier will not back down if challenged. It has high energy levels, too, which means it is not recommended for a home within the city. The Airedale is best exercised out in the countryside, where it can explore and is less likely to come into contact with other dogs. Neutering of male dogs in particular can make them more placid. The Airedale is typically tenacious, just like other terriers.

10. Labradoodle

As the best known of today's so-called "designer dogs," created by the crossing of two distinct breeds, the Labradoodle has become very popular in a relatively short space of time. This is partly due to its friendly and responsive nature.

History

The Labradoodle is the result of a breeding program, which was originally intended to enable blind people to benefit from having a guide dog, even if they suffered from allergies. Wally Conron of the Australian Guide Dog Association pioneered the idea of crossings between the Labrador Retriever (see page 11) and the Standard Poodle (see page 106) for this purpose in the 1980s. The Standard Poodle was an ideal choice, not just because it does not shed, but also because of its natural intelligence, combining with that of the Labrador Retriever, which was traditionally used as a guide dog. As in any crossbreeding, the appearance of the puppies could be very variable, even between those in the same litter, and not all were hypoallergenic.

Buying a Labradoodle

Since the early days, selective breeding between first generation puppies occurred. With Labradoodles now being mated with each other, gradually, a unique appearance has emerged, creating what is now effectively a distinctive breed in its own right. No longer simply viewed as a working companion, the Labradoodle has evolved very much into a dog that is ideal as a family pet, especially if you are obtaining one of these dogs on the basis of its hypoallergenic coat.

CANINE CHARACTERISTICS		NOTES
Personality	Friendly, dependable nature; affectionate	
Size	Height: 17–24 in. (43–61 cm) Weight: 30–77 lb (14–35 kg)	Not standardized in these respects
Exercise	Needs a good walk; likes water and can swim well	Exercise daily with a good walk
At home	Ideal for a home with older children or teenagers	
Behavior	Learns quickly, but can be sensitive; can be taught to respond to hand signs; has plenty of energy	Always provide encouragement
Grooming	Most Labradoodles now have intermediate coats; grooming needs depend on the coat type—coat can be woolly and curled, like a Poodle; fleecy, soft, and wavy; or may resemble a Labrador's coat	
Common health issues	Hip dysplasia, a weakness affecting both parental breeds; Progressive Retinal Atrophy (PRA)	Ensure breeding stock has been screened for these conditions

Labradoodle color
The appearance of the coat is variable, with the Labradoodle's coloration reflecting that of the parent breeds

Thick tail
The tail is relatively long and quite thick

Powerful legs and deep chest
The powerful, straight front legs and a relatively deep chest are often characteristic of these dogs

Dog types for experienced owners, used to training dogs; people without children; and those living in isolated areas.

Rottweiler

Guard Dogs

Black Russian Terrier

Think carefully before acquiring a member of one of the breeds in this section. Although they are typically friendly and loyal to people they know well, they are instinctively suspicious of strangers and so do not take readily to visitors. This can be a particular problem if you have young children, as their friends could easily be intimidated by dogs of this type, and may be reluctant to come to your home.

As might also be expected, the majority of these dogs are large and powerful, and can be difficult to control as a consequence, particularly off the leash. They tend to have a dominant nature and will not back down readily if challenged. This means that outside the home, they can become difficult to control if they meet another, similar type of dog. Nevertheless, they are now far less aggressive than in the past, thanks to the fact that they are kept mainly for show purposes. They are actually very intelligent by nature, as revealed by the fact that the Doberman, for example, is often used by the police. The key here is training. If you do not have experience in this area, it would be better to obtain another type of dog.

Akita

1. Doberman Pinscher

This breed was originally known as the Thuringer Pinscher, after the area of Germany where it was bred, but it was then renamed as the Dobermann Pinscher in 1899, commemorating the name of its creator. In North America, the breed is spelled with just one "n" in "Doberman."

AT A GLANCE

- Instinctively dominant nature
- Sleek appearance
- Powerful build
- Loyal and responsive
- Lively nature
- Athletic

Strong neck
The well-muscled neck broadens into the body

Doberman colors
The coat is black, blue, red, or fawn in color, sometimes with a small white patch on the chest

History

The breed was developed by Louis Dobermann during the 1870s. He used a variety of dogs to create the breed, but no detailed records survive of how this was achieved. What is known is that nonpedigree dogs were used. He started by crossing some of the dogs with German Pinschers. A diverse range of breeds, from the German Pointer to the Greyhound (see page 52), are then thought to have contributed, with guard dogs, such as the Rottweiler (see page 120), also involved. His aim was to develop a breed that looked aggressive, and that could be aggressive if necessary.

Worldwide popularity

The Doberman has now established an international following, and is often kept for working purposes, either as a police dog or a patrol dog, guarding property. It is fierce and bold if challenged, and must be well trained from puppyhood. While remaining wary as far as visitors are concerned, Dobermans can also be affectionate and loyal companions with people they know well. The more gentle side to their nature is reflected by the fact that they have been trained as guide dogs for the blind.

CANINE CHARACTERISTICS		NOTES
Personality	Dominant and intelligent; less aggressive than in the past; very loyal to family members	Encourage socialization from an early age to minimize the risk of conflicts
Size	Height: 24–28 in. (61–71 cm) Weight: 60–100 lb (27–45 kg)	
Exercise	Needs plenty of opportunities to run to prevent boredom	Exercise daily with a good run
At home	Alert guardian; other, more placid breeds are better for a home with young children; not recommended for novice owners	
Behavior	Lively	Involve all older family members in training to prevent the dog from becoming dominant
Grooming	Grooming needs are minimal, thanks to the sleek coat	Brush with a hound glove
Common health issues	Skin ailments; food allergies	Watch for fleas, which can trigger a bad reaction; can use hypoallergenic foods

Rust markings
The Doberman has rust-colored markings above the eyes, on the muzzle and throat, plus the chest, legs, feet, and tail

Catlike feet
The catlike feet are well arched

2. Akita

This Japanese breed is named after Akita Prefecture, a northern part of the island of Honshu, where it was bred. The Akita is a spitz dog, as reflected by its appearance, and its origins probably lie farther to the north in mainland Asia.

AT A GLANCE
- Brave and loyal
- Not especially social with other dogs
- Powerful on the leash
- Moderate grooming needs
- Energetic

History

The Akita was originally kept for dogfighting purposes about 400 years ago. Later, it was valued as a guardian of property, and employed by the police. The breed's bravery was also challenged when it was used for hunting bears and wild boar. It pursued deer, too, and acquired the name of the Japanese Deerhound. The modern transformation of the Akita began during the 1920s, largely due to the efforts of a breeder named Hiroshi Saito. It has now established an international following, with its popularity surging during the 1980s.

A devoted companion

The loyal nature of the Akita is illustrated by one very famous Akita, whose devotion to its owner captured the attention of the whole of Japan. Tokyo professor Eizaburo Ueno commuted to work every day, and was accompanied to and from the local train station by his Akita, named Hachi. In 1925, however, Hachi waited at the station, but his owner never returned. He had died at work. Every day for the next nine years until he died, Hachi went to the station, hoping to be reunited with his owner. A bronze statue was put up there following Hachi's death. The Akita itself is now recognized in Japan as a national monument.

Powerful skull
The broad, powerful skull has a wide muzzle, supported on a thick muscular neck

Plumed tail
The well-plumed tail curves forward, dipping down over the back in true spitz fashion

Shoulders and legs
Short, powerful shoulders link into strong, straight forelegs, with the elbows lying close against the body

Akita color
The Akita can be bred in any color, with markings being well balanced as appropriate if present

CANINE CHARACTERISTICS		NOTES
Personality	Determined, independent, loyal, and affectionate	
Size	Height: 24–28 in. (61–71 cm) Weight: 70–130 lb (32–59 kg)	Dogs are significantly bigger than bitches
Exercise	Needs a long walk or run off the leash	Avoid areas where conflict could arise; be sure that you have full control before letting the dog off the leash
At home	Good guardian; may not live in harmony with a cat	
Behavior	Frequently does not get along with other dogs; not especially responsive to training	Be firm when training
Grooming	Dense double coat; more grooming required in spring when shedding	Brush regularly
Common health issues	Hip dysplasia; eye problems; Acquired Myasthenia Gravis (AMG), an autoimmune disease—symptoms include difficulty in swallowing, excessive salivation, and the dog's bark may also be affected	Ensure breeding stock has been screened for hip dysplasia; watch for symptoms of AMG

3. Rottweiler

The much stockier appearance of the Rottweiler, or "Rottie" as it is sometimes known, serves to distinguish this breed from the Doberman. It has very strong protective instincts and, unfortunately, is now officially regarded as a dangerous breed in some countries.

Broad features
The muzzle is broad with the nose also being broad in appearance

Black coat
The coat is black in color, with markings varying from shades of rust to mahogany

Deep chest
The broad, deep chest extends down to the level of the elbows

Compact feet
The feet are round and compact with hard, thick pads ending in black nails

History

The Rottweiler is named after the town of Rottweil, which lies in southwestern Germany. It was created both to act as a cattle drover, taking cattle to market, and to guard its owner's money, protecting it from thieves by carrying it in a special pouch around the neck. Once cattle started to be moved to market by rail, the Rottweiler's numbers plummeted. It had nearly died out by the early 1900s, but then grew in popularity as a guard dog and was also used by the police, before finally making the transition to the show ring in the 1930s.

Staying in control

The reputation of the Rottweiler has suffered in the hands of those eager to exploit its aggressive side. As a breed, it has received bad press over recent years, but provided that it is properly trained, a Rottweiler can make an excellent companion. It is not a good choice for a home with young children, though, who may tease or even hurt the dog, resulting in an aggressive response. Rottweilers are immensely powerful, and must be taught to walk on the leash from an early age without pulling. Do not allow a Rottweiler to gain the upper hand; this is a breed that must appreciate that it is subservient to family members. Try to involve everyone in the dog's training for this reason.

CANINE CHARACTERISTICS		NOTES
Personality	Bold and intelligent; strong protective instincts; unlikely to be friendly toward visitors	Encourage socialization from puppyhood to avoid this behavior
Size	Height: 22–27 in. (56–69 cm) Weight: 93–110 lb (42–50 kg)	Keep an eye on the dog's weight
Exercise	Can be aggressive toward other dogs when out walking	Neuter young males to curb such behavior; avoid other dogs
At home	Territorial	Involve all older family members in training
Behavior	Brave; will stand its ground if threatened	
Grooming	Smooth coat should appear glossy	Brush when necessary
Common health issues	Susceptible to obesity and associated complications, such as heart disease; weight gain is especially likely after neutering	

4. Bouvier des Flandres

The word "bouvier" means "bovine herder," and describes the primary working role of the Bouvier des Flandres, in terms of working with cattle. The breed also guards other herds, can pull carts, and can be a good family pet.

History

There used to be a number of different localized forms of Bouviers in different parts of Belgium, where they were employed for centuries to work with cattle. As a result of the First World War, however, the majority, such as the Bouvier de Paret, died out. Today, the Bouvier des Flandres is the most common of the two surviving varieties, with the other being the Bouvier des Ardennes. The adaptability of the Bouvier des Flandres aided its survival—it was used to carry messages, for example, among other tasks. The actual origins of the breed are not known, but the Giant Schnauzer (see page 126) and the Beauceron (see page 134) probably played a part in its development. The dog traditionally often had its ears cropped, so they stood up and tapered to small points. If they are not altered in this way, the ears hang down over the sides of the head.

Moving from the farm

This breed first entered the show ring just before the First World War, and is now no longer an uncommon exhibit, particularly at larger shows worldwide. Its facial features, in terms of its very evident eyebrows, plus the longer hair that forms a mustache and beard around the mouth, add to its appeal when seen at close quarters. The dog's powerful physique, determined nature, and reluctance to accept strangers mean that it is important to socialize a puppy from an early age, to reduce its natural caution.

Alert ears
The alert ears are set high. The inner corner of each ear should line up with the outer corner of the eye

Head of hair
The head is relatively large with a mustache and beard of longer hair

Color variety
The coat varies in color from fawn via brindle, "salt and pepper" and gray to black

CANINE CHARACTERISTICS		NOTES
Personality	Intelligent, loyal, and quite calm; not overtly aggressive by nature; unlikely to accept visitors readily	Keep an eye on the dog around visitors
Size	Height: 22–28 in. (56–71 cm) Weight: 60–120 lb (27–54.4 kg)	
Exercise	Needs a good daily run—this is essential	Avoid cattle, as the dog may want to chase them; avoid other dogs, as it may be resentful of them
At home	Very protective	
Behavior	Obedient and responsive to training	Be consistent when training
Grooming	Thick double coat; grooming is very straightforward	Brush and trim when necessary
Common health issues	Hip dysplasia; cataracts	Ensure breeding stock has been screened for these conditions

5. Kuvasz

The unusual name of this Hungarian flock guardian is thought to come from the Turkish word *Kawasz*, meaning "armed guard." This describes the way in which these dogs watch over flocks of sheep, especially after dark when wolves are an increased threat.

AT A GLANCE
- Beautiful appearance
- Healthy appetite
- Large dog
- Training can be difficult
- Often noisy by nature
- Slow to accept strangers

History

The ancestors of Kuvaszok (which is the plural form of Kuvasz) were probably taken to present-day Hungary from Turkey around 900 years ago. As wolves became more scarce, the Kuvasz's role changed, and it became a general guard dog. It almost died out as a result of the Second World War, but its numbers then increased and show recognition in countries on both sides of the Atlantic followed. Although not common today, the future of the breed is more secure again. The Kuvasz's muzzle tapers along its length, which distinguishes it from other similar breeds, such as the Tatra Mountain Sheepdog from Poland, although they do not naturally overlap in terms of their distribution.

Devoted companions

In common with other similar dogs, the Kuvasz is very devoted to its family, but is likely to be reserved, if not hostile toward strangers. Sound training from puppyhood is required to maintain the necessary degree of control. It is equally important at the same time to socialize young Kuvaszok, so they will hopefully grow up to be more tolerant by nature. They are particularly playful at this stage, and learn rapidly. This is also the stage at which to teach these dogs not to bark repeatedly; adults can otherwise sometimes end up being particularly noisy. The coat should be curly, but can sometimes be straight.

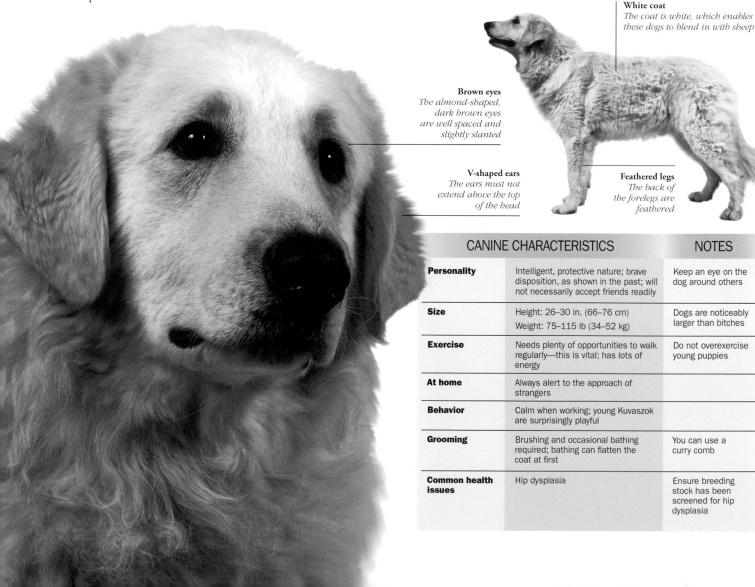

White coat
The coat is white, which enables these dogs to blend in with sheep

Brown eyes
The almond-shaped, dark brown eyes are well spaced and slightly slanted

V-shaped ears
The ears must not extend above the top of the head

Feathered legs
The back of the forelegs are feathered

CANINE CHARACTERISTICS		NOTES
Personality	Intelligent, protective nature; brave disposition, as shown in the past; will not necessarily accept friends readily	Keep an eye on the dog around others
Size	Height: 26–30 in. (66–76 cm) Weight: 75–115 lb (34–52 kg)	Dogs are noticeably larger than bitches
Exercise	Needs plenty of opportunities to walk regularly—this is vital; has lots of energy	Do not overexercise young puppies
At home	Always alert to the approach of strangers	
Behavior	Calm when working; young Kuvaszok are surprisingly playful	
Grooming	Brushing and occasional bathing required; bathing can flatten the coat at first	You can use a curry comb
Common health issues	Hip dysplasia	Ensure breeding stock has been screened for hip dysplasia

6. Bullmastiff

In spite of its size, the Bullmastiff is not an aggressive dog; however, its size means that not only does it require plenty of space, but it is also expensive to feed. It has protective instincts and can make a very effective guardian, as well as a good family dog.

AT A GLANCE
- Very powerful dog
- Training can be problematic
- Well disposed to its immediate family
- Easy to groom
- Independent nature

CANINE CHARACTERISTICS		NOTES
Personality	Placid but determined; quiet nature	
Size	Height: 24–27 in. (61–69 cm) Weight: 100–130 lb (45–59 kg)	Dogs are often significantly bigger than bitches
Exercise	Needs to be walked every day	Avoid exercise in the hottest part of the day to prevent heatstroke
At home	Too big for a home with small children; needs a large area and yard; can become devoted to the family	Check the yard is securely fenced
Behavior	Quite independent in spirit; should not be aggressive	
Grooming	Grooming is straightforward; more frequent grooming during the shedding season is required	Brush when necessary
Common health issues	Hip dysplasia; underactive thyroid; lymphoma cancer; like other large dogs, it may live for less than ten years	Ensure breeding stock has been screened for hip dysplasia

Bullmastiff color
The coat can be fawn, red, or brindle. There may occasionally be a very small area of white on the chest

Dark eyes
Dark, medium-sized eyes contribute to the breed's alert expression

Broad muzzle
The deep and broad muzzle is about a third of the length of the head

Legs and feet
The straight, well-boned forelegs end in medium-sized feet, with black nails. The pads are thick and tough

History

The Bullmastiff was created for a very specific purpose. During the late 1800s, gamekeepers in Britain were being threatened by groups of poachers and needed protection. They then developed the Bullmastiff using both old-style Bulldogs and Mastiffs (see page 124). Bulldogs then were much larger, more active, and aggressive dogs than those of today, while Mastiffs were immensely powerful but relatively placid. Combining both breeds resulted in an effective man-catcher. Faster and more determined, the Bullmastiff was strong enough to overpower and then restrain a person, without inflicting serious injury. Ever since it was first recognized for show purposes during 1924, the breed has been maintained in a pure state.

The contemporary breed

The Bullmastiff today is very friendly, although still powerful. It has changed in some respects, notably in its coloration, with fawn being more common than brindle. As a companion, it still retains its protective instincts and will watch over members of its family with devotion. Training can be a problem, and professional assistance may be needed at an early stage if a puppy starts to be wayward, given the size and strength of the adult Bullmastiff.

7. Mastiff

Even larger than the Bullmastiff, the Mastiff represents an ancient lineage. This is an incredibly powerful dog, and although it will settle well in a home alongside children, its strength means that it will be too strong for children to control.

CANINE CHARACTERISTICS		NOTES
Personality	Devoted, dignified, and determined; courageous and loyal	
Size	Height: 27–30 in. (69–76 cm) Weight: 120–250 lb (54.4–113 kg)	
Exercise	Needs a good walk; not very enthusiastic about running	Exercise with a good daily walk
At home	Alert to the approach of strangers	Keep an eye on the dog around strangers
Behavior	Will respond if there is a threat; training ensures good communication; generally trustworthy with cats	Train firmly and involve all older family members— this is essential
Grooming	Grooming needs are modest, thanks to the short, sleek coat	Watch for localized skin infections in the folds of skin on the head
Common health issues	Hip dysplasia; bloat, leading to gastric torsion	Ensure breeding stock has been screened for hip dysplasia; do not exercise after feeding, as this can cause bloat

History

The Mastiff probably originated in Asia, and was traded along the Old Silk Route, before being taken from the Mediterranean region to Britain. When the Romans arrived there in 55 B.C.E., they were confronted by the dogs. They valued them so highly that they shipped some back to Rome. The Mastiff was used in battle for many centuries and also took part in bear-baiting contests and hunted wolves, but by the early 1900s, it was on the verge of extinction. Attempts to increase its numbers were thwarted as a result of the Second World War, but subsequently, due to some imports of Mastiffs from North America, its numbers rose.

Gentle giants

The Mastiff is still not common today, which is partly due to the cost of its care and also the space that it requires. It is among the heaviest of breeds and has an appetite to match. It is generally calm, good natured, and very loyal. If there is a threat, however, it will instinctively react in an aggressive manner. Like other large breeds, the Mastiff develops slowly, and puppies should be exercised only in moderation for the first two years or so, to guard against joint disorders later in life.

AT A GLANCE

- True heavyweight of the canine world
- Usually only aggressive if challenged
- Expensive to keep
- Friendly nature
- Proper training is essential

Coat color
The coat can be apricot, fawn, or brindle, which shows dark striping. The muzzle, nose, and ears are always black

Muscular neck
The neck is very powerful and muscular and increases in size down to the shoulders

Deep chest
The wide, deep chest is rounded in appearance and extends down to the level of the elbows

8. Scottish Terrier

While the other breeds in this section may be relatively large, do not be fooled by the size or the rather quaint appearance of the Scottish Terrier, or "Scottie." It is an alert and determined guardian that does not take readily to strangers.

History

The bravery of these terriers is such that a small pack of them, kept in Scotland by the Earl of Dumbarton in the late 1800s, were called Diehards, and reputedly led to his regiment, the Royal Scots, being dubbed as "Dumbarton's Diehards." The breed's origins can be traced back to the 1400s. It is closely related to the Skye Terrier, and has been described under a variety of names, including the Highland and Aberdeen Terriers. The breed acquired the latter name in the late 1800s, not only because it was common in this part of Scotland, but also because a breeder named J. A. Adamson became well known for his strain of the terriers at that time. During the 1930s, the Scottish Terrier was one of the most popular breeds in the U.S.

Feisty nature

The Scottish Terrier makes a good watchdog, barking generally only if it detects something of concern. It does not accept strangers readily, and even tends to become more attached to certain members of its immediate family than others. Its brave nature is illustrated in the fact that it was used at one stage for battling badgers in their underground setts. The Scottish Terrier is not generally well disposed to other dogs, although socialization at an early age may help to overcome this to a certain degree.

Pointed ears
The ears are set high on the head, tapering to points

Scottish Terrier colors
Color can be black, wheaten, or brindle. There may be whitish hairs in the coats of black and brindle dogs

Long muzzle
The long muzzle ends with a prominent black nose

Front legs
The forelegs end with rounded feet, which are bigger than the hind feet

CANINE CHARACTERISTICS		NOTES
Personality	Confident by nature; intelligent—adapts well to situations; suspicious of strangers	Keep an eye on the dog around others
Size	Height: 10 in. (25 cm) Weight: 19–23 lb (8.6–10.4 kg)	
Exercise	Enjoys trotting along; agile and fast	Exercise with a daily walk; watch carefully around other dogs, especially terriers
At home	Not ideal for a home with children	
Behavior	Can be stubborn on occasion; may not get along well with cats; independent	Persevere with training
Grooming	Double-layered coat; grooming is essential	Brush weekly; groom professionally every six to eight weeks
Common health issues	Above-average susceptibility to various cancers; bladder cancer most commonly associated with the breed; Scottie Cramp—affects movement usually after exercise	Watch for signs of Scottie Cramp—signs can be temporary spasms

9. Giant Schnauzer

The name of this particular group of dogs derives from the German word *Schnauze*, meaning "snout." This describes the dog's relatively broad muzzle, which is well covered with long hair, forming what is often described as a mustache.

CANINE CHARACTERISTICS		NOTES
Personality	Intelligent and determined; can become dominant; not keen on strangers	Keep an eye on the dog around strangers
Size	Height: 23–28 in. (58–71 cm) Weight: 55–80 lb (25–36 kg)	
Exercise	Needs plenty of exercise and the opportunity to run	Exercise with a good daily walk
At home	Not suitable for an apartment	
Behavior	Energetic; has a loud, intimidating bark; responds well to training, which should begin early in puppyhood	Encourage socialization when young, so the dog becomes familiar with meeting people and other dogs
Grooming	Combing or brushing is essential, particularly for the undercoat; hand stripping required to keep the coat neat	Groom weekly; trim back longer hair around the eyes and ears as required
Common health issues	Hip dysplasia; epilepsy; cancers are a major killer in this breed	Ensure breeding stock has been screened for hip dysplasia

V-shaped ears
The ears are V-shaped, set high, and lie close to the head

Long head
The head is long and rectangular with a powerful muzzle

Oval eyes
The oval, deep set, medium-sized eyes are dark brown

Shoulders and legs
The shoulder blades are long, well muscled but flat, with the forelegs being straight

History

The ancestral form of this breed was the Standard Schnauzer, which was traditionally used to hunt rodents. Bavarian farmers then developed the Giant form to work with cattle, increasing its size by crossings with other native German breeds, including the Rottweiler (see page 120) and Great Dane (see page 82). Giant Schnauzers were traditionally used to drive cattle, but were subsequently used both as police dogs and property guardians, traditionally being kept at breweries. They then became popular as show dogs and also as companions.

At home

The natural intelligence of the Giant Schnauzer has meant that these dogs can settle very well in the home. They adapt well to a family environment, although they are often suspicious of visitors. This may create problems with children and their friends. In the past, the ears of these schnauzers were often cropped to give them a more ferocious appearance, but they are now increasingly left to hang down over the sides of the head. Grooming requirements must not be overlooked—the appearance of the Giant Schnauzer will be improved if its coat is hand stripped at least every six months, to take out loose hairs, rather than having it clipped.

10. Black Russian Terrier

This breed is unusual, having been developed during the Cold War by the Russian Army. Since the breakup of the former Soviet Union, it has become demilitarized and is now quite well known in the West and elsewhere.

AT A GLANCE
- Dense black coat
- New breed
- Very stable temperament
- Impressive appearance
- Sheds very little
- Relatively easy to train

History

The Black Russian Terrier's ancestry involved the input of 17 different breeds, with its coloration probably stemming from the Giant Schnauzer (see page 126). The Airedale Terrier (see page 114) also played a significant early part, as did the Rottweiler (see page 120). The aim was to create a guard dog that was hardy enough to work under extreme weather conditions, and had a dependable temperament. Only in 1957, a decade after the start of the project, were some examples permitted to pass into civilian ownership. Breeders then concentrated on standardizing its appearance.

Adaptability

The Black Russian Terrier, whose name stems in part from its Airedale ancestry, achieved full recognition from the American Kennel Club (AKC) in 2004. It has proved to be a versatile breed, not just excelling in the show ring, but also doing well in obedience and agility competitions, emphasizing its all-around strengths. The only significant drawback for some owners will be the stamina of these dogs, as they need lots of exercise and long walks.

Black coat
This breed is defined in part by its coloration, being black, sometimes with occasional gray hairs

Thick legs
The forelegs are straight and thick in appearance, running parallel to each other

Large feet
The large, rounded yet compact feet have black nails

CANINE CHARACTERISTICS		NOTES
Personality	Intelligent, loyal, responsive; loyal nature; wary of strangers	Keep an eye on the dog around strangers
Size	Height: 26–30 in. (66–76 cm) Weight: 77–154 lb (35–70 kg)	
Exercise	Needs plenty of exercise; has lots of stamina	Exercise with long walks
At home	Eager guardian	
Behavior	Responsive, but needs firm training from puppyhood	Train and keep occupied to prevent boredom and destructive behavior
Grooming	Male dogs have a slight mane of longer hair around the neck; minimal shedding	Brush and comb coat once or twice a week
Common health issues	Hip dysplasia; Progressive Retinal Atrophy (PRA)	Ensure breeding stock has been screened for these conditions

Dog types for people who are looking for more than a placid companion; families with older children; people living on their own, out of cities; and those who have retired early and enjoy walking.

Australian Shepherd

Parson Russell Terrier

Super-smart Dogs

People marvel at the innate intelligence displayed by working dogs such as the Border Collie, but, unfortunately, members of this group are not especially good choices as companions. This is because their working instincts are still so ingrained that they do not settle well in domestic surroundings. What can then happen is that without adequate mental stimulation, the dog becomes bored and destructive, and generally behaves badly. The other thing to bear in mind is that true herding dogs are very energetic and need to be outdoors, rather than cooped up in the home.

Nevertheless, there are some highly adaptable small breeds, such as the Papillon, that make great companions. Terriers are also very resourceful dogs, but less suited to a home with young children, as they can be short-tempered on occasion. Larger breeds with a reputation for intelligence include the German Shepherd Dog and the less well-known Beauceron, as well as the Australian Shepherd, all of which have worked as police dogs, reflecting their versatility. Mongrels, too, bred from dogs of no specific parentage, are known for their resourceful natures and they come in a wide variety of sizes.

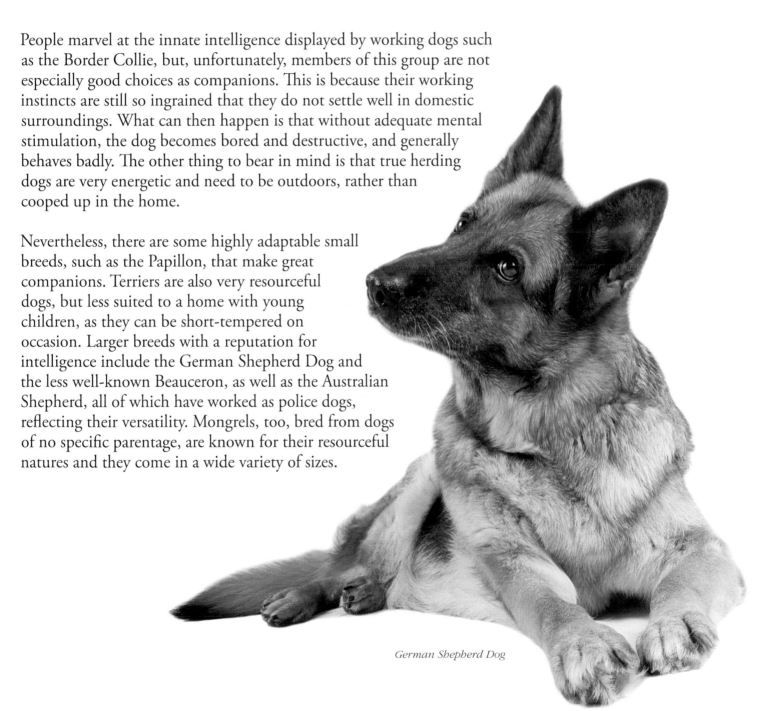

German Shepherd Dog

1. Border Collie

These collies rank among the most intelligent of all dogs, developing an almost intuitive understanding when engaged in farmwork. Down the centuries, shepherds and dogs have evolved a distinctive language for communication, based on whistles and hand signals.

AT A GLANCE
- Highly intelligent
- Very responsive
- Usually a "one person" dog
- Incredible amount of energy
- Hardy nature

History

Named after the region of the Scottish Borders between Scotland and England where it was bred, the Border Collie is still popular as a working sheepdog, there and farther afield. The breed first became more widely known during the 1870s, when sheepdog trials began, and since then, its working skills have been appreciated by much larger audiences on television. The Border Collie only entered the show ring at a late stage, however, not being recognized by the Kennel Club in the U.K. until 1976, having been viewed by devotees primarily as a working dog up to that point.

Nose and muzzle
The nostrils are prominent with the muzzle tapering slightly along its length

Alert expression
The expression is alert and intelligent

Eye color
Brown eyes, irrespective of their shade, are preferred to blue

Compact feet
The feet are oval and compact with strong, arched toes and deep pads

CANINE CHARACTERISTICS		NOTES
Personality	Fairly intense, yet self-contained; not particularly affectionate	
Size	Height: 18–22 in. (46–56 cm) Weight: 27–45 lb (12.2–20.4 kg)	
Exercise	Needs lots of daily exercise; herding instincts are very strong	Keep the dog away from livestock, as it may want to herd them
At home	Must have plenty of space with a good sized yard	Keep the dog occupied to prevent boredom
Behavior	Very focused and determined	Allow time for play sessions—this is important for this intelligent dog
Grooming	Long-coated individuals need more grooming than short-coated	Let mud dry and then brush it out of the coat
Common health issues	Collie Eye Anomaly (CEA); hip dysplasia; epilepsy	Ensure breeding stock has been screened for hip dysplasia; at seven weeks of age, a DNA test is available to check for CEA

Not for all

Unfortunately, the very qualities that make the Border Collie such a compelling breed to watch when it is at work mean that it is far less suitable than many others as a pet. This is because it thrives best when working in the company of a handler. It is not suited to living in a city or even a suburban setting, being a high-energy breed, nor to being left alone for long periods, confined to the home. Its natural intelligence often results in a Border Collie expressing its boredom by becoming destructive if kept under these conditions. In addition, this dog may try to herd other pets, ranging from cats to tortoises. The Border Collie is used to working on a one-to-one basis with its handler and is also not particularly patient with children. Where pet Border Collies can excel, however, is at obedience and agility competitions.

2. German Shepherd Dog

These highly responsive dogs have been trained for many purposes over the years. They have worked as police dogs, guard dogs, search and rescue dogs, and even as guide dogs for the blind, confirming just how well they can adapt to different tasks.

AT A GLANCE
- Versatile worker
- Impressive appearance
- Loyal companion
- Athletic nature
- Learns quickly
- Relatively large breed

History

In various parts of western Europe, there were different strains of working shepherd dog, whose task it was to watch over flocks of sheep, and prevent individuals from straying off. This demanded both concentration and the ability to herd particular sheep back to the flock, without alarming the others. The early German Shepherd Dogs were quite different from those seen today, however, as they did not possess the long, sloping back that typifies the breed that we now see. They had a much more upright stance. In some areas, the German Shepherd Dog was better known as the Alsatian for a long period during the 20th century, being so-called after the region of Alsace where it originated, in the area bordering Germany and France. The name change took place in deference to the anti-German feeling that existed in Britain and elsewhere after the end of the First World War.

Today's breed

The German Shepherd Dog is often described today under the acronym of GSD. It remains by far the most common of this group of European shepherd dogs, although the Belgian breeds (see page 100) are now seen more frequently. As a companion, the German Shepherd Dog is very loyal and responsive, but some individuals can be nervous, particularly if they have not been adequately socialized from an early age. The German Shepherd Dog is strong and athletic, and benefits from plenty of exercise, although areas where sheep are present should be avoided.

Appearance of the head
The head of the male dog has a more masculine appearance than that of the bitch

Alert ears
The ears are held erect when alert, and are moderately pointed at their tips

GSD colors
Strong, rich coloration is preferred, with most colors accepted, apart from blue, white, and liver

Legs and feet
The forelegs are powerful with the feet being short and compact. The toes are well arched with thick pads

CANINE CHARACTERISTICS		NOTES
Personality	Focused yet adaptable; male dogs especially can be strong willed; watchful with strangers	Keep an eye on the dog around strangers
Size	Height: 22–26 in. (56–66 cm) Weight: 65–85 lb (29.4–38.5 kg)	
Exercise	Needs a good walk every day, and exercise off the leash; good jumper and swimmer	Exercise daily and allow time off the leash
At home	Alert guardian; enjoys human companionship	Encourage socialization from an early age
Behavior	Learns quickly; enjoys playing; can be quite dominant by nature	Do not encourage dominant behavior
Grooming	Straightforward brushing required, but long-haired GSDs require more grooming	Brush once or twice a week
Common health issues	Hip dysplasia; pancreatic deficiency, restricting its ability to digest food and leading to weight loss	Ensure breeding stock has been screened for hip dysplasia; treatment is possible for pancreatic problems

3. Parson Russell Terrier

For many years, breeders of Jack Russell Terriers were opposed to having their dogs standardized for show purposes, but ultimately, it was agreed that there could be a standard drawn up for this purpose, with these dogs being registered as Parson Russell Terriers.

History

The origins of the Jack Russell Terrier and ultimately the Parson Russell breed trace back to an Oxford student who spotted a small terrier-type dog accompanying a milkman in the city in 1819. After much discussion, the student was able to persuade the man to part with the dog, who was named Trump. It appears that Trump was probably the result of a mating involving a Black and Tan Terrier and a Wire Fox Terrier (see page 111). When the student, named Jack Russell, left Oxford, for a career in the church, he took Trump with him to the southwest of England, and alongside his passion for fox hunting, he started to develop a terrier lineage. He aimed to ensure that the dogs were small enough to venture into a fox's den and drive it out, but could also run sufficiently fast enough to keep up with the hounds.

Character of the breed

For a relatively small dog, these terriers are very energetic, and they must have a good walk every day. They display boundless curiosity, investigating an area closely as they trot along with you. Their personality is such that they make excellent companions, but they must be well trained and socialized. Otherwise, they may disappear unexpectedly down a burrow, or pick a fight with a much larger dog. Parson Russell Terriers do not take well to being confined. They are very effective at digging and can easily slip under a fence as a result, and they can also jump surprisingly well.

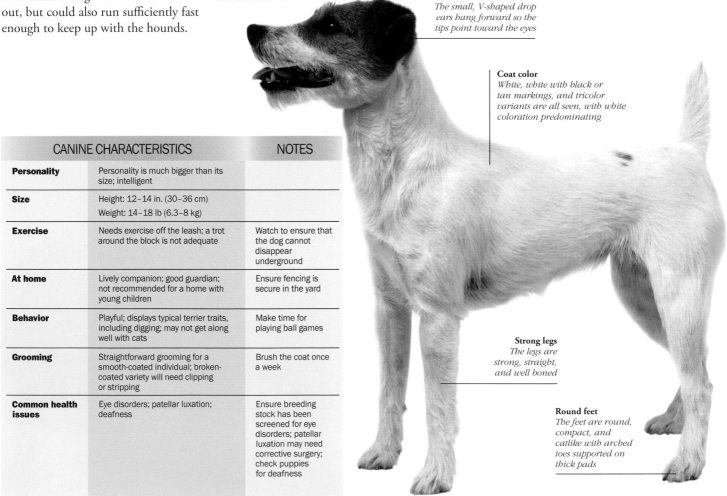

Small ears
The small, V-shaped drop ears hang forward so the tips point toward the eyes

Coat color
White, white with black or tan markings, and tricolor variants are all seen, with white coloration predominating

Strong legs
The legs are strong, straight, and well boned

Round feet
The feet are round, compact, and catlike with arched toes supported on thick pads

CANINE CHARACTERISTICS		NOTES
Personality	Personality is much bigger than its size; intelligent	
Size	Height: 12–14 in. (30–36 cm) Weight: 14–18 lb (6.3–8 kg)	
Exercise	Needs exercise off the leash; a trot around the block is not adequate	Watch to ensure that the dog cannot disappear underground
At home	Lively companion; good guardian; not recommended for a home with young children	Ensure fencing is secure in the yard
Behavior	Playful; displays typical terrier traits, including digging; may not get along well with cats	Make time for playing ball games
Grooming	Straightforward grooming for a smooth-coated individual; broken-coated variety will need clipping or stripping	Brush the coat once a week
Common health issues	Eye disorders; patellar luxation; deafness	Ensure breeding stock has been screened for eye disorders; patellar luxation may need corrective surgery; check puppies for deafness

4. Patterdale Terrier

The British Isles are home to the majority of terrier breeds, some of which remain relatively uncommon. This applies in the case of the Patterdale Terrier, which remains a working dog, not being officially accepted as yet for show purposes.

History

The dog was bred in the Lake District, in the northwest of England. Originally, the area was home to the Fell Terrier, which varied widely in appearance. In 1912, the most distinctive examples provided the foundation stock for what became the Lakeland Terrier, which achieved Kennel Club recognition in the U.K. with its own official show standard. Other breeders wanted to preserve the working-type terriers of the area and evolved a strain of Black Fell Terriers, which were then renamed as Patterdale Terriers, after a small village.

Patterdales today

The breed was created to go underground, either to drive a fox out of its den, so it could then be caught by the waiting hounds, or simply overpower and kill it in its den. Unsurprisingly, the dog has a bold nature, and is not widely kept as a pet, since it retains strong working instincts. These terriers were first taken to North America during the 1970s, where they are still used for hunting. The lack of standardization is apparent in their appearance, with smooth, broken, and rough-coated variants all being recorded. When seeking prey above ground, the Patterdale will crawl on its belly, much as it would within a fox's den, and use whatever cover is available.

CANINE CHARACTERISTICS		NOTES
Personality	Forceful but friendly; intelligent hunting breed; can be stubborn	Start training from the outset
Size	Height: 9–12 in. (23–30 cm) Weight: 9–12 lb (4–5.4 kg)	
Exercise	Needs plenty of opportunities to exercise to guard against boredom	Train the dog carefully to return promptly when called
At home	Not an ideal house pet, but its hardy nature is ideal for someone who is outdoors for much of the day	Encourage travel by car from an early age, so a young Patterdale becomes used to it
Behavior	Bold and tenacious	
Grooming	Appearance can vary significantly, depending on the coat type; regular brushing is required; smooth-coated form is the easiest to look after	Brush at least once a week
Common health issues	Very few problems of any type recorded	

Coat type
Coat type can vary, with smooth, rough, or broken-coated dogs being seen

White patch
A variable white patch on the chest is common

Patterdale colors
Almost all Patterdales are black in color, but occasional bronze, red, liver, chocolate, grizzle, and black and tan individuals occur

Powerful hindquarters
Powerful hindquarters enable these terriers to move through confined spaces

5. Beauceron

The Beauceron possesses an unusual characteristic, which sets it apart from most other dogs. This breed is characterized by the double dewclaws on each of its hind legs. Although these are of no functional significance, they must be present in show dogs.

AT A GLANCE
- Powerful, loyal guardian
- Very determined
- Easy-care coat
- Learns quickly
- Responds to training
- Attractive coloration

History

This ancient French breed of shepherd dog has existed for more than 400 years. It has proved to be an intelligent and versatile working companion, and like many of its kind, has since progressed to undertake a variety of other tasks in the modern world. Virtually nothing is known about its origins today, although it might potentially share a common ancestry with the German Shepherd Dog (see page 131). In common with that breed, both long-coated and short-coated forms of the Beauceron were recognized and the latter became predominant. In 1910, the Beauceron was first seen in the show ring, and it was then used by the French military, both as a messenger dog and also for carrying ammunition, which was strapped to its body.

The matter of markings

In its homeland today, the Beauceron is widely used as a police dog, but it has also become more popular as a show dog in neighboring countries, including Germany. A growing number of these dogs are also kept in North America. Few breeds are more responsive to their owners; its innate intelligence means that it learns rapidly, although consistency in training is very important. It is strong and powerful and if not properly controlled, it can prove to be a distinct liability.

Oval eyes
The eyes are slightly oval and must be dark brown in color. They are set horizontally

Coat length
The coat is slightly longer in length around the neck, compared with the ears and head

Beauceron colors
The coat is black and tan or Harlequin, displaying gray, black, and tan coloration

CANINE CHARACTERISTICS		NOTES
Personality	Intelligent and adaptable; wary of visitors	Keep an eye on the dog around visitors
Size	Height: 24–28 in. (61–71 cm) Weight: 66–100 lb (30–45 kg)	
Exercise	Needs a good walk, as it has lots of energy and plenty of stamina	Exercise with a good daily walk
At home	Protective companion	
Behavior	Learns quickly; slow developer	Use repeated, short training sessions
Grooming	Weather-resistant coat protects against cold and rain	Brush to keep the coat in top condition
Common health issues	Hip dysplasia; Progressive Retinal Atrophy (PRA); bloat, which can be caused by exercising after feeding	Ensure breeding stock has been screened for hip dysplasia and PRA; do not exercise after feeding

6. Papillon

Not all super-smart dogs have a working ancestry, as shown by the Papillon, which is a toy dog. Its name means "butterfly" in French, and describes the appearance of the dog's ears, which have an outline that resembles the shape of the insect.

CANINE CHARACTERISTICS		NOTES
Personality	Happy, friendly disposition; not shy with visitors	
Size	Height: 8–11 in. (20–28 cm)	
	Weight: 7–10 lb (3–4.5 kg)	
Exercise	Needs a good walk around the local park every day; athletic, with plenty of stamina for a small dog; happy to be out with its owner, even when walking to the shops	Exercise with a good daily walk
At home	Suitable for an apartment; adapts quickly to family life; good guardian	
Behavior	Learns quickly; alert; dainty mover	Make time for play and games
Grooming	Lack of an undercoat reduces the risk of matting; regular brushing required	Brush every few days
Common health issues	Progressive Retinal Atrophy (PRA), patellar luxation, affecting the kneecaps; sensitive to anesthetics	Ensure breeding stock has been screened for PRA; patellar luxation may need corrective surgery

Adaptability

The Papillon is a friendly breed, possessing what have been described as feline traits. Its delicate appearance belies the fact that it is actually a robust breed capable of hunting and catching rodents. These small dogs learn quickly, and can be seen today taking part in both obedience and agility competitions. More surprising, perhaps, is the fact that they have even been used as herding dogs, and have a sharp sense of smell, which means they can be good trackers as well. Their balanced, friendly natures have seen them used as therapy dogs, visiting and working with hospital patients. The breed is generally long-lived, and tends to display few signs of aging, both physically and in terms of its character, with older Papillons still being playful.

History

In its original form, the Papillon had ears that lay flat on the sides of the head. This variety still crops up in litters alongside the Papillon, and is called the Phalène, with the breeds together being described as Continental Toy Spaniels. The mutation that gave rise to the characteristic appearance of the Papillon is believed to have arisen in Belgium, about 300 years ago, although alternatively, crossings involving small spitz-type dogs may have introduced the trait in the ears. Papillons rapidly became the most popular form. These small, intelligent, little dogs were highly prized by their aristocratic owners, as reflected by the number that were included in portraits through the centuries by artists, such as Titian and Rembrandt.

Small head
The head is relatively small and slightly rounded across the top of the skull

Big ears
The ears are set on the sides of the head and are either erect or dropped, with rounded tips

Dark eyes
The eyes are dark and round in shape, with the rims of the eyes being dark, too

Papillon colors
The coat is always parti-colored

7. Australian Shepherd

The name of the Australian Shepherd is misleading, as it was created in the U.S., and it has worked with cattle as well as sheep, reflecting its versatility. It has also become much more popular in the show ring over recent years.

AT A GLANCE
- Attractive, individual patterning
- Quiet nature
- Learns quickly
- Eager to please
- Great companion
- Larger breed

Short hair
Hair is shorter on the sides of the face as well as on the lower part of the legs

Aussie colors
The coat is black, red, red or blue merle. It may have white markings and/or tan-colored points

Deep chest
The deep chest extends down

Strong legs
The straight, strong legs end with oval feet that have well-arched toes and thick pads

History

The breed's origins can be traced back to the Pyrenean region in Europe, between France and Spain. During the early 1800s, shepherd families from there migrated to Australia, taking their dogs with them. The evolving bloodline was then augmented by crosses with various types of collies. Subsequently, a number of these dogs were taken to the U.S. during the second half of the 1800s, becoming most common particularly in the area of California, working again with sheep. The breed's versatility has become well recognized today. It has been used for search and rescue work, assisted deaf people, and sniffed out narcotics. Whatever work it undertakes, the Aussie, as it is popularly known, will be devoted to the task for which it has been trained.

The breed today

The Australian Shepherd makes an ideal companion, almost instinctively appreciating what is expected, when in the hands of a sensitive owner. Training is still important though—not least because it helps to build a bond between the dog and its owner. An unusual feature of the Aussie is its coat patterning. This is highly individual, allowing these dogs to be distinguished from some distance away. In some cases, the tail is naturally in the form of a bob, rather than being full length. Recently, in order to make the breed more suited to domestic surroundings, breeders have created a miniature form, which is often called the Mini Aussie, with exactly the same attributes.

CANINE CHARACTERISTICS		NOTES
Personality	Dedicated and active; affectionate; intelligent	
Size	Height: 18–23 in. (46–58 cm) Weight: 35–70 lb (16–32 kg)	
Exercise	Thrives on plenty of exercise; very hardy; energetic	Exercise at least once a day
At home	Ideal in a home alongside older children and teenagers	
Behavior	Learns quickly; adaptable; very responsive; loves playing and chasing toys	Make time for lots of play
Grooming	Very dense, water-repellent undercoat, plus a ruff around the neck; good brushing required, especially when shedding	Brush once or twice a week
Common health issues	Collie Eye Anomaly (CEA); cataracts; epilepsy; underactive thyroid glands	At seven weeks of age, a DNA test is available to check for CEA

8. Collie

Two forms of the Collie exist, based on coat length. Smooth-coated Collies are far less popular, however, even though they are easier to groom than their long-coated counterparts, which were made famous by Lassie.

AT A GLANCE
- Choice of short or long coats
- Attractive coloration
- Elegant appearance
- Very responsive
- Energetic nature
- Playful

CANINE CHARACTERISTICS		NOTES
Personality	Affectionate; can sometimes be short-tempered if pestered by children	Keep an eye on the dog around children
Size	Height: 22–26 in. (56–66 cm) Weight: 50–70 lb (22.7–32 kg)	
Exercise	Needs lots of opportunities to run off the leash—this is important	Avoid areas where sheep are present, as the dog may want to chase them
At home	Playful nature; will chase after balls and flying disks readily	Make plenty of time for lots of energetic play at home
Behavior	Active and thrives on attention— can become bored if not receiving sufficient attention; eager to please; learns quickly	
Grooming	Brushing and combing required for Rough Collies; simple occasional brushing needed for Smooth Collies	Groom regularly
Common health issues	Eye ailments, particularly Progressive Retinal Atrophy (PRA) and Collie Eye Anomaly (CEA); may react badly to some heartworm medication	Ensure breeding stock has been screened for PRA; at seven weeks of age, a DNA test is available to check for CEA

Adaptability

As a working sheepdog over the course of centuries, Collies have proved to be adaptable and intelligent, as reflected by the diverse roles that they have undertaken. In fact, they are now seen primarily in the show ring or simply as companions, rather than in their traditional roles. They still retain their working instincts, however, and have plenty of energy, which means they must have daily exercise if they are not to become bored around the home. Be prepared to groom Rough Collies for longer during the spring, when they are shedding their dense winter coats. The distinctive ruff of long hair between the legs will be less pronounced over the warmer summer months.

Collie ears
The ears are proportionate to the size of the head

Head shape
The head tapers gradually along its length, from the ears to the black nose

History

It is believed that the Collie's ancestry may extend right back to Roman times, when the forerunner of what became the long-coated Rough Collie was introduced to Britain. These dogs were not as tall, and they had shorter muzzles than the Collie of today. These features are believed to have been developed at a much later stage, thanks to crossings involving the Borzoi (see page 67). During the 1860s, Collies became a favorite of Queen Victoria, and this raised their profile. Subsequently, Rough Collies played the role of Lassie in a number of movies and television productions featuring the fictional adventures of the dog. As a result, the breed attained new heights of popularity during the 1940s and 1950s, although today, it is not as widely kept.

Collie color
Coloration can be tricolor, sable and white, blue merle, or white, with some colored markings

9. Staffordshire Bull Terrier

This distinctive, muscular breed has had a bad press, thanks to its links with the notorious Pit Bull Terrier. It has nevertheless become much more popular over recent years, with its intelligence and devotion to its owner being undeniable.

AT A GLANCE
- Very personable
- Training can be demanding
- Often not well disposed to other dogs
- Loyal, protective nature
- Straightforward coat care

CANINE CHARACTERISTICS		NOTES
Personality	Tenacious and strong willed, with a dislike for other dogs; loyal	Neuter male dogs to reduce aggressive behavior
Size	Height: 14–16 in. (36–41 cm) Weight: 24–38 lb (11–17.2 kg)	Do not overfeed the dog, as it can be prone to obesity, especially after neutering
Exercise	Needs time off the leash when out walking, if properly trained; has plenty of stamina	Muzzle the dog if it is likely to be aggressive
At home	Well suited to a family home; frequently gets along well with children; settles well in new surroundings	
Behavior	Lively; often demands attention by jumping up	Do not encourage jumping up behavior
Grooming	Grooming is very straightforward; just brushing required	Check the ears and nails regularly
Common health issues	Eye problems, notably hereditary cataracts and distichiasis, where a second row of eyelashes is present and may rub on the surface of the eye	Ensure breeding stock has been screened for cataracts; distichiasis may require corrective surgery

Staffie colors
Brindle and white examples are common, plus fawn, red, blue, and black, with or without white

Powerful legs
The hind legs are powerful with the tail being low set on the hindquarters

History

Now often known simply as the Staffie, this breed was developed for dogfighting purposes in the early 1800s. It was created initially from crossings between old-style Bulldogs and Black and Tan Terriers, sharing its initial ancestry with the English Bull Terrier breed. Subsequently, during the mid-1800s, in the hands of an enthusiast named James Hinks, the dog was transformed as a result of further crossings with the English White Terrier. It evolved a mastiff-style head, with the small ears set well back on the skull being a legacy of its pugnacious past. Due to its widespread popularity, the Staffordshire Bull Terrier was finally recognized for show purposes in its homeland during 1935.

Socialization

Although relatively small in stature, the Staffie is a surprisingly powerful dog. While it can be very playful, and even gentle, firm training from an early age is essential to prevent the more assertive side of its nature becoming apparent and creating possible problems in later life. Socialization with other dogs from an early age is important, too, as Staffies are not well disposed to other canines, and especially other Staffies. If trained correctly, a Staffordshire Bull Terrier will make an excellent companion, but bear in mind that this is no absolute guarantee that your dog will not prove aggressive in the company of others when you are out for a walk. Always plan to minimize conflict, even if this means teaching your pet to wear a muzzle at times.

Straight legs and padded feet
The forelegs are straight and well spaced with strong, well-padded feet

10. Mongrel

The innate intelligence of the mongrel has been documented by many owners down through the centuries. Mongrels are adaptable dogs, not being bred specifically to undertake particular tasks. They are very enthusiastic and intelligent, and settle well as family pets.

AT A GLANCE
- Unique, individual appearance
- Friendly nature
- Patterned coloration
- Variable coat type
- Differing sizes

History

As long as domestic dogs have existed, so have mongrels, and even today, many people still prefer to have a mongrel as a pet rather than a purebred dog. A mongrel is not a crossbreed, resulting from the mating of two different breeds, but has been the subject of random matings between unrecognized dogs over a number of generations. This helps to explain the diversity in appearance that exists within the group. In general, though, mongrels are less extreme in both appearance and behavior, compared with the variety of purebred dogs. They do not grow to a very large size, nor are they tiny. In the case of a long-haired mongrel, its coat will almost certainly not be as profuse as that of a purebred individual.

What to consider

It can be difficult to determine the likely adult size of a mongrel puppy, but the feet provide a useful clue in this respect. Puppies with large feet are likely to grow up into relatively large adult dogs. The patterning of puppies in a litter will almost certainly be highly individual, but it will remain consistent throughout their lives. Although it is often said that mongrels are healthier than purebred dogs, this is not entirely true, particularly as far as vaccinations are concerned. Mongrels are just as vulnerable to the main killer canine diseases, such as distemper, and their vaccinations must therefore be kept up to date.

CANINE CHARACTERISTICS		NOTES
Personality	Depends on the breeds that originally contributed to its ancestry, and any that may have made a more recent contribution	Encourage socialization from an early age
Size	Height: generally 8 in. (20 cm) or more Weight: weight should correspond to height and build, and to a purebred dog of similar appearance	Mongrels tend to range from average to large; they tend not to be very small
Exercise	Exercise needs depend on the dog's build; hound-type dogs will need a good run every day; smaller terrier-type dogs will appreciate a slower pace	
At home	Training at home is important	Consider that an older mongrel may not be properly house-trained
Behavior	Usually even-tempered, friendly, and quick to learn if socialized from an early age; otherwise, can be withdrawn, and may prove difficult to win the dog's confidence	Seek help from a dog trainer at an early stage if you suspect that the dog has a behavioral problem
Grooming	The coat is usually less profuse than those of purebred dogs; grooming needs depend on the coat type, but not generally a major issue	Brush and comb regularly
Common health issues	Can be afflicted by problems seen in purebred dogs, such as hip dysplasia; a puppy reared in less than ideal conditions may have mites	

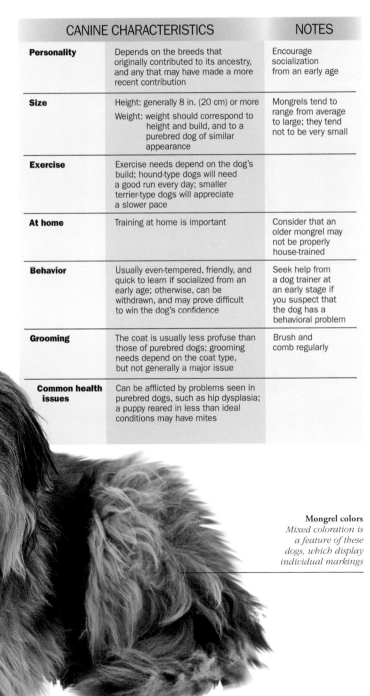

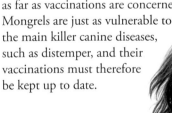

Mongrel muzzle
The muzzle is typically of medium length and width, ending in a black nose. The round, expressive eyes are usually dark

Nail color
The nails in this case are black but can vary in color

Mongrel colors
Mixed coloration is a feature of these dogs, which display individual markings

Dog types for individualists;
romanticists who appreciate the breed's
origins; and people who appreciate talent and
expertise, in whatever form.

Pointer

Newfoundland

Dogs with Talents

Cairn Terrier

Probably from the earliest days of domestication, which began more than 20,000 years ago, people started to keep dogs for particular purposes. Some of these dogs died out, as their working roles disappeared. These include the small Turnspit Dog, which worked in the kitchens of large homes, turning the meat as it cooked over a fire by walking on a treadmill. But even today, there are some highly specialized ancient breeds still in existence, such as the Bloodhound, which is well respected for its incredible tracking skills. Then there is the Italian truffle dog, called Lagotto Romagnolo, which uses its powers of scent to detect highly valuable fungi underground.

It is impossible to generalize about the dogs in this section, except to say that they have all developed a close working relationship with people, which means that they do form a strong bond with those around them. In addition, as working dogs, they tend to be active by nature and therefore need plenty of exercise. Ultimately, however, it will be a matter of delving into the breed's background as much as possible, to see which, if any, of these breeds are likely to be compatible with your lifestyle.

1. Australian Cattle Dog

The Australian Cattle Dog is incredibly tough, and a member of the breed, named Bluey, holds the record for being the longest-lived domestic dog. When Bluey died in 1939, after a lifetime of herding cattle, he was nearly 29½ years old.

CANINE CHARACTERISTICS		NOTES
Personality	Very loyal, rather cautious	
Size	Height: 17–20 in. (43–51 cm)	
	Weight: 30–60 lb (14–27 kg)	
Exercise	Needs plenty of mental and physical exercise—this is essential; usually stays close to its owner when out and off the leash	Exercise with a good daily run and games
At home	Useful guard dog; good companion; develops a strong bond; may try to herd family members by nipping at their heels	Do not encourage the dog to nip
Behavior	Often does not get along particularly well with other dogs; inclined to chew	Encourage socialization from an early age
Grooming	Straightforward brushing required; more frequent grooming needed when shedding	Brush weekly
Common health issues	Progressive Retinal Atrophy (PRA); congenital deafness	Ensure breeding stock has been screened for PRA; check puppies for deafness

Various other breeds, including the Dalmatian (see page 95), which brought added stamina, subsequently contributed to the emerging Australian Cattle Dog breed, and by the 1890s, the dog's appearance had become firmly established.

The breed overseas

During recent years, the Australian Cattle Dog has started to become popular outside its homeland. A characteristic that it shares with its Dingo ancestor is the ability to work without making any noise, although they do possess a distinctive bark. Before obtaining one of these dogs, however, bear in mind the breed's amazing energy and also its enthusiastic working ability. As pet dogs, they have proved themselves a good choice for both obedience and agility competitions. They delight in playing as well, but it can be difficult to find toys that are sufficiently robust to last for long.

History

The ancestors of this breed were developed from crosses between native herding breeds brought from Europe and the Dingo—a feral dog taken to Australia by the early Aboriginal settlers. Dingoes contributed stamina to the breed, which enabled these dogs to work in the harsh, arid surroundings of Australia. Two smooth-coated Collies were also used. This particular bloodline was used to improve an existing strain of cattle dog, known as the Timmon's Biter. It was so-called because it was more aggressive than necessary, and tended to injure the cattle rather than just encourage them to move when required by administering a nip.

Small ears
The relatively small, pricked ears are broad at the base

Muscular neck
The powerful, muscular neck is of medium length and supports the strong skull

Coat color
The coat is either red speckled or blue. It is speckled or mottled, with or without markings that can be blue, black, and tan

Low tail
The tail is set relatively low, extending down to the level of the hocks

2. Basenji

The Basenji is one of relatively few breeds that have been developed in Africa, and ranks as one of the most unusual of all domestic dogs. It is sometimes called the barkless dog, but actually has a yodel-like call. It is a very distinctive, unusual breed and has an attractive appearance.

AT A GLANCE
- Primitive breed
- Long history
- Many unusual behavioral traits
- Felinelike in some respects
- Likes to eat vegetables

History

Striking images of dogs closely resembling the Basenji have been discovered in ancient Egypt, dating back over 4,000 years. The breed was widely kept in areas extending down to the Congo Basin, on the western–central side of Africa, and north into what is now Sudan. The dogs were highly valued by the local tribespeople as hunting companions and were carefully bred. Two early attempts to introduce them to Britain were unsuccessful, as the dogs sadly contracted distemper and died, in an era before vaccinations were available. But a breeder visiting the Belgian Congo discovered some Basenjis and brought a small group back to Britain. These dogs were exhibited at the Cruft's show of 1937, where they caused a sensation because they were so different from the other breeds on view.

Unusual attributes

Some of the Basenji's behavior is very unusual. It grooms itself for long periods, like a cat, and when alert, the loose skin on its forehead wrinkles, so that the dog appears concerned. When on the move, it has an elegant, rather effortless style of trotting, like that of a horse. You may have to be patient to obtain a puppy. Unlike most domestic breeds, a female Basenji only comes into season once a year, so they only produce one litter of puppies annually, as do wild dogs.

Almond-shaped eyes
The dark eyes with dark rims are set obliquely

Muzzle shape
The muzzle is shorter in length than the skull

Curled tail
The tail is tightly curled over the back

Basenji colors
The coat is chestnut red, black, tricolor, or brindled with white areas on the feet, chest and tail tip

CANINE CHARACTERISTICS		NOTES
Personality	Alert; can be aloof; curious and may stand up, supporting itself on its hind legs to get a better view; will not take readily to visitors	Keep an eye on the dog around visitors
Size	Height: 16–17 in. (41–43 cm) Weight: 20–22 lb (9–10 kg)	
Exercise	Needs lots of exercise; capable of jumping well and running fast; energetic; dislikes going out in the rain or snow	Exercise with a good daily walk
At home	Likely to form a very strong bond with the person who is most involved in its care	
Behavior	Instinctively playful; may show an inclination to chase cats	Make time for games and play
Grooming	Simple brushing required	Use a hound glove to give the coat a good gloss
Common health issues	Progressive Retinal Atrophy (PRA), leading to blindness; kidney failure, caused by Fanconi's Syndrome	Ensure breeding stock has been screened for these conditions

3. Bloodhound

As the ancestral form of many of today's scent hounds, the Bloodhound is without a serious rival in terms of following "cold trails" that have been laid hours or even days earlier. Bloodhounds make enthusiastic companions, but sadly, the breed has a short life expectancy.

History

The Bloodhound is a direct descendent of the ancient St. Hubert Hound, which can be traced back to around 600 C.E. A study of early descriptions and portraits of the breed suggests that it has changed little over the course of centuries. In their early days, Bloodhounds were used to track wounded stags, which explains their name, as they would follow the trail of blood. But, subsequently, their tracking skills were employed to pursue human quarry, although Bloodhounds are not aggressive dogs in any way—they are just dedicated to their task. They were already known as "sleuth hounds" for this reason by the late 1200s. Individuals have been known to pursue people on trails for distances of up to 138 miles (220 km), showing their great determination.

Scenting

Unfortunately, the Bloodhound today has become increasingly scarce, largely because its scenting expertise combined with its stamina means that it really needs a spacious rural environment in which to thrive. When pursuing a scent, especially through woodland, it keeps in touch with a melodic deep, baying call. It is usual for Bloodhounds to hunt on their own or work in pairs, sometimes on a leash, but they are occasionally kept in packs. They are social by nature, and disagreements between individuals are rare. It is not just the Bloodhound's greatly enlarged nasal passages that allow it to track a scent. The Bloodhound's ears and skin folds also help keep the scent molecules concentrated and close to the nose.

CANINE CHARACTERISTICS		NOTES
Personality	Generous nature; enthusiastic; friendly; affectionate	
Size	Height: 23–27 in. (58–69 cm) Weight: 80–110 lb (36–50 kg)	Bitches are decidedly smaller than dogs
Exercise	Needs good walks; has almost boundless energy	Exercise at least once a day
At home	Not ideal for a home with toddlers because of the dog's size	
Behavior	Obedience training is difficult, as the dog is unlikely to respond when following a trail	
Grooming	Grooming is very straightforward; can develop quite a strong "doggy odor," and will then need a bath	Brush weekly and check the skin folds regularly for any signs of infection; bathe when necessary
Common health issues	Bloat	Do not exercise after feeding, as this can cause bloat

Bloodhound skull
The skull is narrow in proportion to its width, with a very pronounced occipital peak

Sense of smell
The large, open nostrils aid the Bloodhound's scenting ability

Long ears
The very long, low-set ears fall in folds and have a thin, soft texture

Bloodhound coat
The coat can be black and tan, liver and tan, or red

4. Newfoundland

This gentle giant may actually be the strongest of all breeds. The black-and-white Newfoundland, known as the Landseer, is named after the famous 19th century canine artist, Sir Edwin Landseer, and is sometimes recognized as a separate breed, essentially on the basis of coloration.

AT A GLANCE
- Immensely powerful
- Amenable nature
- Easily trained
- Gets along well with children
- Loves water
- Adaptable

History

The Newfoundland owes its origins to breeds brought from Europe, such as the Great Pyrenees (see page 85), which were probably crossed with indigenous sled dogs in Newfoundland, Canada. Its exact origins are unclear, but certainly before long, it undertook a number of tasks, and was highly valued by the mid-1700s. It is perhaps best known as a water dog for assisting local fisherman by pulling nets ashore, as well as rescuing drowning people. On land, however, it was important as a draft dog and pulled carts of goods.

The breed today

Selective breeding resulted in the Newfoundland becoming increasingly adapted to working in water. This is still evident in the breed today, as reflected by its webbed feet and water-resistant double coat, with its slightly oily texture. It is one of the larger breeds that displays a particular affiliation with children, although its size and strength may be intimidating for a toddler. Effective training is important, as a wayward Newfoundland can be a distinct liability. Luckily, it is very receptive in this respect, and will soon master the basics of what is required.

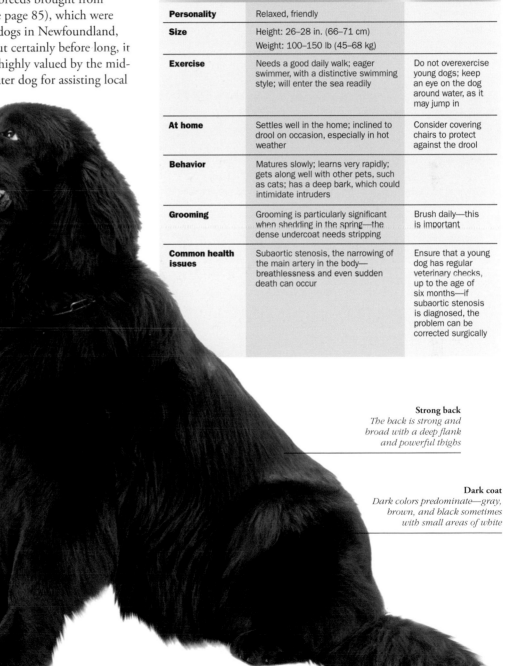

CANINE CHARACTERISTICS		NOTES
Personality	Relaxed, friendly	
Size	Height: 26–28 in. (66–71 cm) Weight: 100–150 lb (45–68 kg)	
Exercise	Needs a good daily walk; eager swimmer, with a distinctive swimming style; will enter the sea readily	Do not overexercise young dogs; keep an eye on the dog around water, as it may jump in
At home	Settles well in the home; inclined to drool on occasion, especially in hot weather	Consider covering chairs to protect against the drool
Behavior	Matures slowly; learns very rapidly; gets along well with other pets, such as cats; has a deep bark, which could intimidate intruders	
Grooming	Grooming is particularly significant when shedding in the spring—the dense undercoat needs stripping	Brush daily—this is important
Common health issues	Subaortic stenosis, the narrowing of the main artery in the body—breathlessness and even sudden death can occur	Ensure that a young dog has regular veterinary checks, up to the age of six months—if subaortic stenosis is diagnosed, the problem can be corrected surgically

Strong back
The back is strong and broad with a deep flank and powerful thighs

Dark coat
Dark colors predominate—gray, brown, and black sometimes with small areas of white

Large feet
The webbed feet are large, corresponding to the body size

5. Pointer

Also known as the English Pointer, this breed is highly valued both as a working gundog and as a companion. The Pointer still retains strong working instincts, possessing great stamina and a need for extensive walks on a regular basis.

CANINE CHARACTERISTICS		NOTES
Personality	Loyal, not really territorial; tolerant	
Size	Height: 23–28 in. (58–71 cm) Weight: 45–75 lb (20.4–34 kg)	
Exercise	Needs long country walks—this is essential	Be aware that Pointers typically walk some distance ahead when off the leash
At home	Gets along well with children; quite happy to sleep for long periods if alternated with spells of exercise	
Behavior	Enjoys playing with flying disks; has some retrieving instincts; young Pointers can be very clumsy	Make time for play
Grooming	Grooming is very straightforward, thanks to the smooth, sleek coat	Use a hound glove to give the coat a good sheen
Common health issues	Hip dysplasia; allergies	Ensure breeding stock has been screened for hip dysplasia

History

Reports of dogs resembling the Pointer can be traced back to the 1600s, but development of the modern breed probably began with the importation of Old Spanish Pointer stock. Steps were then taken to turn the Pointer into a versatile gundog. Crossings with the Greyhound (see page 52) are likely to have improved its pace, compared with its rather ponderous European ancestor, while the use of the Bloodhound (see page 144) increased its scenting skills. The introduction of Foxhound blood contributed to its stamina. Pointers are highly specialized gundogs, working as bird dogs. Their keen scenting skills will locate quarry, but instead of barking, which would scare the bird away, the Pointer freezes, adopting a very distinctive stance, with a front paw raised. Spaniels are then sent into the undergrowth to flush the game out for the waiting guns.

Working traits

This is not a breed that will be happy in urban surroundings—it needs to be kept in a rural area, which is its natural environment. These gundogs are very responsive as far as training is concerned, and their innate ability to point will be apparent even in young, recently weaned puppies. They form strong links with members of the family, and will get along well with children. These are not aggressive dogs by nature, and will live happily in a multidog household and also in the company of cats.

Powerful hindquarters
The muscular hindquarters have long, powerful thighs, which afford good stamina

Coat color
The coat can be liver, lemon, orange, or black. It is either solid colored or has white areas

Oval feet
The oval feet have long toes that are arched and well padded

Jaws and muzzle
The jaws are long and square with a deep muzzle

6. Finnish Spitz

The most striking feature of this breed is its attractive coloration, but it was actually bred to hunt birds in its native Finland, being known there under its local name of Suomenpystykorva. These dogs are now widely kept as companions worldwide.

History

The origins of the Finnish Spitz date back to the early 1800s. It acts like a Pointer, with a unique way of indicating that it has found quarry. At this point, a Finnish Spitz will pause at the bottom of the tree, and utter its very distinctive calls, which sound like a yodel. These can be uttered in intense sequences of up to 160 per minute. It is also said that the way in which it waves its long plumed tail when barking in this fashion effectively hypnotizes a bird, so that it cannot fly off. Finally, the dog moves deliberately around the tree while being watched intently by the bird, which then fails to spot the hunter's approach, with fatal consequences. Especially popular in the southern part of Finland, there was a time late in the 19th century when crossbreeding threatened the Finnish Spitz's future, but a careful breeding program extending for more than 30 years ensured the breed's survival.

In the home

The main drawback of keeping a Finnish Spitz as a pet is reflected by the way the breed works in the field. The Finnish Spitz is likely to be noisy, and will often bark repetitively, although it makes a good watchdog as a consequence. Hardy by nature, it is robust and makes a good family pet—the Finnish Spitz lives well alongside children, although it is less eager to share its home with other dogs.

CANINE CHARACTERISTICS		NOTES
Personality	Sensitive but strong willed; not especially affectionate	
Size	Height: 15–20 in. (38–51 cm) Weight: 31–35 lb (14–16 kg)	
Exercise	Enjoys walks in woodland areas; fairly energetic	Socialize early to minimize disputes with other dogs when out walking
At home	Makes a good family pet	
Behavior	Responds well to positive training methods	Try to discourage repetitive barking from an early stage
Grooming	Grooming must be carried out regularly, especially when shedding; a puppy will not show its adult coloration until it is six months old, maybe even slightly older	Brush undercoat when shedding, especially in spring when it is most profuse
Common health issues	Hip dysplasia; patellar luxation, a weakness affecting the kneecaps; epilepsy	Ensure breeding stock has been screened for hip dysplasia; patellar luxation may need corrective surgery

Curly tail
The high-set tail is plumed and forms a single curl that lies against the thigh

Color tones
Depth of color can vary from deep auburn through to pale honey

Long hair
The coat is longer at the back of the front legs and thighs than elsewhere on the legs

Compact feet
The feet are rounded and compact

7. Chesapeake Bay Retriever

This breed bears the name of the Chesapeake Bay, which lies off the Atlantic coast, lying to the south of Washington, D.C., where it was bred. It has proved to be a very effective retriever, working under what can be very hostile conditions.

History

The Chessie, as it is often known, owes its origins to two Newfoundland puppies that were rescued from a sinking ship off the shore of Maryland in 1807. They ultimately mated with retrievers in the area, and then combined the power and swimming abilities of the Newfoundland (see page 145) with the retrieving skills of the indigenous dogs. Further crosses with Otterhounds and Irish Water Spaniels (see page 113) then took place. The combination worked so well that the dog can retrieve up to 200 ducks a day from the cold waters of the bay.

Unique nature of the breed

The Chessie has powerful hindquarters enabling it to swim well and a large head that sets it apart from other retrievers. These dogs form a very strong affiliation with family members, and make excellent companions, provided that they have enough exercise. Their dense woolly undercoat helps to protect them from the cold, with the water-resistant top coat having an oily texture. Excessive grooming is likely to reduce the undercoat, while regular shampooing will strip out the essential oil from the top coat.

CANINE CHARACTERISTICS		NOTES
Personality	Intelligent; protective; brave—Chessies have been credited with saving drowning children	
Size	Height: 21–26 in. (53–66 cm)	
	Weight: 55–80 lb (25–36 kg)	
Exercise	Needs plenty of exercise, as it has a very powerful body and great stamina; loves swimming	Keep an eye on the dog around water, as it may plunge in
At home	Family friendly	
Behavior	Bares its teeth in a smile when excited; enthusiastic to work, but not the easiest retriever to train; eager participant in agility and obedience competitions	Be patient when training
Grooming	Regular grooming required	Groom with a short-toothed brush about once a week; bathe about three times a year
Common health issues	Eye problems, such as Progressive Retinal Atrophy (PRA) and cataracts; hip dysplasia	Ensure breeding stock has been screened for these conditions

Chessie tail
The medium-length tail is either straight or sometimes slightly curved

Powerful hindquarters
The well-muscled hindquarters aid swimming

Working colors
Color matches the dog's working environment and so the coat should be brown, sedge, or dead-grass colored

Swimming toes
The well-rounded toes have good webbing to aid swimming

AT A GLANCE
- Useful sporting companion
- Unusual appearance
- Great stamina
- Intelligent
- Not particularly easy to train

8. Lagotto Romagnolo

Truffles are sometimes described as "black gold" because of their value. They are a type of fungus that grows underground in association with certain tree roots, and are a sought-after gastronomic delight. In Italy, it was the Lagotto Romagnolo's task to locate them.

History

For many years, this breed's scenting ability outshone its appearance. It is believed to be descended from retrievers that originated in the vicinity of the Ravenna lagoons of Italy more than 500 years ago, with a clear representation of the breed being seen in a painting of 1474. Its truffle-hunting work began in the nearby Romagna hills. The breed's name literally translates as "water dog from Romagna," with *lago* meaning "lake" in Italian. Even today, these dogs can swim very well. It was not until the 1970s, however, that attempts were first made to standardize the breed for show purposes. A club for the breed was set up in 1988 and then a decade later, an international organization was formed, reflecting its increased popularity. Working examples of this breed can be found in many European countries today, ranging from Spain to Scandinavia. The sensitivity of the Lagotto Romagnolo's nose is such that it can locate truffles at least 12 in. (30 cm) below the surface of the soil.

The coat

This breed makes an excellent companion, and can be whitish, orange, or brown in color. Puppies that are brown and white initially are likely to lose their white patches as they grow older. Their coat remains something of a controversial subject, however, but at least some trimming is to be recommended, to keep the hair out of the eyes. If left to grow in a longer style, it becomes matted.

Triangular ears
The ears are quite large and triangular. They are set just above the level of the eyes and are wide at the base

Powerful neck
The neck is relatively short but very powerful and slightly arched

Color variations
Color can vary from off-white to white with orange or brown markings, plus solid brown or solid orange as well as brown roan

Curly coat
The coat is dense and curly, with a woolly texture. It is also waterproof

CANINE CHARACTERISTICS		NOTES
Personality	Determined, intelligent, dedicated	
Size	Height: 16–19 in. (41–48 cm) Weight: 24–35 lb (11–16 kg)	
Exercise	High-energy breed that needs plenty of exercise; enthusiastic swimmer	Exercise daily; keep an eye on the dog around water
At home	Settles well in the home if given enough exercise—can otherwise become bored	
Behavior	Adaptable and playful, retrieves toys readily; eager worker	Make time for play and do not neglect mental stimulation
Grooming	Tight, dense curls must be evident; if trimmed, coat length should be 1–1½ in. (2.5–3.8 cm)	Remove hair in the ear canal
Common health issues	Hip dysplasia; juvenile epilepsy	Ensure breeding stock has been screened for hip dysplasia

9. Nova Scotia Duck Tolling Retriever

The Nova Scotia Duck Tolling Retriever is another highly specialized breed of gundog, named after the Canadian province where it was bred. The description of "tolling" refers to the way in which the dog attracts waterfowl within range of the guns, with "toll" meaning "entice."

History

Hunters would traditionally throw so-called "tolling sticks" into the water for these gundogs to collect, and as they splashed around, the disturbance would attract waterfowl to the spot. The dog would then retrieve any ducks that were subsequently shot. A wide range of different gundogs, and even collies, contributed to the bloodline, with the breed's origins extending back to the 1860s. One of the most obvious distinctions between this breed and other retrievers is its head profile, which is much more elegant and foxlike, although its jaws are still powerful.

Looks and style

The coloring of the Toller, as it is often called, is very distinctive, being a reddish shade that may range from golden through to copper, often broken by small white patches on the body. A very rare chocolate form crops up occasionally. It is the smallest of the retriever breeds, which is probably a reflection of the spaniel input into its ancestry. The Toller has a double-layered coat that provides good insulation when it is working in water. Although not common, it is now represented in many countries besides its Canadian homeland, and makes an excellent companion. It is an active breed and needs plenty of space.

AT A GLANCE
- Stunning coloration
- Attentive
- Easily trained
- Inherently playful nature
- Affectionate companion breed

Broad skull
The skull is broad with the head being slightly rounded while the cheeks are flat

Red coat
Color can be any shade of red, from a golden red through to a dark shade of coppery red

White patches
White markings are present on the chest, feet, and tip of the tail, with a white blaze also present between the eyes

Parallel legs
The forelegs are parallel when seen from the front, with the elbows being close to the body

CANINE CHARACTERISTICS		NOTES
Personality	Affectionate but focused when working	
Size	Height: 17–21 in. (43–53 cm) Weight: 37–51 lb (17–23 kg)	
Exercise	Energetic and needs plenty of exercise; readily splashes about in ponds, lakes, or similar stretches of water	Exercise daily and keep an eye on the dog around water
At home	Good pet for a family; patient with children	
Behavior	Normally quite extroverted by nature; can be reserved in unfamiliar surroundings or with strangers	Make time for play to build a bond between you and the dog; avoid throwing sticks, as these could injure the dog—flying disks are much safer
Grooming	Grooming is particularly important in the spring, and also when shedding	Brush weekly
Common health issues	Hip dysplasia; Progressive Retinal Atrophy (PRA)	Ensure breeding stock has been screened for these conditions

10. Cairn Terrier

There are piles of stones in parts of Scotland that traditionally serve as boundary markers. These piles of stones can also provide retreats for rodents and sometimes even foxes. Farmers in these areas used this small, plucky breed of terrier to evict the unwanted animals.

AT A GLANCE
- Part of Scottish history
- Lively personality
- Keen hunting instincts
- Not particularly friendly toward other dogs
- Suffers from inherited conditions

CANINE CHARACTERISTICS		NOTES
Personality	Determined, curious, alert; intelligent, but not always easy to train	
Size	Height: 10–13 in. (25–33 cm) Weight: 14–18 lb (6.3–8 kg)	Larger, as well as smaller, individuals have been recorded
Exercise	Likes to trot along; can display great stamina, but not a sprinter; likes to be outside exploring, whatever the weather	Exercise with a daily walk or play outside
At home	Likes to explore around both the home and yard regularly	Be aware that the dog may dig outdoors, like many terriers
Behavior	Not always as responsive as might be desired; always on the lookout for vermin	
Grooming	Dead hair should be removed by hand stripping—this is very important, as Cairn Terriers can suffer from skin problems	
Common health issues	Prone to a wide range of hereditary problems, such as cataracts and Von Willebrand's Disease, a blood-clotting disorder	Research is continuing to detect and eliminate such problems, but not all can be detected in this way at present

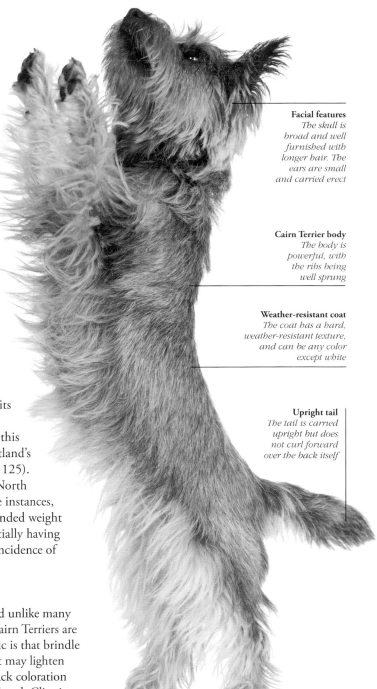

Facial features
The skull is broad and well furnished with longer hair. The ears are small and carried erect

Cairn Terrier body
The body is powerful, with the ribs being well sprung

Weather-resistant coat
The coat has a hard, weather-resistant texture, and can be any color except white

Upright tail
The tail is carried upright but does not curl forward over the back itself

History

The Cairn Terrier represents one of the oldest terrier bloodlines, with its ancestors having lived in the Western Isles and on the Isle of Skye for more than 400 years. Its appearance has altered remarkably little over this period, and it is likely that the dog contributed to the ancestry of Scotland's other native breeds of terriers, including the Scottish Terrier (see page 125). Over recent years, there has been a tendency for the Cairn Terrier in North America to become smaller than its European counterpart. In extreme instances, it may weigh as little as 7 lb (3 kg), which is half the official recommended weight for an adult Cairn Terrier. This trend toward miniaturization is potentially having a longer-term adverse impact on the breed, while also increasing the incidence of genetic weaknesses to which the breed is susceptible.

What to consider

The Cairn Terrier may be a small dog, but it has a large personality, and unlike many other similar terriers, it tends to be more amenable toward children. Cairn Terriers are bred in a relatively wide range of colors, but an interesting characteristic is that brindle Cairns frequently change in appearance as they become older. The coat may lighten in some individuals, becoming more silvery, whereas in other cases, black coloration becomes dominant. Cairn Terriers need to have their coat stripped by hand. Clipping will impact adversely on their distinctive harsh outer coats.

Dog types for extroverted owners; those happy defining beauty on their own terms; and homes with teenage children.

Xoloitzcuintli

Weird and Wonderful Dogs

Chinese Shar-Pei

If it is an unusual appearance that appeals to you when it comes to choosing a dog, then the likelihood is that you will find a breed of interest in this section. But bearing in mind the saying that beauty is very much in the eye of the beholder, do not expect other people—including members of your family!—necessarily to share your enthusiasm for your choice. The Xoloitzcuintli, for example, is a breed that generally draws a strong reaction, whether favorable or adverse, as not everyone appreciates its lack of hair.

Some of these breeds are relative newcomers to the international dog scene, such as the Ibizan Hound and Chinese Shar-Pei, which then became popular in a short space of time, whereas others, like the Norwegian Lundehund, are still rare. Many have a unique working ancestry, with none of these breeds having been evolved primarily as companion dogs in the first instance. Their temperaments and size vary markedly; therefore, it is not possible to generalize in these respects. However, if you consider the purpose for which the breed was originally created, this will give you the best insight into its suitability for your home.

1. Neapolitan Mastiff

As one of the heavyweights of the canine world, this breed has a truly unmistakable appearance. It has been rather cruelly dubbed "the hippopotamus of the canine world." Yet it is quite an active breed in terms of its nature.

AT A GLANCE
- Massive dog
- Huge appetite
- Very powerful dog
- Calm temperament
- Looks fearsome, though relatively placid

History

Neapolitan Mastiffs represent an ancient bloodline that extends all the way back to the time of Alexander the Great, who ruled Greece between 336 and 323 B.C.E. Subsequently, the dogs were taken to Rome, and were used in battle, having acquired a reputation for aggression. Today's lineage is very different in temperament. The efforts of the Italian artist Piero Scanziani (1908–2003) led to them being recognized by the Italian Kennel Club in 1946, and, since then, they have become well known worldwide. There has been a major change in its temperament, too. The aggression has been replaced by a much calmer, more docile nature.

Huge head
The head is massive with a very prominent dewlap and extensive wrinkling of the skin

Thighs and feet
The thighs are very powerful. The hind feet are slightly smaller than the front feet

Large feet
The feet are round and very large with strong, arched toes and dark-colored nails

Coat color
The coat can be gray (blue), black, tawny, or mahogany, sometimes with small white areas and brindling

CANINE CHARACTERISTICS		NOTES
Personality	Loyal; shy with strangers	
Size	Height: 24–31 in. (61–79 cm)	
	Weight: 110–170 lb (50–77 kg)	
Exercise	Not particularly keen on running, except over short distances	Avoid exercise in hot weather, as the dog is susceptible to heatstroke
At home	Needs spacious surroundings; not suitable for a home with small children	
Behavior	Can be clumsy; has a huge reach when standing; tends not to show signs of pain unless it is severe; salivates excessively; learns quickly	Do not leave food within reach on work surfaces; wipe drool off the dog's face when necessary
Grooming	Coat care is straightforward, with just regular brushing required	Watch the skin folds, as these can become infected—wipe these areas with a clean damp cloth
Common health issues	Eye problems; degeneration of the heart muscle; hip dysplasia; bloat; relatively short-lived like many larger dogs	Ensure breeding stock has been screened for eye problems and hip dysplasia

A gargantuan lifestyle

Their huge size means that these dogs are simply too large for many homes, with their powerful tails being able to sweep objects off low tables. They also have massive appetites, which means that feeding them is a very costly undertaking. In common with many other mastiffs, they will also drool around the home, particularly in hot weather, and frequently at mealtimes. Controlling them on the leash requires considerable strength, too, with adequate training being essential to facilitate this task. In return, however, these dogs make great companions, being quite placid by nature, although they still retain a protective streak.

2. Xoloitzcuintli

AT A GLANCE
- Striking appearance
- Ancient breed
- Unique coloration
- Obedient
- Can prove to be hypoallergenic
- No "doggy odor"

The Nahuatl tribe gave these dogs their distinctive name, which is pronounced *sholo-its-quintli*. This translates as "dog of the god Xolotl," a significant figure in Aztec culture. Today, they are known as Xolos and also as Mexican Hairless Dogs.

CANINE CHARACTERISTICS		NOTES
Personality	Friendly; likely to be shy with strangers	
Size	Height: 9–18 in. (23–46 cm) Weight: 5–40 lb (2.2–18 kg)	Three sizes are now recognized: toy, miniature, and standard
Exercise	Lively and enjoys going out for a walk	Be sure that the dog gets enough activity, as it is prone to obesity; use a sweater in cold weather and canine sun block in hot weather
At home	Good family pet; gets along well with children; must be housed indoors; good guardian	
Behavior	Learns rapidly and naturally obedient	
Grooming	Has variable areas of longer hair on the head, lower legs, and tail; care of the spotted variety is more demanding than of those with solid dark coloration	Groom hair; wipe the body with a damp sponge; apply lotion once or twice a month; check that the ears are clean
Common health issues	Vulnerable to skin cancer; may be missing some teeth—this is usual in hairless breeds; very healthy dog, with a long life expectancy of 15 years or so	Keep the dog out of the sun when it is at its hottest

Special care

Love or hate its appearance, once people encounter this breed, they soon fall under its charm. Xolos have very friendly temperaments and are usually very eager to join in with family life, making them excellent companions. Nevertheless, they do need careful management. On hot days, their relative lack of a coat will leave them vulnerable to sunburn, and potentially skin cancer; and over the winter period they will feel the cold and so must wear a suitable sweater or coat, particularly when they are outdoors.

Matching eyes
The almond-shaped eyes are of medium size and must match each other in color

Large ears
The large, thin ears taper to rounded tips. They are set high on the skull

Long muzzle
The muzzle is longer than the skull, with the lips being thin

Xolo color
Xolos can be black, grayish black, slate, liver, red, or bronze in color, often broken with white markings

History

During the pre-Columbian era, it appears that there were a number of different types of essentially hairless dogs being kept in the New World. They were used as bed warmers and were also eaten at times, as well as sacrificed. The Xoloitzcuintli is the best known example of such breeds that still survive. It is not free of hair entirely, with some hair present on the feet and legs, as well as the tip of the tail and the top of the head. In addition, as with other predominantly hairless breeds, there is also a normal-coated variant that sometimes crops up in litters, which is at times described as the Powderpuff. This particular breed was first seen in the U.S. in 1883, but remained very scarce on the international scene until the 1980s.

3. Komondor

These sheepdogs are the largest of Hungary's native dog breeds, and are unmistakable thanks to their corded coat. Their name, pronounced *quman-dur* and meaning "belonging to the Cumans," who invaded Hungary during the 1200s, may reflect their origins.

CANINE CHARACTERISTICS		NOTES
Personality	Attentive and loyal; very aware and can be bold; does not take readily to visitors	Keep an eye on the dog around visitors
Size	Height: 26–30 in. (66–76 cm) Weight: 80–135 lb (36–61 kg)	
Exercise	Needs a good walk every day, as it is a naturally active dog; energetic	Keep the dog away from livestock, as it may interfere with them
At home	Watchful and alert to the approach of strangers	Encourage socialization from an early age
Behavior	Training can be more demanding than with other breeds; has an independent streak	Be patient when training
Grooming	Although soft, a puppy's coat will soon show signs of cording—ultimately, it becomes largely impenetrable; the coat should have corded up by the time a young Komondor reaches two years of age	Train the coat into cords, otherwise it will form large mats
Common health issues	Hip dysplasia	Ensure breeding stock has been screened for hip dysplasia

History

The Komondor's ancestors probably originated in Asia, possibly as early as the 1000s. The breed was already well established in Hungary 500 years ago, and has since changed very little, apart from becoming slightly larger in size. It still serves as a flock guardian, watching over herds of sheep and cattle and protecting them from thieves or predators, such as wolves, with the task of herding traditionally being left to the smaller Puli (see page 64). The Komondor's thick, corded coat actually has a protective function, as it provides a barrier against attack by wolves. Komondor puppies are traditionally brought up with the flocks that they will guard in later life, helping to create a close bond. A similar scenario occurs today when a young Komondor is introduced to the home, where it is likely to prove to be exceptionally loyal.

Strong back
The back is strong and level, with the neck being muscular and slightly arched

Hidden tail
The tail actually hangs down to the level of the hocks, although it may be hidden by the coat

Living with a Komondor

The coat of the Komondor is always whitish, because this coloration enables it to blend in well alongside the sheep that it is responsible for protecting. As well as providing a barrier against attack, the coat is an effective insulator, guarding the Komondor against the cold. It is important to consider the Komondor's temperament, as it tends to be rather independent and not overtly affectionate by nature.

Powerful chest
The chest is very powerful and deep

4. Ibizan Hound

Named after the Mediterranean island where it originated, the Ibizan Hound has a long, narrow neck and huge, upright ears, which are particularly large at the base and set it apart from similar breeds. Its eyes are an attractive amber shade.

AT A GLANCE
- Individual coloration
- A generally healthy breed
- Very fast when pursuing quarry
- More responsive to training than many sight hounds
- Keen hunting instincts

CANINE CHARACTERISTICS		NOTES
Personality	Extroverted; sensitive	
Size	Height: 24–29 in. (61–74 cm)	
	Weight: 45–65 lb (20.4–29.4 kg)	
Exercise	Needs daily exercise; may chase small dogs when off the leash, confusing them with rabbits	Keep away from other dogs, or keep the dog muzzled
At home	Settles well as a family pet	Check fences are secure, as it is capable of jumping well
Behavior	Quiet by nature—barking usually signifies that something is wrong; will get along well with other dogs of similar size; playful; has an independent streak	Offer positive encouragement when training
Grooming	Simple brushing usually suffices; some stripping of the wirehaired variety's coat may be necessary	Brush when necessary
Common health issues	Epilepsy; allergies; deafness; cataracts	Household chemicals can trigger allergies; use hypoallergenic products to wash food bowls and bedding

History

This Ibizan Hound is closely related to other breeds found on islands in this region, including the Pharaoh Hound (see page 102), and shares a common ancestry with them. It is believed that these hounds are all originally descended from ancient Egyptian stock, which was traded through the Mediterranean region by the Phoenicians. Ibizan Hounds remained largely confined to their homeland until the 1950s, although they were kept as hunting dogs in parts of France and Germany beforehand. They then started to become popular as show dogs, both in Europe and farther afield, reaching the U.S. during 1956. They are very effective hunters of rabbits, and are excellent over relatively rough terrain. Ibizan Hounds are regularly used on their own or in couples, although occasionally small packs may be employed. Bitches are preferred for hunting, as they are believed to be better suited to the task.

A stylish companion

The attractive coloration and sleek good looks of the Ibizan Hound have helped to ensure the popularity of the dog, which can usually be distinguished at a glance from the Pharaoh Hound by the large, variable white patches on its body. Some individuals are entirely white. There are two different coat types, with the sleek, smooth-coated variety being by far the most common, compared with its wirehaired counterpart. Although classified as a sight hound, the Ibizan Hound has keen hearing, which can help it to home in on its prey.

Slender neck
The neck is relatively slender yet long and strong, and is carried in a slight arch

Ibizan Hound color
The coat can be white or red in color—either solid or combined. Pale yellowish shades of red are described as "lion" colored

Long legs
The legs are very long, straight, and powerful, and lie very close to the chest

Long tail
The low-set tail is also long, reaching to the level of the hocks, and is very mobile

5. Dandie Dinmont Terrier

This is the only breed of dog named after a fictional character. Its name is taken from that of a character in Sir Walter Scott's novel *Guy Mannering*, which is thought to have been based on a local farmer named James Davidson who kept terriers.

History

Working terrier-type dogs were traditionally kept in parts of northern Britain and Scotland, with the Dandie Dinmont's ancestors originating in the Border area between these two countries. In 1800, Davidson had obtained two of these dogs, called Tarr (meaning Mustard) and Pepper—these were the same names chosen by Scott for the terriers that appeared in his book, effectively confirming the source of his inspiration. After publication, Davidson's terriers soon became known locally as Dandie Dinmont's Terriers, named after a character in Scott's novel. As to whether the breed is descended just from local terriers is, however, still open to debate. Some suggest that the long, low-slung body of the breed reflects a possible link to the Dachshund (see page 53).

Careful management

The unique, distinctive features of the Dandie Dinmont, such as the topknot of hair on its head and the length of its ears were developed further as the breed became a popular show dog. But this breed still retains true terrier attributes, including an eagerness to hunt vermin—in the past, the breed hunted rodents and even rabbits and badgers. The length of the body does leave this particular terrier at risk of developing intervertebral disk problems. In order to minimize the danger, Dandie Dinmonts should always be exercised wearing a harness rather than a collar that pulls on the neck, and you should not encourage them to jump up onto chairs or to climb stairs, as both of these activities can also cause disk problems.

CANINE CHARACTERISTICS		NOTES
Personality	Reserved, especially with strangers	
Size	Height: 8–11 in. (20–28 cm) Weight: 18–24 lb (8–11 kg)	Keep an eye on the dog's weight, as obesity will increase the risk of back problems
Exercise	Trots along happily on its short legs, displaying plenty of stamina; inclined to venture into burrows when out walking	
At home	Settles quite well in an apartment, particularly where there is access to a yard; possesses a bark suggestive of a much larger dog, making it a valuable guard dog	Prevent the dog from climbing stairs by fitting a stair guard; do not allow the dog to jump onto chairs
Behavior	Can be very stubborn, which makes training difficult, and is sometimes possessive of toys; playful	Be patient when training
Grooming	Brushing and combing required; tends not to shed so hand plucking of the coat by a professional groomer is recommended	Groom once a week
Common health issues	Spinal weakness; patellar luxation; epilepsy	Patellar luxation may need corrective surgery

Low-set ears
The ears are set toward the rear of the head and positioned low on the skull

Leg length
The hind legs are longer than the front legs and quite widely spaced apart

Round feet
The feet are rounded, with those on the hind legs being smaller than those on the front legs

Muscular neck
The neck is very muscular and is of medium length, linking well into the shoulders

6. Canaan Dog

This breed is unusual because it is descended from a semiwild population of dogs. It is now recognized as the National Dog of Israel, being the only breed that has been exclusively developed to date in this particular part of the Middle East.

AT A GLANCE
- Highly unusual origins
- Now kept internationally
- Highly adaptable nature
- Variable coloration and patterning
- Can be noisy at times

CANINE CHARACTERISTICS		NOTES
Personality	Focused and adaptable; generally suspicious of strangers	Keep an eye on the dog around strangers
Size	Height: 19–24 in. (48–61 cm) Weight: 35–55 lb (16–25 kg)	
Exercise	Needs regular daily exercise—this is important and will help lessen the dog's wandering instincts	Exercise with a long daily walk
At home	Tends to wander off	Check fencing carefully and ensure that it is secure
Behavior	Alert; easily distracted at times; may display an independent streak; will bark	
Grooming	Regular brushing will suffice; more frequent grooming is important when shedding	Brush once a week
Common health issues	Hip dysplasia; Progressive Retinal Atrophy (PRA); epilepsy	Ensure breeding stock has been screened for hip dysplasia and PRA

History

The ancestors of Canaan Dogs were pariah dogs that lived on the fringes of human settlements and scavenged on whatever leftovers they could find. They have been present in the region for millennia, with some of the oldest remains of domestic dogs being discovered in this area. The Bedouin tribespeople of the Negev Desert have kept such dogs for a very long period of time, and during 1935, when Dr. Rudolphina Menzel was seeking dogs that could be used in military service in the area, she decided to see if these pariah dogs might be suitable to domesticate fully for the purpose. She found that they settled very rapidly in domestic surroundings. She selected dogs that had an appearance like collies in terms of their build, although they do appear more like spitz-type dogs in general appearance, due to their pricked ears and curled tails.

Past and present

Canaan Dogs are now well established as a distinctive breed, but their behavior still reflects aspects of their past. Having originated from a desert region, they seem to drink less than most dogs. Canaan Dogs also display a strong tendency to dig, replicating the way in which they excavate burrows in the sandy desert. There are now very few of their wild relatives still to be found in the desert region, as they were largely wiped out because of fears over rabies, although a few can still be seen around Bedouin encampments.

Slanted eyes
The almond-shaped eyes are dark, with a slight slant

Canaan body
The body is athletic with a moderately deep chest

Bushy tail
The bushy tail may be carried curled over the back when the dog is excited

Legs, feet, and nails
The straight legs end in catlike feet, with nails that match the nose in color

7. Rhodesian Ridgeback

Although first bred in South Africa, the Rhodesian Ridgeback came to prominence in Zimbabwe, formerly known as Rhodesia, accounting for the dog's name. It often accompanied hunters on safari, in search of dangerous quarry, and is sometimes known as the African Lion Dog.

History

The early European settlers in southern Africa brought breeds from Europe, but found that they did not adapt well to the environment. Yet there was a very distinctive African breed, named the Hottentot Dog after the tribe who created it, which thrived there. The Rhodesian Ridgeback was bred from a combination of European breeds, including the Great Dane (see page 82) and the Mastiff (see page 124), crossed with the Hottentot Dog. The resulting breed is bold and courageous.

The ridge

Although the Hottentot Dog no longer exists today, its most distinctive feature—a ridge of hair running down the center of the back—has been transferred into the Rhodesian Ridgeback. The ridge follows a very distinctive pattern, with two whorls of hair, which are called crowns, positioned opposite each other near the shoulders. This creates a fanlike impression, linking into the ridge itself, which continues down the back to the level of the hips. The ridge is formed by the hair growing in different directions down the dog's back. These hounds are now kept worldwide, and are frequently seen at major shows. They thrive where there is space available, particularly on farms or ranches rather than in cities.

Alert expression
The round eyes are relatively well spaced and give an alert, intelligent expression

High-set ears
The ears are set high, being quite wide at the base and taper to rounded points

Rhodesian ridge
The characteristic, clearly defined ridge runs down the center of the back

Strong forelegs
The forelegs are very strong and straight with the elbows being held close to the body

CANINE CHARACTERISTICS		NOTES
Personality	Friendly and brave; sensitive	
Size	Height: 24–27 in. (61–69 cm) Weight: 70–85 lb (32–38.5 kg)	
Exercise	Athletic and needs plenty of opportunities to run off the leash	Ensure that the dog gets enough exercise; otherwise, it may become troublesome
At home	Loyal guardian in domestic surroundings	Socialize from puppyhood to accept visitors
Behavior	Strong willed; needs to be well trained from an early age; not always well disposed toward other dogs	Ensure training is a positive experience
Grooming	Grooming is straightforward; the ridge holds its own shape	
Common health issues	Dermoid sinus, a developmental abnormality, which can be associated with the ridge	Ensure a puppy has been screened by a veterinarian to spot this potentially serious condition

8. Chinese Shar-Pei

By the time that it became known to dog lovers in the West, the Chinese Shar-Pei was on the verge of extinction. Its plight was highlighted in a magazine article written by a Hong Kong dog enthusiast, and this led to the breed being rescued.

CANINE CHARACTERISTICS		NOTES
Personality	Fearless and assertive but can be stubborn; emphasis has been on producing good-natured Shar-Peis in the West; alert to the presence of strangers	Keep an eye on the dog around strangers
Size	Height: 18–20 in. (46–51 cm) Weight: 45–60 lb (20.4–27 kg)	Dogs often have a squarer shape than bitches, and may be larger
Exercise	Needs a good walk every day; energetic	Socialize the dog from puppyhood to reduce aggressive instincts toward other dogs
At home	Loyal guardian	
Behavior	Adaptable, and learns rapidly; has good scenting skills; now being seen not just in agility but also obedience competitions	
Grooming	Grooming is very straightforward; "Shar-Pei" translates roughly as "sandpaper-like coat"	Watch for any infection in the skin folds
Common health issues	Skin problems; entropion, where the eyelids turn inward and rub against the eyeball	Entropion may need corrective surgery

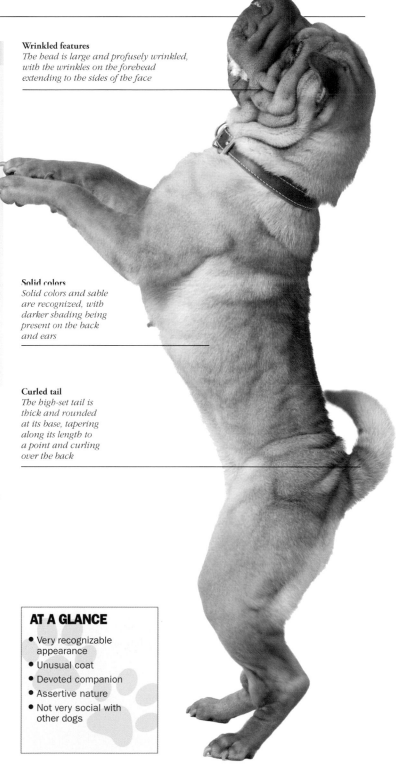

Wrinkled features
The head is large and profusely wrinkled, with the wrinkles on the forehead extending to the sides of the face

Solid colors
Solid colors and sable are recognized, with darker shading being present on the back and ears

Curled tail
The high-set tail is thick and rounded at its base, tapering along its length to a point and curling over the back

History
The origins of the Chinese Shar-Pei extend back over 2,000 years. It is descended from the Han Dog, which was kept as a guardian during the Han Dynasty. It shares its origins with the Chow Chow (see page 60), as reflected by the fact that both breeds have bluish–black tongues. The Shar-Pei ultimately became localized to southern China, where it has undertaken a wide variety of tasks down through the millennia. The breed worked both as a guard dog and as a farm dog to herd stock. It also acted as a vermin killer, but it became best known as a fighting breed. Its wrinkled skin made it difficult for an opponent to gain a grip on its body, while its bristly coat had an unpleasant texture.

Back from the brink
By the time that Western breeders became aware of the breed's plight in the late 1970s, there were probably no more than 60 surviving Shar-Peis. Examples were first taken to the U.S. and Germany. Today, the breed's future is secure, with more than 100,000 Chinese Shar-Peis in North America alone. The Shar-Pei's coat length is naturally variable, ranging from the short "horse coat" up to the much longer brush coat, which measures as much as 1 in. (2.5 cm) long.

AT A GLANCE
- Very recognizable appearance
- Unusual coat
- Devoted companion
- Assertive nature
- Not very social with other dogs

9. Bulldog

The appearance of this breed has altered dramatically over the centuries. Bulldogs are generally placid companion dogs, and are far less athletic than they used to be in the past. They are also significantly smaller, now having shorter legs.

History

As its name suggests, the Bulldog was originally developed to participate in bull-baiting contests, which were popular public spectacles from the 1200s right up until 1835 when they were banned. The dogs were expected to leap onto the bull's head and grip the bull's snout without letting go. The Bulldog's very broad, flattened muzzle, allowed it to anchor itself firmly in place, while being able to breathe without relinquishing its grip. Its relatively small size also helped it to dodge the bull's ferocious horns. Once bull-baiting ceased, it was not long before Bulldogs became popular in the show ring. Over time, their appearance has been modified, compromising their soundness. Breeders are now concentrating on trying to eliminate the health problems that have become inherent in the breed.

The breed today

There is no doubting the appealing personality of today's Bulldog—it is a very friendly dog. As with other breeds with a flattened face, however, it is susceptible to heatstroke in warm weather and it should be exercised only in the relative cool of the morning and evening, and never around midday. It is quite common for Bulldogs to snore, because of the shape of their noses. Other types of Bulldogs have now been developed, but these more closely resemble the original form of the breed, not just in terms of stature, but also in terms of temperament, as they tend to be more assertive by nature.

Bulldog eyes
The eyes are situated relatively low down in the skull, well away from the ears

Color varieties
Brindle, white, red, fawn, fallow, and piebald variants are all recognized

Black nose
The large, broad, black nose's tip is set deeply between the eyes

Deep lips
The very deep lips cover the jaws on the sides

CANINE CHARACTERISTICS		NOTES
Personality	Affectionate; placid and good natured	
Size	Height: 12–14 in. (30–36 cm) Weight: 40–50 lb (18–22.7 kg)	Keep an eye on the dog's weight, as obesity should be avoided
Exercise	Happy with a walk around the park; ambles, does not race	Avoid exercise in the hottest part of the day
At home	Not suited to an apartment; good with children and other pets, including cats; likes human company and likes to spend time with family members	Be sure to spend time with the dog
Behavior	Not very active, but will explore around the home	
Grooming	Coat care is straightforward, with a weekly brushing being adequate	Watch that the skin folds do not become infected, and check that nails do not become overgrown
Common health issues	Has a higher incidence of hip dysplasia than any other breed; congenital heart ailments are also a significant issue; large heads mean that puppies may need a Caesarean birth	Ensure breeding stock has been screened for hip dysplasia; puppies must receive a thorough veterinary check

10. Norwegian Lundehund

The name of this Norwegian breed reflects the purpose for which it was created, *lunde* being the Norwegian word for "puffin." These seabirds used to be highly prized for food, but catching them when they came ashore to nest required particular skill, which is where this breed became especially useful.

History

Few breeds are more specialized than the Norwegian Lundehund. It has even evolved additional toes that help it to maintain its balance when clambering around on cliffs. Its forelegs are also very flexible, as is its neck, enabling it to reach easily into the puffins' burrows. Even its pricked ears can be folded down, to protect them not just against the elements but also from soil in these surroundings. Records of the breed extend back over 400 years, but as nets started to be widely used for catching the birds, the Norwegian Lundehund began to decline significantly in numbers. Outbreaks of the deadly disease distemper also affected its numbers, so that by 1963 just six examples of the breed survived, of which five shared the same mother. Since then, however, the Norwegian Lundehund has been saved from extinction by a careful breeding program. There are now around 350 out of an estimated total population of up to 1,500 individuals being kept in the U.S., where it was first seen in 1987.

Future prospects

The breed's popularity continues to increase, although it is no longer used for hunting in its homeland, where puffins are now a protected species. It makes a lively companion, and is completely unique in many respects. Its relatively small size means that it is not difficult to accommodate, and it thrives in domestic surroundings. It will almost certainly start to excel in both agility and obedience contests in the near future.

CANINE CHARACTERISTICS		NOTES
Personality	Lively and curious; intelligent; affectionate	Socialize early to prevent nervousness later
Size	Height: 12–16 in. (30–41 cm) Weight: 13–20 lb (6–9 kg)	Weigh the dog regularly and keep a record so that you can watch for Lundehund Syndrome (see below)
Exercise	Active and appreciates going out for walks—this is also significant as house-training is often difficult	
At home	Diet is very important, both to prevent or help to address Lundehund Syndrome	
Behavior	Sensitive to noise; alert and noisy by nature; barks frequently; has hunting instincts for small animals and birds; strong pack instincts; gets along well with others of its own kind	Be aware that the dog may hide food and return to eat it later
Grooming	Regular brushing will suffice; sheds heavily, especially in spring, losing its winter coat	Check that the nails do not become overgrown
Common health issues	Lundehund Syndrome, a digestive disorder said to afflict all members of the breed, although not all exhibit symptoms	Diarrhea, vomiting, or failure to gain weight, in the case of puppies—are all potential warning signs

Triangular ears
The triangular, broad ears are usually carried upright but are very flexible

Rib shape
The ribs are set well back and give good chest capacity, although they are not barrel shaped

Front feet
Six toes should be present on each front foot, with eight supporting pads present

Hind feet
The hind feet are oval, with at least six toes present—four extend to the ground, supporting the dog's weight

The Human Selector

Here are some points that you need to consider about yourself before choosing your dog. You have mulled over the various responsibilities of caring for a dog and rightly decided that the benefits are well worth the commitment. But which type will you choose? The domestic dog, *Canis lupus familiaris*, is more varied in physical features and behavior than any other land mammal, so it is not an easy decision. The questions below will help you to review your lifestyle. Then you can think about what dog might suit you.

Is this the first time you have owned a dog?

NO, I'VE ALWAYS HAD A DOG	I HAD A DOG GROWING UP, BUT NOT SINCE	YES, I'M AN ABSOLUTE BEGINNER
See most dogs, but especially Border Collie, German Shepherd Dog, Mongrel, Parson Russell Terrier	See most dogs, but especially Collie, English Setter, Miniature Schnauzer	See Boston Terrier, Golden Retriever, Pug, Schipperke, Tibetan Spaniel

Do you have any other pets?

NO, AND I ONLY WANT ONE	I HAVE A CAT	YES, SEVERAL
See most dogs, but especially Australian Cattle Dog, Bull Terrier, Kerry Blue Terrier	See Beagle, Border Terrier, Lhasa Apso, Pekingese, Shih Tzu	See Brittany, Cavalier King Charles Spaniel, Clumber Spaniel, Coton de Tulear, Spinone Italiano

Do you or does anyone you live with have pet allergies?

NO, I'M ALLERGY FREE	ONE OF US IS MILDLY ALLERGIC	YES, I'M VERY ALLERGIC
See most dogs, but especially Borzoi, Neapolitan Mastiff, Old English Sheepdog	See most dogs, but especially Airedale Terrier, Bedlington Terrier, Bichon Frisé, Irish Water Spaniel, Wire Fox Terrier	See Chinese Crested Dog, Curly-coated Retriever, Labradoodle, Poodle, Portuguese Water Dog

Do you have children or are you planning a family?

NO, I LIVE ALONE	NO, IT'S JUST THE TWO OF US	YES, TWO CHILDREN AND ONE ON THE WAY
See most dogs, but especially Bichon Frisé, Bulldog, Gordon Setter, Irish Setter	See most dogs, but especially Australian Shepherd, Beauceron, Papillon, Whippet	See Beagle, Bearded Collie, English Toy Spaniel, Miniature Schnauzer

NOW PUT TOGETHER 5 POINTS FOR EVERY LEFT-HAND ANSWER, 3 POINTS FOR EVERY CENTRAL ANSWER, AND 1 POINT FOR EVERY RIGHT-HAND ANSWER

15 or more A wide range of dog types will suit you, and your living situation will accommodate most of them.

10 or more There is a perfect dog for you, but you will have to be more careful selecting a breed that suits your specific needs.

Less than 5 You will need to think very carefully about having a dog. Although some dogs will suit you better than others, all dogs need some attention and affection. A dog should not be brought into an environment that is too restricted by your busy lifestyle.

Before you make your final decision, consider your own personality.

Are you seeking a soul mate as a companion?

Are you security conscious?

If you have a special talent, perhaps you would like a dog with unique skills of its own?

If you're creative and have spare time, you might like a dog you can groom to your heart's content.

If you're quirky and an independent thinker, an unusual dog might suit you best. Use the chart opposite and see if you can find the perfect dog for you!

Progressively more important →

THINGS THAT I HAVE		
Money	On a budget? See Affenpinscher, Bolognese, Chihuahua	With some money? See Dalmatian, Golden Retriever, Spinone Italiano	With money to spare? See Anatolian Shepherd Dog, Great Dane, Neapolitan Mastiff
Time	Time is tight? See French Bulldog, Italian Greyhound, Japanese Chin	Most evenings free? See Chow Chow, Dandie Dinmont Terrier, Hamiltonstövare	A whole lot of time? See Afghan Hound, Old English Sheepdog
Space	Bijou living? See Pekingese, Pomeranian, Silky Terrier	With some space? See Beauceron, Border Collie, Mongrel	With acres of space? See Alaskan Malamute, Bloodhound, Irish Wolfhound
Fitness	Prefer to spend time on the sofa? See Pekingese, Pug, Shih Tzu, Whippet	Enjoy a good walk? See Siberian Husky, Welsh Corgi	Always on the go? See Dalmatian, Lurcher, Pointer, Weimaraner

Progressively more important →

THINGS THAT I WANT		
A smart dog	Fun and cute more important? See Bulldog, Dachshund, Greyhound, Pekingese, Pug, Scottish Terrier	Intelligence quite important? See Basenji, Newfoundland, Pharaoh Hound, Rhodesian Ridgeback	Intelligence very important? See Border Collie, Mongrel, Papillon
A social dog	Spend lots of time alone? See Black Russian Terrier, Dogue de Bordeaux, Kuvasz, Mastiff	Will meet people sometimes? See Cavalier King Charles Spaniel, Coton de Tulear, Soft-coated Wheaten Terrier	Always around others? See Bearded Collie, Boxer, Irish Setter, Vizsla
An easy care dog	Lots of time for grooming? See Afghan Hound, Havanese, Keeshond, Komondor, Maltese, Old English Sheepdog	Don't mind a bit of work? See Spinone Italiano, Whippet	Easy care a must? See Bichon Frisé, Irish Water Spaniel, Labradoodle
A guard dog	Would prefer a friendly companion? See Boston Terrier, Brittany, English Setter, Miniature Schnauzer	Want a vocal watchdog? See Belgian Shepherd Dog, Canaan Dog, German Shepherd Dog, Scottish Terrier	Will be your home security? See Akita, Bouvier des Flandres, Doberman Pinscher, Rottweiler
A dog to pamper	No desire for a pampered pooch? See Bedlington Terrier, Curly-coated Retriever, Wire Fox Terrier	Will pamper when you're in the mood? See Afghan Hound, Borzoi, Chinese Shar-Pei, Puli	Clothes, bows, and all? See Cocker Spaniel, Maltese, Poodle, Samoyed, Shih Tzu
A working dog	Would rather have a companion? See Basset Hound, Chow Chow, Greyhound, Pekingese, Pug, Shih Tzu	Want an eager workmate? See Great Dane, Labrador Retriever, Rottweiler, Samoyed, Siberian Husky	Must earn its keep? See Border Collie, Boxer, Mastiff, Newfoundland, Saint Bernard
A quiet dog	Love to hear your dog all day? See Beagle, Chihuahua, German Shepherd Dog, most terriers	Think there's always time for quiet? See Bernese Mountain Dog, Greyhound, Lhasa Apso, Pug	Can't bear the barking? See Basenji, French Bulldog, Great Dane, Whippet
A fragrant dog	Love outdoorsy smells? See Bulldog, Cocker Spaniel, Old English Sheepdog, Saint Bernard	Don't mind normal doggy aromas? See Affenpinscher, Boxer, Dalmatian, Lurcher, Weimaraner	Can't bear pet smells? See Chihuahua, Labradoodle, Lhasa Apso, Shih Tzu, Whippet
A dog for tricks	Who needs a performing dog? See Bloodhound, Bulldog, Dachshund, Greyhound, Mastiff, Pug	Want a playmate? See Mongrel, Patterdale Terrier, Staffordshire Bull Terrier	Want to perform for crowds? See Australian Shepherd, Border Collie, Golden Retriever, Shetland Sheepdog

The Dog Selector

The following chart provides some insights into choosing a breed, although a number of factors can affect the suitability of a dog. Puppies, generally, are more likely to settle without problems than older dogs whose backgrounds may be unknown or disturbed. Within each group, certain breeds are highlighted with a special star (✪) as potentially being the most suitable for specific situations, depending on your living arrangements.

THE DOG SELECTOR						
BREED	**Likes exercise**	**Grooming requirements**	**Ease of training**	**Suitable for older owners**	**Suitable for families with young children**	**Suitable for families with teenagers or empty-nesters**
Affenpinscher	★★	★★	★★	★★★	★★★	★★
Afghan Hound	★★★	★★★	★	★	★	★★★
Airedale Terrier	★★★	★★★	★	★	★	★★★
Akita	★★★	★★	★★	★	★	★★★
Alaskan Malamute	★★★	★★	★★	★	★	★★★
Anatolian Shepherd Dog	★★★	★★	★★	★	★	★★★
Australian Cattle Dog	★★★	★	★★	★	★★	★★★
Australian Shepherd	★★★	★★	★★★	★★	★★	✪
Basenji	★★★	★	★★	★★	✪	★★★
Basset Hound	★★★	★	★	★	★★	★★★
Beagle	★★★	★	★	★	★★	★★★
Bearded Collie	★★★	★★★	★★★	★	★★	★★★
Beauceron	★★★	★	★★	★	★	★★★
Bedlington Terrier	★★	★★★	★★	★★	★★	★★★
Belgian Shepherd Dog	★★★	★★	★★	★★	★★	★★★
Bernese Mountain Dog	★★★	★★	★★	★	✪	★★★
Bichon Frisé	★	★★★	★★	★★★	✪	★★★
Black and Tan Coonhound	★★★	★	★	★	★	★★★
Black Russian Terrier	★★★	★★★	★★★	★★	✪	★★★
Bloodhound	★★★	★★	★	★	★	★★★
Bolognese	★	★★	★★	★★★	★★	★★
Border Collie	★★★	★★	★★★	★	★	★★★
Border Terrier	★★★	★★★	★★	★★	★★	★★★
Borzoi	★★★	★★	★	★	★	★★★
Boston Terrier	★★	★	★★	★★★	★★	★★★
Bouvier des Flandres	★★★	★★	★★	★	★	✪
Boxer	★★★	★	★★	★	★	✪
Brittany	★★★	★★	★★★	★★	★★	★★
Bulldog	★	★	★★	★★★	✪	★★
Bullmastiff	★★★	★	★★	★	★	★★★
Bull Terrier	★★★	★	★	★	★★	★★★
Cairn Terrier	★★	★★	★★	✪	★★	★★
Canaan Dog	★★★	★★	★★	★★	★★	★★★
Cavalier King Charles Spaniel	★	★★	★★	★★★	✪	★★

BREED	Likes exercise	Grooming requirements	Ease of training	Suitable for older owners	Suitable for families with young children	Suitable for families with teenagers or empty-nesters
Cesky Terrier	★★	★★	★★	★★	★★	✪
Chesapeake Bay Retriever	★★★	★★	★★★	★	★★	★★★
Chihuahua	★★	★★	★★	★★★	★★	★★
Chinese Crested Dog	★★	★★★	★★	✪	★★	★★★
Chinese Shar-Pei	★★	★★	★★	★	★	✪
Chow Chow	★★★	★★	★	★	★	★★
Clumber Spaniel	★★★	★★	★★★	★	★★	★★★
Cocker Spaniel	★★★	★★	★★★	★	★★	★★★
Collie	★★★	★★	★★★	★★	★	★★★
Coton de Tulear	★	★★★	★★	✪	★★★	★★
Curly-coated Retriever	★★★	★★★	★★	★	★★	★★★
Dachshund	★★	★★	★★	★★★	★	★★★
Dalmatian	★★★	★	★★	★	★★	★★★
Dandie Dinmont Terrier	★★	★★★	★★	✪	★★	★★
Doberman Pinscher	★★★	★	★★	★	★	★★★
Dogue de Bordeaux	★★★	★	★★	★	★	★★★
English Setter	★★★	★★	★★	★	★★	★★★
English Toy Spaniel	★	★★	★★	★★★	✪	★★
Finnish Spitz	★★★	★★★	★★	★★	★★	★★★
French Bulldog	★	★	★★	★★★	✪	★★
German Shepherd Dog	★★★	★★	★★★	★	★	★★★
German Shorthaired Pointer	★★★	★	★★★	★	★	★★★
Giant Schnauzer	★★★	★★★	★★★	★★	★★	★★★
Golden Retriever	★★★	★★	★★★	★	★★	★★★
Gordon Setter	★★★	★★	★★	★	★★	★★★
Great Dane	★★★	★	★★	★	★	✪
Greater Swiss Mountain Dog	★★★	★★	★★	★	★	★★★
Great Pyrenees	★★★	★★	★★	★	★	★★★
Greyhound	★★★	★	★★	★★	★★	★★★
Hamiltonstövare	★★★	★	★★	★	★★	★★★
Havanese	★	★★★	★★	★★★	★★★	★★
Ibizan Hound	★★★	★★	★★	★	★★	★★★
Irish Setter	★★★	★★	★★	★★	★★	✪
Irish Water Spaniel	★★★	★★	★★	★★	★★	★★★
Irish Wolfhound	★★★	★★	★★	★	★	★★★
Italian Greyhound	★★	★	★★	★★★	★★	★★★
Japanese Chin	★	★★	★★	✪	★★	★★
Keeshond	★★★	★★★	★★	★★	★★	★★★
Kerry Blue Terrier	★★	★★★	★	★	★	★★★
Komondor	★★★	★★	★★	★	★	★
Kuvasz	★★★	★★	★★	★	★	★★★
Labradoodle	★★★	★★	★★★	★★	★★★	✪
Labrador Retriever	★★★	★	★★★	★	★★	✪
Lagotto Romagnolo	★★★	★★★	★★	★★	★★	★★★
Lhasa Apso	★★	★★★	★★	★★★	★★★	★★
Löwchen	★★	★★★	★★	✪	★★★	★★
Lurcher	★★★	★★	★★	★★	✪	★★★
Maltese	★	★★	★★	★★★	✪	★★

BREED	Likes exercise	Grooming requirements	Ease of training	Suitable for older owners	Suitable for families with young children	Suitable for families with teenagers or empty-nesters
Mastiff	★★★	★	★★	★	★	★★★
Miniature Pinscher	★★	★	★★	★★★	★★	★★★
Miniature Schnauzer	★★	★★★	★★	★★	★★	★★
Mongrel	★★	★★	★★	★★★	★★★	★★★
Neapolitan Mastiff	★★★	★★	★★	★	★	★★★
Newfoundland	★★★	★★★	★★	★	★	✪
Norwegian Elkhound	★★★	★★	★★	★★	★★	★★★
Norwegian Lundehund	★★★	★★	★★	★★★	★★	★★★
Nova Scotia Duck Tolling Retriever	★★★	★	★★★	★	★	★★★
Old English Sheepdog	★★★	★★★	★★	★	★	★★
Papillon	★★	★★	★★	★★★	✪	★★★
Parson Russell Terrier	★★★	★★	★★	✪	★	★★★
Patterdale Terrier	★★★	★★	★★	★★	★	★★★
Pekingese	★	★★	★★	✪	★★	★★
Petit Basset Griffon Vendéen	★★★	★★	★	★	✪	★★★
Pharoah Hound	★★★	★	★★	★★	★★★	★★★
Pointer	★★★	★	★★★	★★	★★	★★★
Pomeranian	★★	★★	★★	★★★	★★	★★
Poodle	★★	★★★	★★	★★★	★★★	★★★
Portuguese Water Dog	★★★	★★	★★	★★	★★★	★★★
Pug	★	★	★★	✪	★★	★★★
Puli	★★	★★★	★★	★★	✪	★★
Rhodesian Ridgeback	★★★	★	★★	★	★	★★★
Rottweiler	★★★	★	★★	★	★	★★★
Saint Bernard	★★★	★★	★★	✪	★★	★★★
Saluki	★★★	★★	★	★	★★	★★★
Samoyed	★★★	★★	★★	★	★★	✪
Schipperke	★	★★	★★	★★★	★★	★★★
Scottish Deerhound	★★★	★★	★	★	★	★★★
Scottish Terrier	★★	★★	★	✪	★	★
Shetland Sheepdog	★★	★★	★★	★★★	★★	★★★
Shih Tzu	★	★★★	★★	✪	★★★	★★
Siberian Husky	★★★	★★	★★	★	★	★★★
Silky Terrier	★	★★★	★★	★★★	★★	★★
Soft-coated Wheaten Terrier	★★	★★★	★	★★	★★	★★★
Spinone Italiano	★★★	★★	★★	★	★★	✪
Staffordshire Bull Terrier	★★★	★	★	★	★	★★★
Tibetan Mastiff	★★★	★★	★★★	★	★	★★
Tibetan Spaniel	★★	★★★	★★	★★★	★★	★★★
Tibetan Terrier	★★	★★	★★	★★	★★	★★
Toy Manchester Terrier	★★	★	★★	★★★	★★	★★★
Vizsla	★★★	★★	★★★	✪	★★	★★★
Weimaraner	★★★	★★	★★★	★★	★★	★★★
Welsh Corgi	★★	★★	★★	★★	★	★★
Whippet	★★★	★	★★	★★	★★★	★★★
Wire Fox Terrier	★★★	★★★	★	★★★	★	★★★
Xoloitzcuintli	★★	★★	★★	★★★	✪	★★★
Yorkshire Terrier	★	★★★	★★	★★★	★★	★★

Glossary

Addison's Disease a disorder of the adrenal glands, which are positioned in the body above the kidneys. This disorder is most common in young bitches. It causes a shortfall in the output of the hormone aldosterone, which maintains the balance between potassium and sodium. Symptoms in the dogs affected may vary from sudden collapse to vomiting and diarrhea, plus increased thirst.

Apple dome a description given to the distinctive shape of the Chihuahua's head, which has an applelike appearance.

Belton a description given to the English Setter and its distinctive coat flecking. The term was coined by one of the leading early **breeders**, Sir Edward Laverack, with the name being derived from a town in Northumberland, in northern England, where setters with this type of coat were relatively common, in the breed's early days.

Biscuit a brownish color, which is associated with some sled breeds in particular.

Blenheim chestnut and white coloration. Blenheim is one of four color varieties associated with both the Cavalier King Charles Spaniel and the English Toy Spaniel.

Bloat an accumulation of gas in the stomach, which is a particular problem in narrow-chested, large breeds, such as the Greyhound. Avoid feeding your dog prior to exercise as this is a predisposing factor that can trigger this potentially life-threatening condition.

Blue eye a description used for the clouding of the cornea over the surface of the eye, which is a symptom of canine adenovirus type 1, or an adverse reaction to the use of the live vaccine of this type, which was a particular problem in the Afghan Hound. New vaccines have since been developed to avoid this adverse side effect in this breed.

Brachycephalic syndrome (Brachycephaly) a condition associated with some breeds of dog, defined by the short, wide appearance of the head. It is typically recognized when the width of the head is at least 80 percent or more of the length. The Pug is considered an extreme example. Other similar breeds include the Pekingese, Bulldog, and Boxer.

Breeching a term used to describe the short hair present on the rump, which extends down the hind legs.

Breeder a person who has puppies, usually on a regular basis, and who may exhibit dogs, having evolved his or her own distinctive bloodlines of a particular breed. Breeder is also sometimes used to describe a dog kept for breeding.

Brindle the appearance resulting from a combination of light and dark hairs in the coat, often resulting in a streaky patterning that is less distinct in long-coated dogs.

Brisket the area of the chest between the forelegs.

Canine Inherited Demyelinative Neuropathy (CIDN) an inherited disease affecting the nervous system of the Tibetan Mastiff. Signs emerge in puppies of about six weeks old, resulting in weakness and paralysis of the hind legs. There is no treatment and affected dogs usually die by four months old.

Cerebellar ataxia a condition that can be triggered by a variety of causes, including an inherited genetic defect, toxins, or injury to the cerebellum—the part of the brain concerned with balance and coordination. The severity of signs varies. A number of breeds can be affected and the condition may be diagnosed by an MRI scan. DNA testing is starting to be used to identify genetic carriers.

Cherry Eye a condition caused by a prolapse of the gland of the third eyelid, causing a swollen, red area to appear at the inner corner of the eye. Surgical correction will be required to treat it.

Chondrodysplasia a genetic disease affecting the legs, which leads to deformities in affected puppies, although healthy dogs may carry the gene responsible.

Collie Eye Anomaly (CEA) an inherited condition that tends to be most common in **pastoral breeds**. It can cause blindness in some but not all cases. Young puppies should be given an ophthalmic examination at around eight weeks of age to check for signs of the condition.

Croup the part of the spinal column known as the sacrum, which is present in the lumbar region, plus the pelvic girdle.

Dapple a description applied to the Dachshund. Dappling does not refer to any specific color but rather the contrast between light and dark areas in the coat. Chocolate and tan dapples are one of the rarest forms.

Dewlap the fold of skin that hangs down near the throat and runs back in the direction of the neck. This is a particular feature of mastiff-type breeds.

Diabetes mellitus a disease that affects the cells of the pancreas, which produce the hormone insulin, resulting in abnormal blood sugar levels. Some breeds such as the Keeshond, Samoyed, and Cairn Terrier are among the most vulnerable to the disease.

Distichiasis the abnormal positioning of the eyelashes, causing them to rub on the surface of the eye, resulting in irritation, as reflected by redness in the white area of the eye.

Drop ears ears that hang down the sides of the dog's head, as in breeds such as the Bloodhound. Drop ears serve to protect the sensitive inner part of the ear from injury when the dog is in undergrowth.

Ectropion a condition affecting the eyelids. The eyelids in this case are directed outward, away from the eyes. This condition most commonly affects the lower eyelid. It may cause no ill effects, but can result in conjunctivitis and tear staining. It is relatively common in breeds such as the Saint Bernard and Cocker Spaniel. Treatment for the condition is surgery.

Entropion a condition affecting the eyelids. The eyelids in this case fold inward. This condition usually affects the lower lids, with the eyelashes themselves rubbing against the cornea, causing intense irritation. Breeds such as the Chow Chow, Bullmastiff, and Bloodhound especially are most likely to be affected by entropion. Surgical correction is likely to be required to treat the condition.

Fawn a pale shade of color—the dilute form of red.

Field trial a working competition, for breeds such as retrievers, spaniels, and other pointing or flushing breeds.

Flyball a canine sport that began in California during the 1960s. Teams of dogs compete against each other. The dogs run in relays, with each dog catching a tennis ball, which is released when the dog jumps onto a spring-loaded pad, before taking the ball back to its handler.

Gastric torsion twisting of the stomach. It is associated with **bloat** and is sometimes synonymous with it. Deep-chested dogs are most at risk of suffering from gastric torsion, with the Great Dane being particularly vulnerable. Rapid veterinary examination is absolutely essential if the problem is suspected.

Grizzle grayish coloration created by a mixture of black and white hairs in the coat. This coloration can create a bluish-gray or iron-gray appearance. It is effectively a **roan** type of coat.

Harlequin a coat variant—the term is used to describe the black and white coloration of the Great Dane, for example. White should predominate in the coat with black occurring in the form of patches.

Hemeralopia a condition often referred to as day blindness where bright light causes the blurring of vision. It can be an inherited condition in the Alaskan Malamute, and can also arise as a side effect of certain anti-convulsants.

Hip dysplasia a condition affecting many breeds in which malformation of the hip joints can cause lameness and even arthritis.

Hock the dog's tarsal joint, located in the hind leg. This is the equivalent of the human ankle.

Hound glove a piece of grooming equipment that slips over the hand. It is used to groom dogs—typically hounds. Depending on the material that the glove is made of, the glove gives a good gloss to the coat.

Hydrocephalus a defect often described as "water on the brain." This is a hereditary defect, and is most commonly seen in the Chihuahua. It is caused by an accumulation of cerebrospinal fluid. Apart from creating an abnormal dome-shaped appearance of the head, other signs, such as seizures and mobility problems, may be evident in those afflicted.

Hypothyroidism a condition resulting from an abnormally low output of hormones produced by the thyroid glands in the neck, which help to regulate the body's metabolism. Lethargy, weight gain, and loss of hair, particularly on the tail, are common signs of the condition, often becoming evident in dogs of around five years old. It is most common in certain breeds, such as the Doberman and Irish Setter. The condition is easily treated with tablets.

Inguinal hernia when part of the abdominal contents extends through the inguinal ring, in the area of the rear leg close to the body wall, resulting in swelling here. This is most common in **intact** bitches—the size of the hernia varies. It can be life threatening and needs to be repaired by surgery.

Intact a term used to describe a dog or bitch that has not been neutered.

Lemon a very pale shade of yellow, or a wheaten color.

Mask a darker area on the face that extends from the nose up the muzzle for a variable distance, depending on the individual dog or breed.

Merle a color combination consisting of a base color, such as black or reddish–brown offset with contrasting reddish or lighter blue coloring, resulting in a mottled or speckled effect. This is a relatively common feature in **pastoral breeds**, and is linked with the merle gene.

Mismarked a description given to dogs that have markings that should not be present. These may be seen in solid-colored individuals, such as a black Labrador Retriever that might show tan markings as well, or equally in patterned breeds.

Outcrossing the process of breeding involving dogs that are not closely related. The opposite of inbreeding.

Parti-colored areas of the coat that are differently colored. Parti-colored is often used to describe "pied" dogs, which have dark and white patches of color on their coats.

Pastoral breed a breed whose traditional function was to herd livestock, such as sheep, cattle, or even reindeer. Pastoral breeds include the various shepherd dogs and collies, and some breeds, such as the Bergamasco, which also acted as flock guardians.

Patellar luxation a weakness of the patellas (kneecaps), which is relatively common in many small breeds of dog. Signs of patellar luxation become apparent usually between four and six months of age, with the kneecap becoming dislocated. Symptoms vary from mild to severe lameness, and can trigger osteoarthritis. Patellar luxation is likely to require surgery.

Pointing the posture adopted by pointer breeds, indicating the presence of game in the vicinity. The dog freezes, with its foreleg raised.

Prick ears raised ears, which are a feature of some breeds, although dogs generally tend to prick their ears when excited.

Prince Charles the term used to describe the tricolored form of the Cavalier King Charles Spaniel or the English Toy Spaniel, which is black and white with tan markings.

Progressive Retinal Atrophy (PRA) a condition affecting the retina, where the image is formed at the back of each eye. The condition causes a loss of vision with signs first becoming apparent in darkened surroundings. A variety of breeds, such as the Samoyed and Tibetan Terrier, are susceptible to the condition.

Prolapsed eyeballs eyeballs that become protruded from their sockets. This condition is particularly linked to the Pekingese breed.

Renal dysplasia a disease resulting from a congenital developmental problem with the kidneys, resulting in typical signs of kidney failure, such as weight loss and increased thirst. The Shih Tzu and Standard Poodle are among the breeds most likely to be affected by the disease.

Roan a combination of white and colored hairs in the coat, which will not become paler with age. Different forms of roan are recognized, such as red roan, depending on the dog's coloration.

Ruby the term used to describe the chestnut color of both the Cavalier King Charles and English Toy Spaniels.

Saddle the area over the back, which is dark in color, standing out from the rest of the coat. The saddle is often a feature seen in **scent hounds**.

Scent hound a member of the hound group relying primarily on its sense of smell rather than its eyesight to track its quarry. Typical examples include the Beagle and Basset Hound.

Scottie Cramp a genetic problem associated with the Scottish Terrier, causing abnormalities in the gait of an affected individual, which typically last about 10 minutes. Treatment with tranquilizers may help, along with a Vitamin E supplement.

Seal a variable color, closely associated with terrier breeds, which may create a blackish appearance in some lights, but is distinguishable because the individual hairs have tan tips.

Setting the way in which a setter indicates the presence of game. The word is derived from the old English word "set," meaning to "sit."

Sight hound a hound group member that hunts largely by eyesight, recognizing its quarry from some distance away. Examples of sight hounds include the Greyhound and Afghan Hound.

Slipped stifle this is another term for **patellar luxation**, with the patella overlying the stifle or knee joint.

Socialization the process whereby young dogs are introduced to others of their own kind, with the aim being to prevent them from being nervous and potentially aggressive as they grow older.

Splashed a term used to describe **parti-colored** dogs, which have darker areas on the top and sides of the body, and white underparts, as seen, for example, in the Siberian Husky.

Stifle joint the equivalent to the knee joint.

Stopper pad the non-weight-bearing pad at the back of each foreleg, located relatively close to the ground at the level of the accessory carpal bone.

Syringomyelia a condition caused by the presence of a cavity or cyst within the spinal cord, being associated particularly with the Cavalier King Charles Spaniel.

Treeing a term used to describe the way in which coonhounds drive their quarry up into trees.

Von Willebrand's Disease an inherited disorder that interferes with the blood-clotting system. This disorder is most commonly associated with the Doberman Pinscher.

Withers the highest point of the shoulder, and the point that serves as the standard benchmark when measuring the height of dogs.

Wobbler Syndrome a problem affecting the cervical (neck) vertebrae, causing the bones to press on the spinal cord and resulting in an unsteady gait. Particularly associated with the Great Dane, but can afflict other large breeds, too. Wobbler Syndrome may require surgery.

Further Resources

Further Reading
Alderton, David. *Hounds of the World.*
Stoeger Publishing Company, 2002.

Alderton, David. *Smithsonian Handbooks:*
Dogs. Dorling Kindersley, 2002.

Alderton, David. *Top to Tail: The 360°*
Guide to Picking Your Perfect Pet. David
& Charles, 2006.

American Kennel Club, The. *The Complete*
Dog Book. Ballantine Books, 2006.

Canadian Kennel Club, The. *The*
Canadian Kennel Club Book of Dogs.
Gazelle Book Services, 1989.

De Prisco, Andrew & Johnson, James B.
Canine Lexicon. T.F.H. Publications, 1993.

Fergus, Charles. *Gun Dog Breeds: A*
Guide to Spaniels, Retrievers, and Pointing
Dogs. The Lyons Press, 2002.

Gagne, Tammy. *Designer Dogs* (Animal
Planet Pet Care Library). T.F.H.
Publications, 2008.

Glover, Harry. *Toy Dogs.* David & Charles,
1977.

Horner, Tom. *Terriers of the World.* Faber
& Faber, 1984.

Jackson, Frank. *The Dictionary of Canine*
Terms. Crowood Press, 1996.

Kennel Club, The. *The Kennel Club's*
Illustrated Breed Standards. Ebury Press, 2003.

Kern, Kerry. *The Terrier Handbook.*
Barron's Educational Series, 2005.

Larkin, Peter & Stockman, Mike. *The*
Complete Dog Book. Lorenz Books, 1997.

Morris, Desmond. *Dogs: The Ultimate*
Dictionary of Over 1,000 Dog Breeds.
Trafalgar Square Publishing, 2008.
Plummer, David Brian. *The Working*
Terrier. Boydell and Brewer, 1978.

Sanderson, Angela. *The Complete Book*
of Australian Dogs. Currawong Press, 1987.

Wilcox, Bonnie & Walkowicz, Chris.
The Atlas of Dog Breeds of the World.
T.F.H. Publications, 1995.

Yamazaki, Tetsu & Kojima, Toyoharu.
Legacy of the Dog: The Ultimate
Illustrated Guide to Over 200 Breeds.
Chronicle Books, 1995.

Major breed registries in North America
American Kennel Club
260 Madison Avenue, New York,
NY 10016, U.S.A.
www.akc.org

Canadian Kennel Club
200 Ronson Drive, Suite 400, Etobicoke,
Ontario M9W 5Z9, Canada
www.ckc.ca

Continental Kennel Club
P.O. Box 1628, Walker, LA 70785, U.S.A.
www.continentalkennelclub.com

National Kennel Club Inc.
134 Rutledge Pike, P.O. 331, Blaine,
Tennessee 37709, U.S.A.

www.nationalkennelclub.com
United Kennel Club
100 East Kilgore Road, Kalamazoo,
MI 49002-5584, U.S.A.
www.ukcdogs.com
Universal Kennel Club International
101 W Washington Avenue, Pearl River,
NY 10954, U.S.A.
www.universalkennel.com

World Kennel Club
P.O. Box 60771, Oklahoma City,
OK 73146, U.S.A.
www.worldkennelclub.com

World Wide Kennel Club Ltd.
P.O. Box 62, Mount Vernon, NY 10552,
U.S.A.
www.worldwidekennel.qpg.com

**Major breed registries in Europe, Africa,
Asia, and Australia**
Australian National Kennel Council
P.O. Box 815, Dickson ACT 2602,
Australia
www.ankc.org.au

Fédération Cynologique Internationale
Place Albert 1er, 13 B-6530 Thuin,
Belgium
www.fci.be

Irish Kennel Club, The
Fottrell House, Harold's Cross Bridge,
Dublin 6W, Ireland
www.ikc.ie

Kennel Club, The
1–5 Clarges Street, Piccadilly, London,
W1J 8AB, England
www.thekennelclub.org.uk

Kennel Club of India, The
No. 28 (89) AA Block, First Street, Anna
Nagar, Chennai 600 040, Tamil Nadu, India
www.thekci.org

Kennel Union of Southern Africa, The
P.O. Box 2659, Cape Town 8000, South
Africa
www.kusa.co.za/home.php

New Zealand Kennel Club
Prosser Street, Private Bag 50903,
Porirua 5240, New Zealand
www.nzkc.org.nz

Index

Page numbers in **bold** indicate main entries.

A

Addison's Disease 169
Affenpinscher 25, **78**, 166
Afghan Hound 57, **58**, 166, 169, 172
African Lion Dog see Rhodesian Ridgeback
Airedale Terrier **114**, 127, 166
Akita **119**, 166
Alaskan Malamute **91**, 166, 170
Alsatian see German Shepherd Dog
American Cocker Spaniel 17
American Kennel Club (AKC) 10, 17, 36, 127
Anatolian Shepherd Dog 81, **83**, 166
apple dome 169
August, Grand Duke Karl 96
Australian Cattle Dog **142**, 166
Australian Shepherd 129, **136**, 166
Australian Terrier 74

B

Barbet 113
Basenji **143**, 166
Bassett Hound 36, **55**, 166, 171
Beagle 21, **22**, 166, 171
Bearded Collie 21, **23**, 166
Beauceron 121, 129, **134**, 166
Bedlington Terrier 18, 62, **109**, 166
Belgian Sheepdog 100
Belgian Shepherd Dog **100**, 166
belton 169
Berner Sennenhund see Bernese Mountain Dog
Bernese Mountain Dog 86, **90**, 166
Bichon Frisé **112**, 166
biscuit 169
Black and Tan Coonhound **42**, 166
Black and Tan Setter see Gordon Setter
Black and Tan Terrier 28, 50, 132, 138

Black Russian Terrier **127**, 166
Blenheim 19, 35, 169
bloat 169, 170
Bloodhound 42, 84, 96, 141, **144**, 146, 166, 170
blue eye 169
Bobtail see Old English Sheepdog
Bohemian Terrier see Cesky Terrier
Bolognese 40, **77**, 112, 166
Border Collie 129, **130**, 166
Border Terrier **79**, 166
Borzoi **67**, 88, 98, 137, 166
Boston Terrier **10**, 166
Bouvier des Ardennes 121
Bouvier des Flandres **121**, 166
Boxer 21, **24**, 166, 169
Brachycephalic syndrome 169
Brachycephaly 169
breeching 169
breeder 169
brindle 169
brisket 169
Brittany **34**, 166
Bulldog 10, 24, **162**, 166, 169
Bullmastiff **123**, 124, 166, 170
Bull Terrier 10, 21, **28**, 114, 166

C

Cairn Terrier **151**, 166, 170
Canaan Dog **159**, 166
Canine Inherited Demyelinative Neuropathy (CIDN) 169
Cáo de Água see Portuguese Water Dog
Cavalier King Charles Spaniel 19, **35**, 166, 169, 171, 172
cerebellar ataxia 169
Cesky Terrier **51**, 167
Cherry Eye 169
Chesapeake Bay Retriever **148**, 167
Chihuahua 45, **46**, 167, 169, 170
Chinese Crested Dog **108**, 167
Chinese Shar-Pei 153, **161**, 167
chondrodysplasia 169
Chow Chow **60**, 161, 167, 170
Clumber Spaniel **36**, 167
Cocker Spaniel **17**, 36, 167, 170
Collie **137**, 142, 167
Collie Eye Anomaly (CEA) 169

Conron, Wally 115
Continental Toy Spaniel 135
Coton de Tulear 33, **38**, 167
croup 169
Curly-coated Retriever **110**, 167
Czesky Terrier see Cesky Terrier

D

Dachshund **53**, 76, 158, 167
Dalmatian 28, 93, **95**, 142, 167
Dandie Dinmont Terrier 51, 71, **158**, 167
dapple 170
Deerhound 99
dewlap 170
diabetes mellitus 170
Dingo 142
distichiasis 170
Dobermann, Louis 118
Doberman Pinscher 117, **118**, 167, 170, 172
Dogue de Bordeaux 24, **87**, 167
drop ears 170

E

ectropion 170
English Cocker Spaniel 17
English Foxhound 42
English Pointer see Pointer
English Setter **39**, 167, 169
English Springer Spaniel 39
English Toy Spaniel 17, **19**, 35, 167, 169, 171
English Toy Terrier 50
entropion 170
Épagneul Breton see Brittany

F

fawn 170
field trial 170
Finnish Spitz **147**, 167
flyball 170
French Barbet 37
French Bulldog **47**, 167

G

gastric torsion 170
German Pinscher 76, 118

German Pointer 118
German Shepherd Dog 129, **131**, 134, 167
German Shorthaired Pointer 21, **26**, 167
Giant Schnauzer 25, 121, **126**, 127, 167
Golden Retriever 21, **30**, 167
Gordon Setter **65**, 167
Graham, Captain George 88
Gray Elkhound see Norwegian Elkhound
Great Dane 81, **82**, 126, 160, 167, 170, 172
Greater Swiss Mountain Dog **86**, 167
Great Pyrenees **85**, 145, 167
Greyhound 18, 41, 45, 48, **52**, 67, 99, 118, 146, 167, 169, 172
Griffon Bruxellois 78
Griffon Vendéen 27
grizzle 170
Groenendael see Belgian Shepherd Dog
Grosser Schweizer Sennenhund see Greater Swiss Mountain Dog

H

Hamilton, Count Adolph 31
Hamiltonstövare 21, **31**, 167
harlequin 170
Havanese 33, **40**, 112, 167
hemeralopia 170
hip dysplasia 170
hock 170
Horák, František 51
hound glove 170
hydrocephalus 170
hypothyroidism 170

I

Ibizan Hound 153, **157**, 167
inguinal hernia 171
intact 171
Irish Kennel Club 63
Irish Setter 30, **98**, 167, 170
Irish Water Spaniel 110, **113**, 148, 167
Irish Wolfhound 62, 81, 82, **88**, 167

Italian Greyhound 18, **48**, 50, 76, 167
Italian Kennel Club 154

J

Jack Russell Terrier 132
Japanese Chin **49**, 167

K

Keeshond 9, **16**, 167, 170
Kennel Club (UK) 130, 133
Kerry Blue Terrier **62**, 167
King Charles Spaniel see English Toy Spaniel
Komondor 64, **156**, 167
Kuvasz **122**, 167

L

Labradoodle **115**, 167
Labrador Retriever 9, **11**, 39, 110, 115, 167, 171
Laekenois 100
Lagotto Romagnolo 141, **149**, 167
Landseer 145
Laverack, Sir Edward 39, 169
lemon 171
Lhasa Apso 29, 43, **75**, 167
Little Lion Dog see Löwchen
Löwchen **59**, 167
Lurcher **99**, 109, 167

M

Malinois 100
Maltese **72**, 77, 167
Manchester Terrier 18, 50, 71
mask 171
Mastiff 123, **124**, 160, 168
merle 171
Mexican Hairless Dog see Xoloitzcuintli
Miniature Pinscher **76**, 168
Miniature Schnauzer 21, **25**, 168
mismarked 171
mongrel 129, **139**, 168

N

Neapolitan Mastiff **154**, 168
Newfoundland **145**, 148, 168
Norwegian Elkhound **103**, 168

Norwegian Lundehund 153, **163**, 168
Nova Scotia Duck Tolling Retriever **150**, 168

O

Old English Sheepdog 43, 57, **61**, 168
Old Spanish Pointer 98, 146
Oorang Airedale 114
Otterhound 148
outcrossing 171

P

Papillon 129, **135**, 168
Parson Russell Terrier **132**, 168
parti-colored 171, 172
pastoral breed 169, 171
patellar luxation 171, 172
Patterdale Terrier **133**, 168
Pekingese 13, 14, **29**, 70, 168, 169, 171
Persian Greyhound see Saluki
Petit Basset Griffon Vendéen **27**, 168
Phalène 135
Pharaoh Hound **102**, 157, 168
Pit Bull Terrier 138
Pointer **146**, 168
pointing 26, 146, 171
Polish Lowland Sheepdog 23
Pomeranian 25, **73**, 168
Poodle **106**, 107, 110, 113, 115, 168, 171
Portuguese Water Dog **107**, 168
prick ears 171
Prince Charles 19, **35**, 171
Progressive Retinal Atrophy (PRA) 171
prolapsed eyeballs 171
Pug 9, **13**, 47, 168, 169
Puli **64**, 156, 168
Pyrenean Mountain Dog see Great Pyrenees

R

Red Setter see Irish Setter
renal dysplasia 171
Rhodesian Ridgeback **160**, 168

Riehl, Georg 25
roan 170, 171
Rottweiler 118, **120**, 126, 127, 168
Rough Collie 15, 137
Ruby 19, 35, 171

S

saddle 171
Saint Bernard **84**, 168, 170
Saito, Hiroshi 119
Saluki 93, **101**, 168
Samoyed 57, 60, **66**, 168, 170, 171
scent hound 22, 31, 95, 144, 171
Schipperke **12**, 168
Schott, Heinrich 25
Scottie Cramp 172
Scottish Deerhound 33, **41**, 88, 168
Scottish Terrier 51, **125**, 151, 168
seal 171
Sealyham Terrier 51
Segugio Italiano 37
setting 39, 65, 172
Shetland Sheepdog 9, **15**, 168
Shih Tzu 21, **29**, 168, 171
Siberian Husky 93, **94**, 168, 172
sight hound 48, 52, 67, 88, 93, 99, 101, 157, 172
Silky Terrier **74**, 168
Skye Terrier 71, 74, 125
slipped stifle 172
socialization 172
Soft-coated Wheaten Terrier **63**, 168
Spanish Pointer 26, 39
Spinone Italiano **37**, 168
splashed 172
Springer Spaniel 17
Staffordshire Bull Terrier **138**, 168
stifle joint 172
stopper pad 172
Suomenpystykorva see Finnish Spitz
syringomyelia 172

T

Tatra Mountain Sheepdog 122
Tervuren 100

Tibetan Mastiff 60, 88, **89**, 168, 169
Tibetan Spaniel **14**, 70, 168
Tibetan Terrier **43**, 64, 75, 168, 171
Toy Manchester Terrier **50**, 168
treeing 172
Tweed Water Spaniel 30

V

Vizsla **97**, 168
Von Willebrand's Disease 172

W

Water Spaniel 39
Wavy-coated Retriever 30
Weimaraner **96**, 168
Welsh Corgi **54**, 168
Whippet 9, **18**, 109, 168
Willison, Gwendoline 23
Wire Fox Terrier **111**, 132, 168
withers 172
Wobbler Syndrome 172

X

Xoloitzcuintli 153, **155**, 168

Y

Yorkshire Terrier **71**, 74, 168

Z

Zwergpinscher see Miniature Pinscher

Acknowledgments

Marshall Editions would like to thank the following for their kind permission to reproduce their images.

Key: **t** = top **b** = bottom **c** = center **r** = right **l** = left

Front cover: Shutterstock/Eric Isselée; **back cover:** Shutterstock/Nata Sdobnikova; **inside front flap:** Shutterstock/Eric Isselée; **inside back flap:** Shutterstock/Marina Jay

Pages: 1 Warren Photographic/Mark Taylor; 2–3 Warren Photographic/Jane Burton; 4l Shutterstock/Todd Taulman; 4t Shutterstock/Sparkling Moments Photography; 5 Shutterstock/Lobke Peers; 7 Shutterstock/Photosign; 8l Shutterstock/GLYPHstock; 8r Shutterstock/Erik Lam; 9 Shutterstock/Eric Isselée; 10 iStock/Rhys Hastings; 11t Warren Photographic/Jane Burton; 11b Warren Photographic/Jane Burton; 12 Marc Henrie Photography; 13 Warren Photographic/Jane Burton; 14 Shutterstock/Erik Lam; 15 Warren Photographic/Jane Burton; 16 Shutterstock/Michal Napartowicz; 17 Warren Photographic/Jane Burton; 18 Shutterstock/Kostudio; 19 DK Images/Dave King; 20l Shutterstock/Tstockphoto; 20r Shutterstock/Somer McCain; 21 Shutterstock/Elliot Westacott; 22 Warren Photographic/Jane Burton; 23 Warren Photographic/Mark Taylor; 24 Warren Photographic/Jane Burton; 25 Alamy/Petra Wegner; 26 Warren Photographic/Mark Taylor; 27 DK Images/Tracy Morgan; 28t Shutterstock/Eric Isselée; 28b Warren Photographic/Jane Burton; 29–30 Warren Photographic/Jane Burton; 31 DK Images/Tracy Morgan; 32 Warren Photographic/Mark Taylor; 33 Shutterstock/Chris Alcock; 34–35 Warren Photographic/Jane Burton; 36 DK Images/Tracy Morgan; 37 DK Images/Dave King; 38 Shutterstock/Eric Isselée; 39 DK Images/Jerry Young; 40 Shutterstock/Viorel Sima; 41 DK Images/Tracy Morgan; 42–43 DK Images/Tracy Morgan; 44l Shutterstock/Eric Isselée; 44r Shutterstock/Snaprender; 45l Shutterstock/Alexia Khruscheva; 45r Shutterstock/Eric Isselée; 46 Warren Photographic/Jane Burton; 47t /Eric Isselée; 47b Corbis/Barry Lewis/In Pictures; 48 DK Images/Dave King; 49 Shutterstock/Eric Isselée; 50 Corbis/Pat Doyle; 51 DK Images/Tracy Morgan; 52 Shutterstock/Eric Isselée; 53 Warren Photographic/Jane Burton; 54–55 Warren Photographic/Jane Burton; 56 Shutterstock/Steamroller Blues; 57 Shutterstock/Dina Magnat; 58 Shutterstock/Eric Isselée; 59 DK Images/Tracy Morgan; 60t Shutterstock/Eric Isselée; 60b Warren Photographic/Mark Taylor; 61 DK Images/Dave King; 62 Marc Henrie; 63 Getty Images/DK Images/Dave King; 64 DK Images/Tracy Morgan; 65 Alamy/Petra Wegner; 66 Shutterstock/Alexia Khruscheva; 67 Warren Photographic/Jane Burton; 68l Shutterstock/Marina Jay; 68c Shutterstock/Erik Lam; 69 Shutterstock/Tish1; 70–71 Warren Photographic/Jane Burton; 72 Shutterstock/Eric Isselée; 73 Warren Photographic/Jane Burton; 74 Shutterstock/Phil Date; 75 Alamy/Life On White; 76 Shutterstock/Konstantin Gushcha; 77 Alamy/Juniors Bildarchiv; 78t Warren Photographic/Jane Burton; 78b DK Images/Tracy Morgan; 79 Warren Photographic/Jane Burton; 80 Shutterstock/Eric Isselée; 80–81 Shutterstock/grafica; 82–83 Shutterstock/Eric Isselée; 84 Warren Photographic/Jane Burton; 85 Marc Henrie; 86 Alamy/Petra Wegner; 87 Shutterstock/Eric Isselée; 88 Alamy/Arco Images GmbH; 89 DK Images/Tracy Morgan; 90 DK Images/Jerry Young; 91 Shutterstock/Eric Isselée; 92t Shutterstock/Tomas Skopal; 92b Shutterstock/Laila Kazakevica; 92–93c Shutterstock/Joe Gough; 92–93b Shutterstock/Jakub Pavlinec; 94–95 Warren Photographic/Jane Burton; 96 Shutterstock/Eric Isselée; 97 Warren Photographic/Jane Burton; 98 Shutterstock/Erik Lam; 99 Warren Photographic/Jane Burton; 100 Alamy/Petra Wegner; 101 Warren Photographic/Jane Burton; 102 DK Images/Tracy Morgan; 103 Alamy/DK Images; 104t Shutterstock/Cynoclub; 104b Shutterstock/Asharkyu; 104c Shutterstock/Vnlit; 105 Shutterstock/Jacqueline Abromeit; 106 Shutterstock/WilleeCole; 107l Alamy/Juniors Bildarchiv; 107r Alamy/Juniors Bildarchiv; 108 Warren Photographic/Jane Burton; 109 Corbis/DK Images; 110 DK Images/Tracy Morgan; 111 DK Images/Dave King; 112t Warren Photographic/Mark Taylor; 112b Warren Photographic/Mark Taylor; 113 DK Images/Tracy Morgan; 114 Shutterstock/vnlit; 115 Getty Images/DK Images; 116l Shutterstock/Paul Cotney; 116r Shutterstock/Eric Isselée; 117 Shutterstock/Eric Isselée; 118t Warren Photographic/Jane Burton; 118b DK Images/Tracy Morgan; 119 Shutterstock/Eric Isselée; 120 Warren Photographic/Jane Burton; 121 Shutterstock/Eric Isselée; 122 DK Images/Tracy Morgan; 123 & 124t Warren Photographic/Jane Burton; 124b DK Images/Dave King; 125 Warren Photographic/Jane Burton; 126 Shutterstock/Eric Isselée; 127 Alamy/Arco Images GmbH; 128 Shutterstock/Eric Isselée; 129 Shutterstock/Nikolai Tsvetkov; 130–131 Warren Photographic/Jane Burton; 132--133 DK Images/Tracy Morgan; 134 Shutterstock/Eric Isselée; 135 Warren Photographic/Jane Burton; 136t Shutterstock/Photosign; 136 Shutterstock/Eric Isselée; 137t Warren Photographic/Jane Burton; 137b DK Images/Tracy Morgan; 138–139 Warren Photographic/Jane Burton; 140tl Shutterstock/Eric Isselée; 140 & 141c Shutterstock/Tad Denson; 141tr Shutterstock/Perrush; 142–143 DK Images/Dave King; 144 DK Images/Tracy Morgan; 145 Alamy/Vario Images GmbH & Co.KG; 146–147 DK Images/Tracy Morgan; 148t Warren Photographic/Jane Burton; 148b Warren Photographic/Jane Burton; 149 DK Images/Tracy Morgan; 150 Alamy/Petra Wegner; 151 Shutterstock/Perrush; 152 Shutterstock/Nikuwka; 153 Shutterstock/Eric Isselée; 154 Alamy/Image Register 044; 155 Corbis/Yann Arthus-Bertrand; 156 DK Images/Tracy Morgan; 157 DK Images/Tracy Morgan; 158 Corbis/Yann Arthus-Bertrand; 159 DK Images/Tracy Morgan; 160 Alamy/Arco Images GmbH; 161 Shutterstock/Luchschen; 162l Warren Photographic/Jane Burton; 162r Shutterstock/Eric Isselée; 163 Alamy/DK Images; 165 Shutterstock/Erik Lam.